XML Processing
with Python

D1529831

ISBN 0-13-021119-2

90000

9 780130 211194

⟨!CFG:OIM⟩ Charles F. Goldfarb Series on Open Information Management

"Open Information Management" (OIM) means managing information so that it is open to processing by any program, not just the program that created it. That extends even to application programs not conceived of at the time the information was created.

OIM is based on the principle of data independence: data should be stored in computers in non-proprietary, genuinely standardized representations. And that applies even when the data is the content of a document. Its representation should distinguish the innate information from the proprietary codes of document processing programs and the artifacts of particular presentation styles.

Business data bases—which rigorously separate the real data from the input forms and output reports—achieved data independence decades ago. But documents, unlike business data, have historically been created in the context of a particular output presentation style. So for document data, independence was largely unachievable until recently.

That is doubly unfortunate. It is unfortunate because documents are a far more significant repository of humanity's information. And documents can contain significantly richer information structures than data bases.

It is also unfortunate because the need for OIM of documents is greater now than ever. The demands of "repurposing" require that information be deliverable in multiple formats: paper-based, online, multimedia, hypermedia. And information must now be delivered through multiple channels: traditional bookstores and libraries, the World Wide Web, corporate intranets and extranets. In the latter modes, what starts as data base data may become a document for browsing, but then may need to be reused by the reader as data.

Fortunately, in the past ten years a technology has emerged that extends to documents the data base's capacity for data independence. And it does so without the data base's restrictions on structural freedom. That technology is the "Standard Generalized Markup

Language" (SGML), an official International Standard (ISO 8879) that has been adopted by the world's largest producers of documents and by the World Wide Web.

With SGML, organizations in government, aerospace, airlines, automotive, electronics, computers, and publishing (to name a few) have freed their documents from hostage relationships to processing software. SGML coexists with graphics, multimedia, and other data standards needed for OIM and acts as the framework that relates objects in the other formats to one another and to SGML documents.

The World Wide Web's HTML and XML are both based on SGML. HTML is a particular, though very general, application of SGML, like those for the above industries. There is a limited set of markup tags that can be used with HTML. XML, in contrast, is a simplified subset of SGML facilities that, like full SGML, can be used with any set of tags. You can literally create your own markup language with XML.

As the enabling standard for OIM of documents, the SGML family of standards necessarily plays a leading role in this series. We provide tutorials on SGML, XML, and other key standards and the techniques for applying them. Our books vary in technical intensity from programming techniques for software developers to the business justification of OIM for enterprise executives. We share the practical experience of organizations and individuals who have applied the techniques of OIM in environments ranging from immense industrial publishing projects to websites of all sizes.

Our authors are expert practitioners in their subject matter, not writers hired to cover a "hot" topic. They bring insight and understanding that can only come from real-world experience. Moreover, they practice what they preach about standardization. Their books share a common standards-based vocabulary. In this way, knowledge gained from one book in the series is directly applicable when reading another, or the standards themselves. This is just one of the ways in which we strive for the utmost technical accuracy and consistency with the OIM standards.

And we also strive for a sense of excitement and fun. After all, the challenge of OIM—preserving information from the ravages of technology while exploiting its benefits—is one of the great intellectual adventures of our age. I'm sure you'll find this series to be a knowledgeable and reliable guide on that adventure.

About the Series Editor

Dr. Charles F. Goldfarb is the father of markup languages, a term that he coined in 1970. He invented the SGML language in 1974 and later led the team that developed it into the International Standard on which both HTML and XML are based. He serves as editor of the Standard (ISO 8879) and as a consultant to developers of SGML and XML applications and products. He is based in Saratoga, CA.

About the Series Logo

The rebus is an ancient literary tradition, dating from 16th century Picardy, and is especially appropriate to a series involving fine distinctions between things and the words that describe them. For the logo, Andrew Goldfarb incorporated a rebus of the series name within a stylized SGML/XML comment declaration.

The Charles F. Goldfarb Series on Open Information Management

As XML is a subset of SGML, the Series List is categorized to show the degree to which a title applies to XML. "XML Titles" are those that discuss XML explicitly and may also cover full SGML. "SGML Titles" do not mention XML per se, but the principles covered may apply to XML.

XML Titles

Goldfarb, Pepper, and Ensign
- SGML Buyer's Guide™: Choosing the Right XML and SGML Products and Services

Megginson
- Structuring XML Documents

Leventhal, Lewis, and Fuchs
- Designing XML Internet Applications

DuCharme
- XML: The Annotated Specification

Jelliffe
- The XML and SGML Cookbook: Recipes for Structured Information

McGrath
- XML by Example: Building E-commerce Applications

Goldfarb and Prescod
- The XML Handbook™ Second Edition

Floyd
- Building Web Sites with XML

Morgenthal and la Forge
- Enterprise Application Integration with XML and Java

McGrath
- XML Processing with Python

SGML Titles

Ensign
- $GML: The Billion Dollar Secret

Rubinsky and Maloney
- SGML on the Web: Small Steps Beyond HTML

McGrath
- ParseMe.1st: SGML for Software Developers

DuCharme
- SGML CD

General Titles

Martin
- TOP SECRET Intranet: How U.S. Intelligence Built Intelink—The World's Largest, Most Secure Network

XML
Processing
with Python

■ Sean McGrath

Prentice Hall PTR, Upper Saddle River, NJ 07458
www.phptr.com

Library of Congress Cataloging-in-Publication Data

McGrath, Sean
  XML processing with Python / Sean McGrath.
    p. cm.
  ISBN 0-13-021119-2 (pbk.)
    1. XML (Document markup language) 2. Python (computer program language) I.
Title.
QA76.76.H94 M3885 2000
005.7'2--dc21

                              00-026326

Editorial/Production Supervision: Patti Guerrieri
Acquisitions Editor: Mark L. Taub
Editorial Assistant: Michael Fredette
Marketing Manager: Kate Hargett
Manufacturing Manager: Alexis R. Heydt
Cover Design: Anthony Gemmellaro
Cover Design Direction: Jerry Votta
Series Design: Gail Cocker-Bogusz

© 2000 Prentice Hall PTR
Prentice-Hall, Inc.
Upper Saddle River, NJ 07458

Prentice Hall books are widely used by corporations and government agencies for training,
marketing, and resale.

The publisher offers discounts on this book when ordered in bulk quantities. For more information, contact:
Corporate Sales Department. Phone: 800-382-3419; FAX: 201-236-7141; E-mail: corpsales@prenhall.com;
or write to: Prentice Hall PTR, Corp. Sales Dept., One Lake Street, Upper Saddle River, NJ 07458.

All products or services mentioned in this book are the trademarks or service marks of their respective companies or
organizations.

Printed in the United States of America

10 9 8 7 6 5 4 3 2 1

ISBN 0-13-021119-2

Prentice-Hall International (UK) Limited, *London*
Prentice-Hall of Australia Pty. Limited, *Sydney*
Prentice-Hall Canada, Inc., *Toronto*
Prentice-Hall Hispanoamericana, S.A., *Mexico*
Prentice-Hall of India Private Limited, *New Delhi*
Prentice-Hall of Japan, Inc., *Tokyo*
Pearson Education Asia Pte. Ltd.
Editora Prentice-Hall do Brasil, Ltda., *Rio de Janeiro*

For my daughter Áine—who, like both Python and XML, is young, well designed, and full of promise.

Contents

Foreword

XML is not a programming language . . . it is a markup language.

Python, on the other hand—like Java, C++, and Perl—is a programming language. As such, it is designed to *do* things to data. Programming languages have verbs like "read," "write," "compare," and . . . well . . . "do." They can also *describe* data to some extent, but not as well as a markup language.

That's because a markup language like XML is designed *solely* to describe data—any data that could occur in a paper document, which is virtually any data at all. When properly used, the data descriptions can be very rich indeed. Not just bare-bones datatype information, like "string" or "integer," but also detailed metadata about the schema, structure, and semantic properties.

Moreover, XML data is completely neutral and can be processed with any tools, in any system environment, and with any programming language.

As a result, XML presents the programmer with enormous opportunity for creating powerful applications and Web sites that integrate and visualize data, however created and wherever found.

But realizing that opportunity can involve a lot of work. That's why you'll want to program in a language that supports full access to everything in an XML representation—and that makes it easy and natural to process what you find.

Enter Python, the programming language preferred by many of the world's leading XML experts. Among them is Sean McGrath, Chief Technology Officer of mobile Internet company Propylon, one of the developers of XML, and a consultant with fifteen years of markup language experience. Sean's enthusiasm for Python led him to develop the powerful Pyxie open-source library—included on this book's CD-ROM—that adds full XML support to Python's intrinsic text and data manipulation facilities. You'll learn Pyxie from this book, along with all that a programmer needs to get started with Python and put it to practical use.

As author of *XML By Example: Building E-commerce Applications* and *ParseMe.1st: SGML for Software Engineers*, Sean has taught tens of thousands of programmers to develop markup language applications. In *XML Processing with Python,* he shows you how easily you can create your own—and how much fun you can have working with Python!

Charles F. Goldfarb

Saratoga, CA

May, 2000

Introduction

ML is everywhere on the Web these days. Structured data of all shapes and sizes such as financial transactions, news feeds, health care records, even HTML is metamorphosing into XML. There is just no getting away from it!

I'm glad actually. The fact that XML is everywhere is a fundamentally *good thing* in my opinion.

Why? Well, thanks to XML, the Web is in transition from an enormous repository of display-oriented, unstructured, low-level data (HTML) into a repository of structured, heterogenous, content-oriented information (XML). This new, improved World Wide Web, housed on a bedrock of XML, presents programmers with awesome opportunities for innovative software development.

This suits me just fine because software development is what I like to do—even more than writing books about software development.

The fact that the "L" in XML stands for "Language" has been the source of some confusion. It is important to remember that XML is a *data representation* technology. It is *not*, by any stretch of the imagination, a programming language. Its strength lies in its ability to simply and cleanly represent complex hierarchical data structures. As you know, XML is a World Wide Web Consortium (W3C) recommendation for structured data representation. There is no such thing as a W3C-recommended XML programming language. Choice of a programming tool is entirely within the hands of the individual developer. In making a selection, an embarrassment of riches presents itself to us. We have the Java™ programming language, Perl, Tcl, C++, C, JavaScript™, Visual Basic™, Delphi™, and of course Python. Each language has its benefits and its drawbacks as an XML-processing tool.

How to choose?

Well, choosing a programming language is an inexact science at best and is influenced by many factors that are technical, commercial, emotional, futuristic and political in nature. Even serendipity has a role to play.[1]

For my part, standing here (actually sitting here) at the start of the 21st century, I can safely say, without fear of contradiction, that *no* programming language I know comes close to Python for XML processing.

"Strong words," you may say, but then again, I am only speaking about the languages I know, not the ones I don't.[2]

Enough said! We are not here to engage in programming language wars—that is what Usenet is for. Suffice it to say that Python is a solidly engineered, general-purpose programming language with a natural affinity for text processing in general and XML processing in particular. Mix XML and Python together and you have an explosive cocktail of information representation and information processing power.

In my opinion . . .

---

[1] I came across Python in 1994 quite by accident!

[2] I have programming experience in all the languages mentioned above, though.

1.1 | Purpose of This Book

This book has essentially one purpose: To give you all the information, explanations, working examples, and software packages (on the accompanying CD-ROM) you need to start writing XML-processing applications in Python *fast*.

This book will not slow you down with intricate technical details of either Python or XML. That is not to say that these things are not important! They are very important, but they are not discussed in this book. The reason for this omission is that I believe a pragmatic treatment of a subject such as Python/XML is the best way to become productive quickly. I believe that comprehensive coverage of the details too early on in the exploration of a topic like this just gets in the way. So, in this book, comprehensive coverage takes second place to working examples of real-world Python/XML programming. I will provide plenty of pointers to more detailed information for those of you who wish to dig deeper.

1.2 | The Pyxie Open Source Project

This book heralds the beginning of the Pyxie project—an Open Source software development initiative aimed at fully developing Python's potential as an XML-processing platform.

By the time you read this, the Pyxie project will have been launched at `http://www.pyxie.org`. It contains all the source code from this book along with more demo programs and applications for Windows and Linux.

There is a mailing list for Pyxie. To subscribe, send e-mail to `pyxie-request@starship.python.net` with the word `subscribe` in the body of the e-mail.

Get involved!

1.3 | Prerequisites

This book assumes that you have a high-level understanding of the ideas and syntax of XML. In particular, it would be helpful if you know the following:

- What an *element* is
- What *start-tags* and *end-tags* look like
- What the term "well formed XML" means
- What a *DTD* (Document Type Definition) is for

If you feel the need to brush up your XML, you might like to read my book *XML by Example—Building eCommerce Applications* available in this series.

This book assumes that you have some previous programming experience in a high-level language. Some exposure to object-oriented programming is desirable but not critical. If you have any exposure at all to the Java programming language, Perl, awk, Tcl, C++, C, JavaScript, Visual Basic, Delphi, or shell scripting languages, you are in good shape to attack this book.

If your programming background is minimal, fear not! Python is a ridiculously easy programming language to learn. Indeed, it makes an excellent first programming language for those approaching the discipline afresh.

If you are a seasoned programmer in one or more languages, I believe you will be pleasantly surprised at how easy, natural, and (okay, I'll say it) *beautiful* Python is.

1.4 | How to Read This Book

This book is intended to be read from start to finish. One of the techniques I have used to avoid long tracts of narrative about Python language features or support libraries is that I explain them as they pop up in the course of writing real programs.

As a consequence, skipping material might lead to gaps in the presentation of Python features. Even if you are very familiar with the subject matter in a section of the book, please give it a high-level scan to ensure that you pick up on any Python nuggets buried inside.

If your background is Java, you might like to read Appendix A before continuing. It introduces Python from a Java programming language perspective. Similarly, you might like to read Appendix B at this point if your background is in the Perl programming language.

1.5 | A Note about Platforms

My day-to-day programming environment is a mixture of Windows NT™ 4.0 and Red Hat® Linux 6.0. These are the two platforms that the software presented in this book has been developed and tested on.

Although the book focuses on Windows NT and Linux, the Python programs in the book and in the CD-ROM's root directory should run just fine on any Win32 or Unix® platform. There will obviously be the usual assortment of differences to do with default installation directories, differing shells, and so on. I have not attempted to cover all the eventualities in this book. To do so would make it twice as long and ten times more tedious to read.

1.6 | Structure of Code Samples

All examples of XML, program code, operating system commands, and so on are typeset in a fixed-width font. They may occur in the middle of a line `like this` or as a block of lines:

```
CD-ROM reference=1001.txt
Like this
And this
```

Every code sample in the book has a code reference number associated with it, such as the one in the example above (1001.txt). Each reference number corresponds to a filename in the book subdirectory of the accompanying CD-ROM. As well as being able to access the relevant file directly, you will find a linked set of HTML pages on the CD-ROM that will allow you to find a particular file easily. Point your Web browser at index.html on the CD-ROM and follow the link from there. This means that anything you find in the code samples will be easily available to you via cut-and-paste from the text files. You will not have to resort to typing anything.

Whenever an operating system command is illustrated in a section not specifically devoted to Windows or Linux, the command line will have a Windows-style C> prompt. Typing a file, for example, is denoted with a type command as shown here.

```
CD-ROM reference=1002.txt
C>type foo.xml
```

On Linux, your prompt will almost certainly be different, and you will use the cat command to type out a file.

Occasionally in Linux-specific sections, an indication of a command prompt is required. In these cases, a simple $ prompt is used like this:

```
CD-ROM reference=1003.txt
$cat foo.xml
```

1.7 | And Finally . . .

I am a programmer who learns best by example. If this is a reasonable description of how you learn best, you are in the right place.

If you have read this far, you will have surmised that this book is going to take a no-nonsense, snappy, and purposeful approach to XML processing with Python.

Ready? Let's go to work . . .

Installing Python

When learning a new language or software application, I like to have it installed and up and running on my machine so that I can "doodle" as I read. In anticipation of the possibility that you might like to doodle too, we start by getting Python and the XML package for Python up and running on your machine. We attack Python installation in this chapter and the installation of the XML package in the next chapter.

2.1 Getting a Python Distribution

Python is freely available in both source code and compiled form for nearly every hardware platform you can imagine. The center of activity in the Python world is http://www.python.org, and this is the place to go for up-to-the-minute Python information.

For your convenience, compiled distributions of Python version 1.5.2 for both Windows and Linux (Red Hat and Debian) are supplied on the accompanying CD-ROM.

2.2 | Installing the Software

Windows On the CD-ROM you will find windows `py152.exe`. This is a self-extracting setup program that will do all the work required to get Python up and running on any Win32 platform, that is, Windows 95™, Windows 98™, Windows 2000™, or Windows NT.

When you run `py152.exe`, you will see the introductory screen shown in figure 2–1.

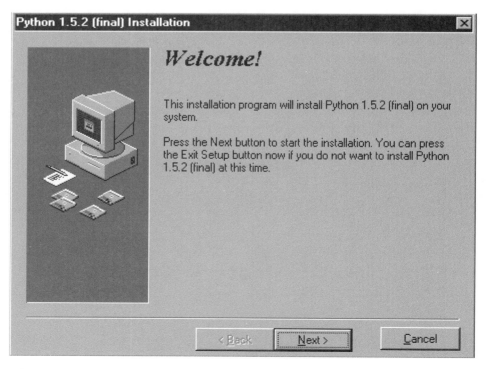

Figure 2–1   Python Windows Installation screen 1.

Click `Next`; the next screen asks you to select a destination directory, as shown in figure 2–2.

The default behavior is to install Python as part of the `Program Files` directory hierarchy. Installing Python to that location has the advantage that it is the Microsoft recommended destination for application software.

It has the disadvantage that you end up with long directory names for frequently visited locations such as Python's documentation directory `\Program Files\Python\Doc` or Python's tools directory `\Program Files\Python\Tools`. Depending on the Win32 platform or application you are using, it may be necessary to add double quotes to filenames to deal with the space between `Program` and `Files`, for example,

```
CD-ROM reference=2001.txt
cd "\Program Files\Python\Doc"
```

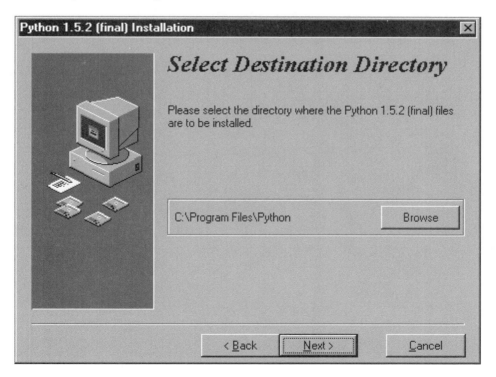

Figure 2–2 Python Windows Installation screen 2.

A subdirectory called \Python is another popular choice. Your call.
In this example installation, I have opted for the default directory
\Program Files\Python. Having clicked Next, you are asked to
select the components you want to install, as shown in figure 2–3.

Unless disk space is very tight, I suggest you install everything. At the
very least, you need the Python interpreter and library. The Tcl/Tk option
allows you to decide whether or not you wish the Python installation
to install the Tcl/Tk scripting language and GUI widget set.

The reason for this installation option is that Python provides an
interface to the Tk GUI building toolkit. This popular Python module
is known as Tkinter. The Tk GUI toolkit is part of a scripting lan-

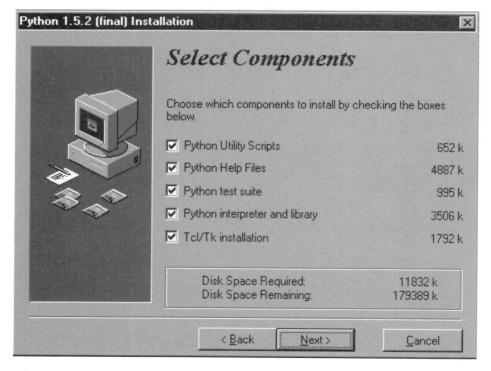

Figure 2–3   Python Windows Installation screen 3.

guage, known as `Tcl`, developed by John Ousterhout (`http://www`
`.scriptics.com`). Although Python has interfaces to numerous GUI
toolkits, the `Tk` toolkit has historically been favoured in the Python community. Python's integrated development environment, known as `idle`,
is based on Tk. If you want to be able to run `idle` or you want to develop
GUI applications with Python's Tk interface, then you should install this
component. You will not need `Tk` to run the programs in this book.

Having selected your components, click `Next`; the final question
you need to answer is presented, as shown in figure 2–4.

Here, you can decide where you would like the shortcuts to appear
under `Programs` in your start menu. Shortcuts are created to allow
you to run `Idle` and to run Python itself. There is also a handy
shortcut for accessing the Python documentation. The documentation for Python is supplied in HTML format, so you will need a Web
browser to view it.

Figure 2–4 Python Windows Installation screen 4.

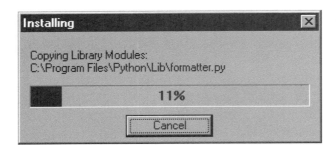

Figure 2–5   Python Windows Installation screen 5.

The documentation is also available in compiled HTMLHelp format on the CD-ROM in the file `windows/pythlp.chm`. This form of the Python documentation is the work of Hernán Martinez Foffani and Dale Nagata.

Clicking `Next` causes the installation to begin. Some minutes will pass as the installation program copies all the necessary files to your chosen installation directory, as shown in figure 2–5.

If you selected Tcl/Tk in your component selection earlier, you will now be asked if you want to install the Tcl/Tk package, as shown in figure 2–6.

If you say yes, the Tcl/Tk installation program runs. At this point you have one install program (`py152.exe`) that has called another

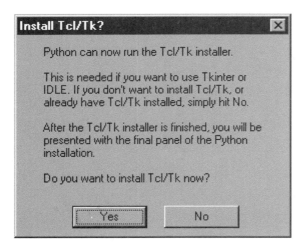

Figure 2–6   Python Windows Installation screen 6.

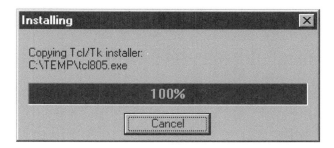

Figure 2–7   Python Windows Installation screen 7.

(`tcl805.exe`). If you happen to be switching around windows at this point (with `Alt-Tab`, for example) you will see that the main Python install program is still running. Its window looks like that in figure 2–7.

This window will remain until you finish the Tcl/Tk installation, the first screen of which is shown in figure 2–8.

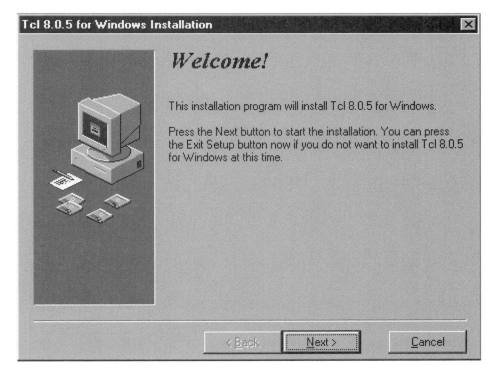

Figure 2–8   Tcl/Tk Installation screen 1.

As with the main Python install, the first step is to pick a destination directory, as shown in figure 2–9.

Unless disk space is very tight, I suggest selecting "full installation" from the screen shown in figure 2–10.

A full install only costs 5 megabytes. You can save some disk space by not installing the same scripts (roughly 500K) and the help files (roughly 1800K). Choose the custom installation option (see figure 2–10) if you want to deselect these components for installation.

That is pretty much it; click Next and installation will proceed apace, as shown in figure 2–11.

If you have opted to install the Tcl/Tk component, you will be asked to reboot Windows so that changes made can take effect.

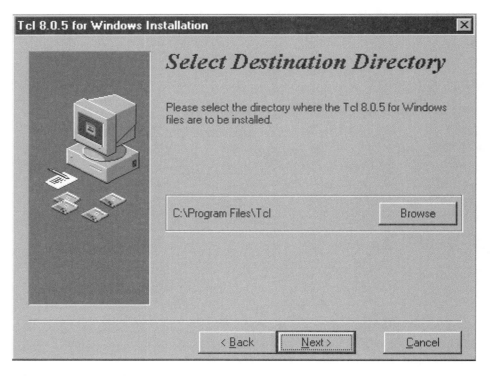

Figure 2–9   Tcl/Tk Installation screen 2.

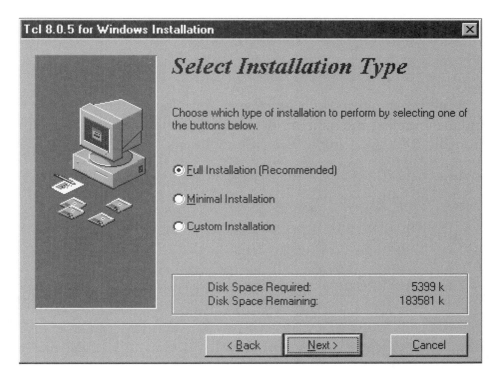

Figure 2–10 Tcl/Tk Installation screen 3.

Note: *Python treads lightly on Windows. By this I mean that it does not make extensive use of the registry and does not use anything more Windows-specific than a dynamically linked library. Python is also available in a form that deeply integrates it with Windows and makes an excellent Win32 system programming environment. This enhanced Python for Windows is known as PythonWin and is the work of Mark Hammond. It is also available on the CD-ROM accompanying this book, in the file* windows win32all-125.exe. *If you plan on doing Windows-specific programming such as MFC, COM, ActiveX™, and so on, you should consider installing this after installing the main Python distribution.*

None of the programs in this book makes use of the Windows-specific functionality of PythonWin, but all the example programs will work just fine with PythonWin.

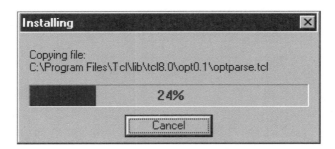

Figure 2–11   Tcl/Tk Installation screen 4.

To be able to invoke Python from the command line, you need to add the Python directory to your path. On Windows 95 and 98, you can do this by adding a line to your `autoexec.bat`. For example:

```
CD-ROM reference=2002.txt
path=%path%;"c:\program files\python"
```

On higher versions of Windows, you can add Python to your path by changing the `path` environment variable, which is available under Settings-Control Panel-System Properties-Environment.

To compile Python from the sources, you will need the file `pyth152.tgz` from the root directory of the CD-ROM.

Detailed instructions are provided in the `PCbuild/readme.txt` file. You will need Microsoft Visual C++ version 5 to use the project files provided. For other C compilers, instructions are provided in the `PC/readme.txt` file.

In summary, you need to open the workspace file `pcbuild.dsw` and build the `python15` and `python` projects in that order.   ■

Linux   On the CD-ROM you will find an RPM called `python-1.5.2-2.i386.rpm`, created by Oliver Andrich. A Debian™ package `python-base-1.5.1-7.deb` is also provided.

The 6.0 version of Red Hat Linux ships with Python version 1.5.1 preinstalled. To install Python 1.5.2 by updating the existing 1.5.1 Python to 1.5.2, execute the command:

```
CD-ROM reference=2003.txt
rpm -U python-1.5.2-2.i386.rpm
```

To compile Python from the sources, you will need the file `py152.tgz` from the root directory of the CD-ROM.

Detailed build instructions are provided in the `readme` file. In summary, having unpacked the distribution, you need to execute `./configure`, followed by `make`. ■

2.3 | Testing the Python Installation

The first thing we will do is prove that Python is installed correctly on your machine. Type `python` at your system's command prompt and press the RETURN key. On Windows, you should see something like this:

```
CD-ROM reference=2004.txt
Python 1.5.2 (#0, Apr 13 1999, 10:51:12) [MSC 32 bit (Intel)]
>>>-
```

On Linux, you should see something like this:

```
CD-ROM reference=2005.txt
Python 1.5.2 (#1, Apr 18 1999, 16:03:16)   [GCC pgcc-2.91.60
19981201
(egcs-1.1.1)  on linux2]
Copyright 1991-1995 Stichting Mathematisch Centrum, Amsterdam
>>>
```

The cursor should be flashing just to the right of the three greater than signs (>>>). This is Python's command prompt. You are now running Python interactively, and it is waiting for you to type in a command.

Let's do some simple math. At the Python command prompt, type

```
CD-ROM reference=2006.txt
1 + 2
```

and press the Return key. Python responds with (surprise, surprise):

```
CD-ROM reference=2007.txt
3
```

From here on, we will drop the use of "at the Python command prompt, type" and instead indicate that something should be entered on the command line by showing Python's >>> prompt like this:

```
CD-ROM reference=2008.txt
>>> 1 + 2
3
```

Let us now get Python to print a string for us:

```
CD-ROM reference=2008.txt
>>> print "Hello World"
```

Python responds with (shock, horror!):

```
CD-ROM reference=2010.txt
Hello World
```

Before we declare Python "up and running" on your machine, we will test to see if it can successfully locate some of the software modules that ship with Python. Having executed the following commands interactively,

```
CD-ROM reference=2011.txt
>>> import xmllib
>>> import os
>>> import sys
>>> print os.pathsep
>>> print sys.platform
```

you should see this on the Windows platform,

```
CD-ROM reference=2012.txt
;
win32
```

and you should see this on the Linux platform,

```
CD-ROM reference=2013.txt
:
linux2
```

By now, you may have guessed that the `os.pathsep` variable contains the string used to separate directory names in environment variables such as `path`. Here is my path on Windows. Notice the semicolon separator between the directory names.

```
CD-ROM reference=2014.txt
PATH=C:\WINNT\system32;C:\WINNT;C:\WIN32APP\TOOLKIT;c:\utils;
  c:\emacs\bin;"c:\program files\Python"
```

Here is my path on Linux. Note the colon separator between the directory names.

```
CD-ROM reference=2015.txt
PATH=/usr/bin:/usr/local/bin:/bin:/usr/bin:/usr/X11R6/bin
```

Now let us exit Python and return to the operating system shell. We can do that in a number of ways, some platform dependent, some not. Let's look at the platform-dependent ways first.

- You can type ^Z and press Return. (This is the "end of file" character on Windows.)

  Windows

- You can type F6 and press Return. (This causes a ^Z character to be entered.)

- You can type Ctrl-Break.

- You can type ^D. (This is the "end of file" character on Unix.)

  Linux

- You can type ^C. This is Python's interrupt command. It can also be used to stop executing Python programs.

- Python comes with a large collection of code *modules* that you can use in your programs. One of those modules, known as the `sys` module, provides a function for exiting a program. It can be used as follows:

```
CD-ROM reference=2016.txt
>>> import sys
>>> sys.exit()
```

We will be returning to the concept of *modules* in chapter 5, "Just Enough Python."

- You can raise an exception, known as SystemExit, as follows:

```
CD-ROM reference=2017.txt
>>> raise SystemExit
```

We will be returning to exceptions and exception handling later on in the book.

2.4 | Using a Python Program File

In the examples so far, we have used Python interactively by typing commands at the >>> command prompt for immediate execution. To wrap up the Python-existence proof, we will execute the same commands, but this time execute them from a file. Create a file foo.py in some convenient location with the following contents:

```
CD-ROM reference=2018.txt
print 1+2
print "Hello World"
```

At the command prompt of your system, type python foo.py and press Enter. The following output should appear:

```
CD-ROM reference=2019.txt
3
Hello World
```

You should now be back at your system's command prompt.

On Linux, a technique known as "pound bang"[1] can be used by many scripting languages, so that you can avoid having to type in, say,

```
CD-ROM reference=2020.txt
python foo.py
```

and instead, simply type

```
CD-ROM reference=2021.txt
foo.py
```

Here is what you do. Edit the file `foo.py` you created above and add this as the first line:

```
CD-ROM reference=2022.txt
#! /usr/bin/env python
```

As far as Python is concerned, this line is a comment because it starts with the # character. However, the Unix shell uses this line to find the program that will execute the script.

Change the permissions of the file so that it is an executable file.

```
CD-ROM reference=2023.txt
chmod +x foo.py
```

Now, execute the Python program by simply typing in its name:

```
CD-ROM reference=2024.txt
foo.py
```

```
3
Hello World
```

The above invocation assumes that `foo.py` is on your path. If you are in the same directory as `foo.py`, you may get the following message:

```
CD-ROM reference=2025.txt
foo.py: Command not found.
```

---

[1]It is called "pound bang" because of the nicknames for the # and ! characters commonly used in Unix circles.

If this happens, then the current directory is not in your path. Type this instead:

```
CD-ROM reference=2026.txt
./foo.py

3
Hello World
```

Any line or part of a line that begins with a # is ignored by Python—it is a comment. So, you can add "pound bang lines" for use on Unix without affecting the portability of your scripts to some other platform such as Windows. On Windows, the line will simply be ignored.   ■

Windows   On Windows it is possible to avoid having to type

```
CD-ROM reference=2027.txt
python foo.py
```

and instead simply type

```
CD-ROM reference=2028.txt
foo.py
```

On Windows, the .py file extension is associated with the Python executable program Python.exe. The Python install program creates this association on your behalf. Let's try it:

```
CD-ROM reference=2029.txt
C>foo.py

3
Hello World
```

Unfortunately, there is a problem with using this technique if you attempt to capture the output of a Python program using "shell redirection." Shell redirection is a common and very useful thing, so an explanation is in order. Execute the following command:

```
CD-ROM reference=2030.txt
C>Python foo.py > first.txt
```

Now, type the file `first.txt` to the screen. You will see that it has captured the output of the Python program:

```
CD-ROM reference=2031.txt
3
Hello World
```

Now, try executing the program like this:

```
CD-ROM reference=2032.txt
C>foo.py > first.txt
```

The command will seem to have worked okay, but look at the contents of the file `first.txt`.

```
CD-ROM reference=2033.txt
C>type first.txt
```

Nothing! This is not a bug in Python! It is simply a consequence of how Windows works. Programs invoked by means of their file association do not have an associated "output stream" on which to produce output.

Bottom line: leaving out the Python command name and just typing in the name of the Python program will cause difficulties if you are trying to redirect output to a file or to another program. My advice is to not use this facility on Windows and to always explicitly provide `python` as the name of the program to be invoked.

As you become more familiar with Python and start to read Python code, you will find that many programs begin with a line like this:

```
CD-ROM reference=2034.txt
#! /usr/bin/env python
```

Any line or part of a line that starts with a # is ignored by Python—it treats the text after # as a comment. The above syntax is used on Unix systems to associate scripts with the program that will execute them. The comment is harmless on Windows.

2.5 | In Conclusion

At this point, Python should be up and running on your machine. If you have problems getting it to work, please refer to the troubleshooting section of `http://www.pyxie.org`.

If you have Tcl/Tk installed, you might like to play with `idle`. You will find that it has an interactive mode similar to the ordinary interactive mode but with some very useful features added. I will leave it up to you to find out what these neat features are. You can use `idle` instead of the plain vanilla interactive mode with the samples in this book.

Windows users might like to install Mark Hammond's PythonWin now that Python is up and running. They will find it on the CD-ROM (`\windows\win32all-125.exe`). As with `idle`, PythonWin provides a Python interactive mode that can be used instead of the plain interactive mode with the samples in this book.

Installing the XML Package

The core Python 1.5.2 distribution ships with XML support in the form of a library known as `xmllib`—a simple, small, nonvalidating XML parser written in Python by Sjoerd Mullender. However, the bulk of the XML support for Python is in an add-on package developed and maintained by Python's XML special interest group (Python XML-SIG `http://www.python.org/sigs/xml-sig/`). It is this add-on package that we are most interested in, so let's get it up and running on your machine.

For your convenience, compiled distributions of the XML package for both Windows and Linux are supplied on the accompanying CD-ROM.

On the CD-ROM you will find windows `pythonXML.exe`. This is a Windows installation program for the XML package, created by Christian Tismer.

Windows

When you execute the program, you should see the introductory screen shown in figure 3–1.

If you click `Next` to continue the installation, you will be prompted for an installation directory. The default directory will be an `xml` sub-directory of your main Python directory, as shown in figure 3–2.

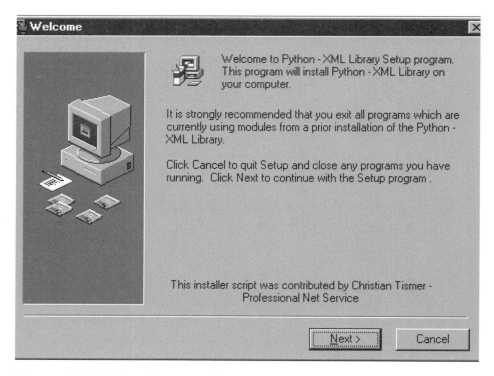

Figure 3–1 XML package installation screen 1.

The program can make a complete backup of any files overwritten during the installation. To enable the creation of a backup, select the Yes option in the screen shown in figure 3–3.

The installation will proceed without asking any further questions, as shown in figure 3–4. ▪

Linux   On the CD-ROM you will find an RPM called `python-xml-0.5.1-2.i386.rpm`. Install this RPM with the command:

```
CD-ROM reference=3001.txt
rpm -i python-xml-0.5.1-2.i386.rpm
```

The package will be installed into your `site-packages` subdirectory which, if you have Python installed in the default location, is at `/usr/lib/python1.5/site-packages`. ▪

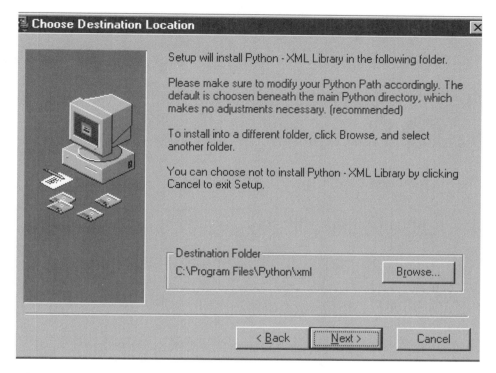

Figure 3–2 XML package installation screen 2.

Also on the CD-ROM you will find `unix/xml-0_5_1.tgz`. This is the source code for the XML package so that you can recompile from scratch if you prefer. The `readme` in the archive contains instructions for doing this. In summary, you need to execute `make -f Makefile.pre.in boot` followed by `make install`.

3.1 | Testing the XML Package Installation

Over the course of this book, we will be visiting pretty much every part of the XML package. Our focus here is on running a couple of simple tests to make sure the package is installed correctly on your machine.

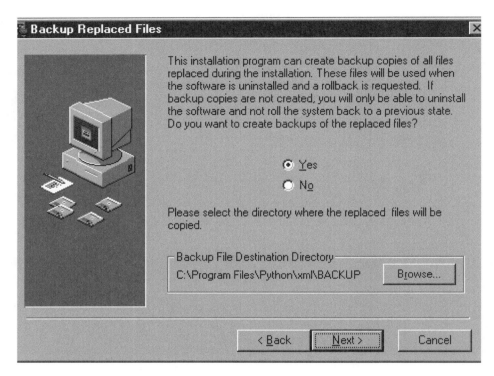

Figure 3–3 Creating a backup before installing the XML package.

3.2 | Testing the pyExpat Module

The `pyExpat` module is a Python module based on James Clark's nonvalidating XML parser written in C and known as `expat`. The `expat` XML parser is the basis for XML support in the Mozilla browser and in other scripting languages, including Perl and Tcl. For more information on `expat`, see `http://www.jclark.com`.

On the CD-ROM you will find a Python program `testpyexpat.py`. Executing `testpyexpat.py` should produce the following output:

```
CD-ROM reference=3002.txt
Element Employee has started
```

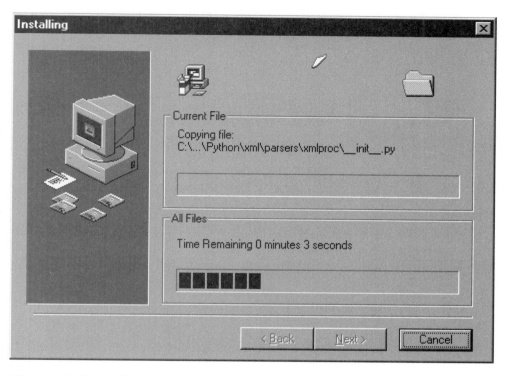

Figure 3–4 Installing the XML package.

```
Element Name has started
Element Given has started
Element Given has ended
Element Family has started
Element Family has ended
Element Name has ended
Element Extension has started
Element Extension has ended
Element Employee has ended
```

If this does not work, please refer to the troubleshooting section of
http://www.pyxie.org.

3.3 | Testing SAX Support

SAX is an acronym we will be using a lot in this book. It stands for Simple API for XML. An application programming interface (API) is simply a collection of named operations that a program can perform to interface with a system.

SAX is a standardized API for interfacing to XML parsers. By using SAX, you can change the XML parser used in a program *without* having to modify the program itself. Much more on SAX later on. Here, we just want to make sure it works on your machine.

On the CD-ROM you will find a Python program `testsax.py` that performs a simple test of the SAX part of the XML package. Executing `testsax.py` should produce the following output:

```
CD-ROM reference=3003.txt
Element Employee has started
Element Name has started
Element Given has started
Element Family has started
Element Extension has started
```

Table 3.1   Components in XML package

Component	Description
DOM	An implementation of the W3C's Document Object Model, by Stéfane Fermigier and Andrew Kuchling.
SAX	An implementation of the Simple API for XML, by Lars Marius Garshol.
PyExpat	A Python module providing access to James Clark's `expat` XML parser, by Jack Jansen.
xmlproc	A validating XML parser written in Python, by Lars Marius Garshol.

If this does not work, please refer to the troubleshooting section of `http://www.pyxie.org`.

The main components of the XML package covered in this book are listed in table 3.1.

At this point, the XML package should be up and running on your machine. You may want to take a moment to peruse the contents of the `xml` subdirectory. A number of demonstration programs are provided in the `demo` subdirectory; you may like to play with these a little before moving on.

Tools of the Trade

4

A s XML continues to flood the planet, XML utilities such as parsers, editors, and viewers are beginning to rank right up there alongside text editors and zip archivers in terms of indispensable utility programs for software developers. In this chapter, we look at some utility programs I have created for working with XML.

4.1 The XMLN and XMLV Parsing Utilities

xmln is a nonvalidating XML parsing utility built on top of James Clark's expat. xmlv is a validating XML parsing utility built on top of Richard Tobin's rxp parser. Executable versions plus the source code for both utilities, as well as the expat and rxp distributions, can be found on the CD-ROM.

So, what do these utilities do and why might you want to use them? Read on . . .

4.1.1   *Purpose of XMLN and XMLV*

The idea behind the creation of `xmln` and `xmlv` is to have validating and nonvalidating XML parsing utilities that (a) generate simple output suitable for input into other programs and (b) fit on a single floppy disk for easy deployment wherever your XML work takes you.

Secondary considerations included making the utilities easy to install and fast. Thanks to the excellence of the `expat` and `rxp` parsers, these goals were easily achieved. Each executable stands alone both on Windows and on Linux. Furthermore, no setup process is required. Just copy and run!

4.1.2   *The PYX Notation*

The output format from the utilities is purposely kept very simple. A line of output is generated for each of the following constructs discovered in an XML document:

- Start of an element
- End of an element
- An attribute
- Character data
- A processing instruction

The first character of each line serves to indicate what type of line it is, as shown in table 4.1.

To give you an idea of the output format, here is a simple XML document along with the output created by parsing it with `xmln`.

```
CD-ROM reference=4001.txt
C>type people.xml

<Person sex="male">
```

```
<?foo bar?>
<FamilyName>Mc Grath</FamilyName>
<GivenName>Sean</GivenName>
<e-mail>sean@digitome.com</e-mail>
</Person>
```

Table 4.1   Line-type indicators

First character	Construct
(	Start-tag
)	End-tag
-	Character data
A	Attribute
?	Processing Instruction

C>**xmln people.xml**

```
(Person
Asex male
-\n
?foo bar
-\n
(FamilyName
-Mc Grath
)FamilyName
-\n
(GivenName
-Sean
)GivenName
-\n
(e-mail
-sean@digitome.com
)e-mail
-\n
)Person
```

The output makes it easy to see exactly what the XML parser has made of the file. The simple, line-oriented output format is also suitable for input into a whole variety of text-processing tools—including Python, of course. We will see some examples later on in this chapter. Let's get the utilities installed on your machine first.

4.1.3   *Installing XMLN*

Windows   On the CD-ROM you will find `windows/xmln.exe`. Copy it to some suitable directory—preferably one that is on your path so that you can invoke `xmln` from any directory. I keep mine in a directory called `\utils`, which I have added to my path and which is heavily stocked with little utility programs such as `xmln`. ■

Linux   On the CD-ROM you will find `linux/xmln`. Copy it to some suitable directory such as `/usr/local/bin`. ■

4.1.4   *Installing XMLV*

Windows   On the CD-ROM you will find `windows/xmlv.exe`. Copy it to some suitable directory on your machine—the same directory that contains `xmln`, for example. ■

Linux   On the CD-ROM you will find `linux/xmlv`. Copy it to some suitable directory such as `/usr/local/bin`. ■

4.1.5   *Using XMLN*

The `xmln` utility provides a quick and easy way to parse and tokenize arbitrary, well-formed XML files. The easiest way to invoke `xmln` is to specify a filename on the command line.

```
CD-ROM reference=4002.txt
C>type sean.xml
```

```
<Person>
```

```
<FamilyName>Mc Grath</FamilyName>
<GivenName>Sean</GivenName>
<e-mail>sean@digitome.com</e-mail>
</Person>
```

C>**xmln sean.xml**

```
(Person
-\n
(FamilyName
-Mc Grath
)FamilyName
-\n
(GivenName
-Sean
)GivenName
-\n
(e-mail
-sean@digitome.com
)e-mail
-\n
)Person
```

As you can see, xmln has parsed the file, split it into its component parts in terms of start-tags, end-tags, and data. These separate tokens have been output one per line.

xmln can also process XML data arriving on standard input via a pipe.

```
CD-ROM reference=4003.txt
```
C>**type sean.xml | xmln**

```
(Person
-\n
(FamilyName
-Mc Grath
...
```

The ellipsis in the output means that only the first few lines of data content have been reproduced.

Shell redirection also works as you would expect.

```
CD-ROM reference=4004.txt
```

```
C>xmln < sean.xml

(Person
-\n
(FamilyName
-Mc Grath
...
```

One final point about xmln: it understands wildcards on Windows. (On Unix, the operating system looks after filename wildcard expansion, but on Windows, each application has to deal with it itself.) This feature can be very useful when all you want to determine is whether or not XML files in a collection are well formed. Both xmln and xmlv write normal output to "standard output," and write error messages to "standard error." So, by redirecting standard output, you will simply see any error messages.

Here is an sample invocation of xmln in which the two XML files test.xml and sean.xml in a directory are parsed with a single command.

CD-ROM reference=4005.txt

```
C>type test.xml

<Greeting>
Hello World
</Greeting>

C>type sean.xml

<Person>
<FamilyName>Mc Grath</FamilyName>
<GivenName>Sean</GivenName>
<e-mail>sean@digitome.com</e-mail>
</Person>

C>xmln *.xml
(Person
-\n
(FamilyName
-Mc Grath
)FamilyName
```

```
-\n
(GivenName
-Sean
)GivenName
-\n
(e-mail
-sean@digitome.com
)e-mail
-\n
)Person
(Greeting
-\n
-Hello World
-\n
)Greeting
```

To do a validation check only, we can dispense with standard output. The syntax for doing this is slightly different between Windows and Linux.

```
CD-ROM reference=4006.txt
C>xmln *.xml >nul
```

Windows

```
CD-ROM reference=4007.txt
$xmln *.xml >/dev/null
```

Linux

To test the validation check, we introduce an error into the file sean.xml.

```
CD-ROM reference=4008.txt
C>type sean.xml

<!DOCTYPE Person SYSTEM "Person.dtd">
<Person>
<FamilyName>Mc Grath</FamilyName>
<GivenName>Sean</GivenName>
<e-mail>sean@digitome.com</e-mail>
</PErson>
```

Note the incorrect capitalization in the `Person` end-tag. XML is case sensitive and therefore treats `Person` and `PErson` as different element type names.

Windows

```
CD-ROM reference=4009.txt
C>xmln *.xml > nul

File:'sean.xml' Error:'mismatched tag' on line '6'
```

Linux

```
CD-ROM reference=4010.txt
$xmln *.xml > /dev/null

File:'sean.xml' Error:'mismatched tag' on line '6'
```

4.1.6 *Using XMLV*

`xmlv` can be invoked in exactly the same way as `xmln` and produces exactly the same PYX notation as output. The difference between them is that `xmlv` contains a validating XML parser. It will therefore generate an error message if any of XML's validity constraints are violated. The main thing you will notice is that it complains if it cannot locate a DTD. To be accurate, `xmlv` will downgrade the parse to a nonvalidating parse if it cannot find a DTD.

```
CD-ROM reference=4011.txt
C>type sean.xml

<Person>
<FamilyName>Mc Grath</FamilyName>
<GivenName>Sean</GivenName>
<e-mail>sean@digitome.com</e-mail>
</Person>

C>xmlv sean.xml

Warning: Document has no DTD, validating abandoned
```

```
 (detected at end of prolog of document
file:/C:/xpp/sean.xml)
(Person
-\n
(FamilyName
-Mc Grath
)FamilyName
-\n
(GivenName
-Sean
)GivenName
-\n
(e-mail
-sean@digitome.com
)e-mail
-\n
)Person
```

Here is a DTD suitable for parsing `sean.xml`.

```
CD-ROM reference=4012.txt
C>type person.dtd

<!ELEMENT Person (FamilyName,GivenName,e-mail)>
<!ELEMENT FamilyName (#PCDATA)>
<!ELEMENT GivenName (#PCDATA)>
<!ELEMENT e-mail (#PCDATA)>
```

Here is `sean.xml` changed to reference this DTD.

```
CD-ROM reference=4013.txt
C>type sean.xml

<!DOCTYPE Person SYSTEM "Person.dtd">
<Person>
<FamilyName>Mc Grath</FamilyName>
<GivenName>Sean</GivenName>
<e-mail>sean@digitome.com</e-mail>
</Person>
```

With the DTD in place, `xmlv` will parse the file without comment.

```
CD-ROM reference=4014.txt
```

```
C>xmlv sean.xml

(Person
-\n
(FamilyName
-Mc Grath
)FamilyName
-\n
(GivenName
-Sean
)GivenName
-\n
(e-mail
-sean@digitome.com
)e-mail
-\n
)Person
```

4.2 | Simple XML-Processing Tasks with XMLN and XMLV

The line-oriented output of xmln and xmlv lends itself to processing with simple, common shell utilities such as wc, grep and awk. Unix users already have these as part of the standard Unix toolset. For Windows users, the GNU versions of the grep and awk utilities can be found in the windows subdirectory of the CD-ROM.

In the following sections, xmln is used to perform useful work by combining its ability to parse and tokenize XML with generic line-oriented text-processing tools. In all cases, xmlv could just have easily been used to perform a validating parse.

In the examples that follow, we illustrate various processing tasks on the following XML file.

```
CD-ROM reference=4015.txt
C>type staff.xml

<staff>
<department name="Technical">
```

```
<person>
<title>Technical Director</title>
<name>
<given>Sean</given>
<family>Mc Grath</family>
</name>
<email>sean@digitome.com</email>
<web>http://www.digitome.com/sean.html</web>
</person>
<person>
<title>Senior Software Engineer</title>
<name>
<given>Neville</given>
<family>Bagnall</family>
</name>
<email>neville@digitome.com</email>
<web>http://www.digitome.com/neville.html</web>
</person>
<person>
<title>Software Engineer</title>
<name>
<given>Noel</given>
<family>Duffy</family>
</name>
<email>noel@digitome.com</email>
<web>http://www.digitome.com/noel.html</web>
</person>
<person>
<title>Software Engineer</title>
<name>
<given>John</given>
<family>Coleman</family>
</name>
<email>john@digitome.com</email>
<web>http://www.digitome.com/john.html</web>
</person>
</department>
</staff>
```

4.2.1 *Task 1: Count the Number of Employees*

We know that each employee element will start with a start-tag token of the form "(person" and an end-tag token of the form

")person". We can use `grep` to output lines that match either of these two patterns. Both will give us the correct result.

Windows

```
CD-ROM reference=4016.txt
C>xmln staff.xml | grep (person

(person
(person
(person
(person


C>xmln staff.xml | grep )person
)person
)person
)person
)person
```

Linux

It is a good idea to use quotes to make sure the shell does not misinterpret the parentheses.

```
CD-ROM reference=4017.txt

$xmln staff.xml | grep "(person"

(person
(person
(person
(person
$xmln staff.xml | grep ")person"
)person
)person
)person
)person
```

By inspection, the answer we are looking for is 4 because there are four lines of output. We can get a numeric answer in a number of ways. First, we could use the common `wc` utility to count the lines.

Windows

```
CD-ROM reference=4018.txt
C>xmln staff.xml | grep (person | wc -l
```

4

```
CD-ROM reference=4019.txt
$xmln staff.xml | grep "(person" | wc -l
```

Linux

4

The `grep` command has a `-c` option that will do the work for us by counting the number of matches.

```
CD-ROM reference=4020.txt
C>xmln staff.xml | grep -c (person
```

Windows

4

```
C>xmln staff.xml | grep -c )person
```

4

```
CD-ROM reference=4021.txt
$xmln staff.xml | grep -c "(person"
```

Linux

4

```
$xmln staff.xml | grep -c ")person"
```

4

4.2.2 *Task 2: Strip Tags and Output Data Content Only*

The PYX notation signals data content by means of lines beginning with the "-" character. Our first shot at a `grep` pattern to output data content might be this:

```
CD-ROM reference=4022.txt
C>xmln staff.xml | grep "-"
```

However, this command does not ensure that the matching lines have the "-" character at the beginning of the line, and so we may get *false positive* pattern matches.

```
CD-ROM reference=4023.txt
C>type foo.xml

<Appendix-Item>
Hello World
</Appendix-Item>

C>xmln foo.xml | grep "-"

(Appendix-Item
-\n
-Hello World
-\n
)Appendix-Item
```

The element type name `Appendix-Item` contains a minus sign and thus has caused two false matches in the above output.

We can instruct `grep` to *anchor* the pattern to the beginning of the line with the "^" character. Since any line that starts with a "-" is guaranteed to be character data, this approach removes the false positive hits.

```
CD-ROM reference=4024.txt
C>xmln foo.xml | grep "^-"
-\n
-Hello World
-\n
```

Here is what happens when we use the above `grep` pattern with the `staff.xml` file.

```
CD-ROM reference=4025.txt
C>xmln staff.xml | grep "^-"
-\n
-\n
-\n
-Technical Director
-\n
-\n
```

```
-Sean
-\n
-Mc Grath
-\n
-\n
-sean@digitome.com
-\n
-http://www.digitome.com/sean.html
...
```

Note the number of lines that consist of nothing but \n. This is PYX notation indicating a new line in the input XML. XML, unlike HTML, considers all such new line indicators to be significant, and the XML parser passes them to the application.

We are nearly there. All we need now is some way to strip the first character from each line—the "-". One way to do this is to use the awk utility. awk is a simple scripting language that originated with the Unix text processing system. awk in many ways paved the way for the development of languages like Python.

awk automatically processes its input, line-by-line. This makes it ideal for command-line "one liners" that process PYX. By "one-liners" I mean programs that fit on a single line passed to awk as a command-line parameter. The GNU version of awk, known as gawk, is provided on the accompanying CD-ROM for Windows users. If you are using Unix, you almost certainly already have awk and perhaps gawk as well on your machine.

First, we need to address a small but important difference in the syntax required for awk one-liners between Windows and Linux.

Here is the Windows version of the awk one-liner to print out the data content of an XML file. It uses the substr function to remove the first character from each line. Note the double quotes that surround the gawk command string.

Windows

```
CD-ROM reference=4026.txt
C>xmln staff.xml | grep "^-" | gawk "{print substr($0,2)}"

\n
\n
\n
```

```
Technical Director
\n
\n
Sean
\n
Mc Grath
\n
\n
sean@digitome.com
\n
http://www.digitome.com/sean.html
```

Here is the Linux version of the awk one-liner to print out the data content of an XML file. Note the single quotes—not double quotes—surrounding the gawk command string. The use of single quotes is necessary to ensure that the shell does not attempt to interpret $0 as a reference to an environment variable.

Linux

```
CD-ROM reference=4027.txt
$xmln staff.xml | grep '^-' | gawk '{print substr($0,2)}'
```

Note the $0 variable in the above Awk program. In awk, the $0 variable refers to the entire current line of input.

4.2.3   *Task 3: Generate a Report Showing the Nested Structure of an XML Document*

This task is a little more involved but can still be made to fit on one line with awk. This is approaching the size when the Awk script really belongs in a file to be invoked with the -f option! Personally, once I begin to feel an urge to put an Awk program in a file, I switch to Python; I would urge you to do the same. More on that point later in this chapter. Here is the program.

```
CD-ROM reference=4028.txt
C>xmln staff.xml | gawk "/^\(/ {pad++} /^\)/ {pad—}
{for(x=pad;x>0;x—)printf FS; print NR,$0}"

  (staff
```

```
 -\n
  (department
  Aname Technical
  -\n
   (person
   -\n
    (title
    -Technical Director
   )title
   -\n
    (name
    -\n
     (given
     -Sean
    )given
    -\n
     (family
     -Mc Grath
    )family
    -\n
    ...
```

Notice that each line has been indented to reflect the hierarchical structure of the XML document. The program works by incrementing a variable called `pad` for every start-tag and decrementing it for every end-tag. Each line of output is then preceded by a number of spaces equal in value to the `pad` variable.

4.2.4 *XML Report Writing with Awk*

Awk can do arithmetic—which can be very useful for simple XML report writing tasks. Consider the problem of working out the total cost of the items in the following stock file.

```
CD-ROM reference=4029.txt
C>type stock.xml

<stock>
<item name = "widget" cost = "10"/>
<item name = "grommit" cost = "34"/>
<item name = "doodaa" cost = "12"/>
</stock>
```

Let us start by inspecting the PYX output of `xmln`.

```
CD-ROM reference=4030.txt
C>xmln stock.xml

(stock
-\n
(item
Acost 10
Aname widget
)item
-\n
(item
Acost 34
Aname grommit
)item
-\n
(item
Acost 12
Aname doodaa
)item
-\n
)stock
```

Notice that lines containing attribute information start with the letter "A." The name of the attribute starts immediately after the A and ends with the first space. The rest of the line contains the attribute value.

Note also that the cost attribute precedes the name attribute in the output even though cost comes after name in the item start-tags of the XML file. The order in which attributes appear in a start-tag is not significant in XML. However, it is useful if they always appear in the same order in an output notation such as PYX. Both xmln and xmlv sort the attributes into alphabetical order prior to output.

Here is an awk one-liner that prints out the name and value of the attributes in the above file.

```
CD-ROM reference=4031.txt
C>xmln stock.xml | gawk "/^A/ {print substr($1,2),$2}"

cost 10
name widget
cost 34
```

```
name grommit
cost 12
name doodaa
```

In English, this command means "generate PYX from the file `stock.xml` using `xmln`. Pipe the PYX output into `gawk`. For every line of PYX that starts with an 'A' character, execute the print statement."

Note the use of the `$1` and `$2` variables. These refer to the first word and the second word in the current input line, respectively. The `print` statement uses the `substr` function to strip off the first character A from the first word, which yields the attribute name. The `$2` variable refers to the attribute value.

We can arrange to print out just the values associated with `cost` attributes by expanding the match pattern to include the name `cost`.

```
CD-ROM reference=4032.txt
C>xmln stock.xml | gawk "/^Acost/ {print $2}"

10
34
12
```

Finally, we need a variable to keep track of the cumulative total cost.

```
CD-ROM reference=4033.txt
C>xmln stock.xml | gawk "/^Acost/ {total+=$2} END {print
  total}"

56
```

Here is how it works. Awk programs consist of a collection of pattern/action pairs. Formatting script over multiple lines makes the structure of the program clearer. See the comments below for an explanation of how the script works.

```
CD-ROM reference=4034.txt
/* If any input line matches the pattern ^Acost execute
  {total +=$2} */
/^Acost/ {total+=$2}

/* At the end of the file, the magic END pattern is matched.
```

```
    When this happens, print out the accumulated total */
END {print total}
```

4.2.5   *A Word about One-Liners*

It is such good fun writing one-liners that even the most conscientious software developer can end up producing utterly impenetrable code! If you start using Awk for this sort of processing and see your scripts heading for more than a few lines of code, stop! It will be much easier to understand, debug, and maintain your code if you write it in Python.

That said, one-liners are a very useful tool. They will serve you well in XML processing *as long as* you do not stretch the length of a line too far.

4.3 | The GetURL Utility—A Web Resource Retriever in Python

On machines with Internet or intranet connections, it is useful to be able to point the `xmln` and `xmlv` utilities at arbitrary URLs. Python has excellent support for Internet protocols. The following simple program retrieves the contents of an arbitrary URL and outputs its contents on standard output.

```
CD-ROM reference=4035.txt
C>type geturl.py

"""
Simple utility to retrieve a URL and print
its contents to standard output.
"""
import sys
import os
from urllib   import urlretrieve, urlcleanup

def geturl(url):
    try:
            filename,headers = urlretrieve(url)
```

```
        print open(filename,"r").read()
    finally:
        urlcleanup()

if __name__ == "__main__":
    geturl(sys.argv[1])
```

Here is an example of the `geturl` utility in action. You simply give it a URL and it does the rest.

```
CD-ROM reference=4036.txt
C>python geturl.py http://www.digitome.com/Hello.xml

<?xml version = "1.0" encoding="ISO-8859-1"?>
<Greeting>
Hello World
</Greeting>
```

The `xmln` and `xmlv` utilities can work with XML content provided on standard input, so it is easy to pipe the contents of an arbitrary URL into them.

```
CD-ROM reference=4037.txt
C>python geturl.py http://www.digitome.com/Hello.xml | xmln

(Greeting
-\n
-Hello World
-\n
)Greeting
```

Of course, `geturl` can also be used to create local copies of Internet resources.

```
CD-ROM reference=4038.txt
C>python geturl.py http://www.digitome.com/Hello.xml >
Hello.xml
C>type Hello.xml
<?xml version = "1.0" encoding="ISO-8859-1"?>
<Greeting>
Hello World
</Greeting>
```

4.4 | The PYX2XML Utility: Converting PYX to XML

The pyx2xml utility program converts PYX notation to XML. This utility greatly facilitates the development of XML to XML conversion programs. Combined with awk and other Unix line-oriented utilities, it is capable of a surprising amount of useful work.

```
CD-ROM reference=4039.txt
"""
Convert PYX to XML
"""
import string

def PYXDecoder(s):
    """
    Decode the escaped line ends and tabs in PYX notation.
    """
    s = string.replace(s,"\\n","\n")
    s = string.replace(s,"\\t","\t")
    return s

def pyx2xml(fo):
    """
    Treat contents of file object fo as PYX.
    Create XML output.
    """
    L = fo.readline()
    while L:
        if L[0] == "(":
            # Grab element type name.
            etn = L[1:-1]
            # Process any attributes that follow.
            attrs = {}
            L = fo.readline()
            while L[0] == "A":
                # An attribute - grab name and value
                  parts.
                i = string.index (L," ")
                aName = L[1:i]
                aValue = PYXDecoder(L[i+1:-1])
                # Store in dictionary.
                attrs[aName] = aValue
                L = fo.readline()
```

```
        if len(attrs)==0:
            # No attributes -> simple start-tag
            sys.stdout.write("<%s>" % etn)
        else:
             # Attributes present, separate with
               spaces.
            sys.stdout.write ("<%s " % etn)
            for (a,v) in attrs.items():
                sys.stdout.write ('%s = "%s"' %
                  (a,v))
            sys.stdout.write (">")
        continue
    if L[0] == ')':
        # End-tag
        etn = L[1:-1]
        sys.stdout.write ("</%s>" % etn)
    elif L[0] == '-':
        # Character data
        sys.stdout.write (PYXDecoder(L[1:-1]))
    elif L[0] == '?':
        # Processing instruction
        target = L[1:i]
        data = L[i+1:-1]
        sys.stdout.write ("%s %s?" % (target,data))
    L = fo.readline()

if __name__ == "__main__":
    import sys
    if len(sys.argv)==1:
        pyx2xml(sys.stdin)
    else:
        pyx2xml(open(sys.argv[1],"r"))
```

Here is an example of "round tripping" an XML file through PYX and back to XML again.

```
CD-ROM reference=4040.txt
C>type small.xml

<small>
A small <b>XML</b> file
</small>

C>xmln small.xml | python pyx2xml.py
<small>
A small <b>XML</b> file
<small>
```

Here is an example of how a combination of awk and pyx2xml can be used for XML-aware search and replace. The Awk program below uses PYX notation to turn the element type name small into the element type name large.

```
CD-ROM reference=4041.txt
C>type small2big.awk

/* convert PYX for small start-tag to PYX for big start-tag
*/
/\(small/ {print "(big"; getline}

/* convert PYX for small end-tag to PYX for big end-tag */
/\)small/ {print ")big";getline}

/* for all other records, print the record unchanged */
{print $0}
```

The following pipe illustrates how the combination of xmln, awk, and the pyx2xml utility get the job done.

```
CD-ROM reference=4042.txt
C>xmln small.xml | awk -f small2big.awk | python pyx2xml.py

<big>
A small <b>XML</b> file
</big>
```

4.5 | The C3 Utility: An XML Document Editor/Viewer in Python

It is very useful during XML program development to be able to see the tree structure of an XML file. The C3 is a Python utility that is part of the Pyxie Open Source Project that does exactly that. It is implemented with the wxPython cross-platform GUI toolkit, which we will use extensively in this book.

The wxPython toolkit is a wrapping of the cross-platform GUI toolkit for C++ programmers, which is called wxWindows. The wxPython toolkit is the work of Robin Dunne (`http://alldunn.com/wxPython`). The wxWindows toolkit is the work of Julian Smart (`http://www.wxwindows.org`). Before executing the C3 application, we will need to get wxPython up and running on your machine.

4.5.1 *Installing wxPython and the C3 XML Editor/Viewer*

On the CD-ROM, you will find `windows/wxPython-2-1b3.exe`. This is the wxPython installation program.

Windows

This is a self-extracting distribution program. When you run it you should see the following setup screen (figure 4–1).

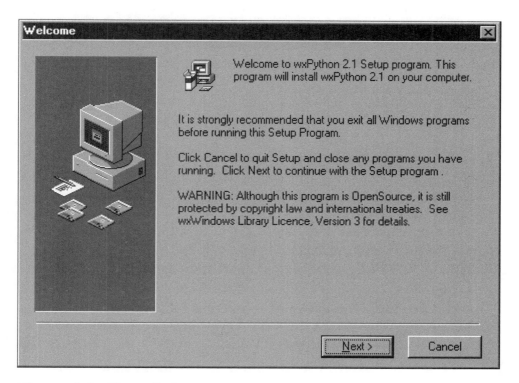

Figure 4–1   The wxPython setup process.

Figure 4–2   Selecting a directory for wxPython.

The installation program first seeks out the location of Python on your machine and offers to install wxPython as a subdirectory of that location. Unless you have good reason not to, this is a sensible place to put wxPython (see figure 4–2).

That is basically it. Clicking the Next button causes the installation process to commence. See figure 4–3.

You may like to run the wxPython demonstration program to get a feel for the capabilities of wxPython. A wxPython menu has been added to the start menu. In this menu you will find a Run the DEMO option. Alternatively, you can execute demo.py from the wxpython/demo directory. ■

Linux   On the CD-ROM you will find linux/wxPython-2-1b1-2-i386.rpm. To install this RPM, execute the command:

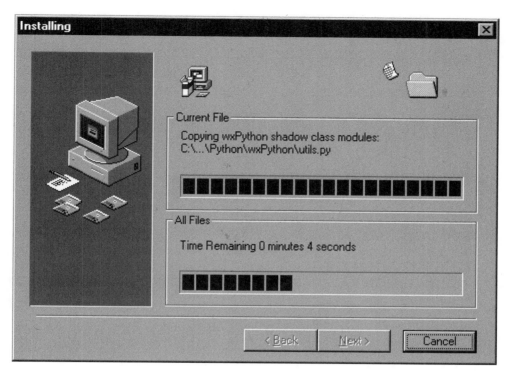

Figure 4–3   The wxPython installation in progress.

```
CD-ROM reference=4043.txt
rpm wxPython-2_161-2_i386.rpm
```

The software will be installed into your /usr/lib/python1.5/ site-packages directory in a subdirectory called wxPython.

You may want to run the demonstration program demo/demo.py to get a feel for the capabilities of wxPython.

The remaining task is to simply copy the c3.py utility from the CD-ROM to some suitable location on your hard disk. You might like to load some of the XML files from the CD-ROM to test out C3.

When c3.py runs, it displays a split pane window, as shown in figure 4–4.

An XML file is opened from the File-Open dialog in the normal way. When first displayed, the entire structure is collapsed to the root element in a tree structure in the left-hand pane. See figure 4–5.

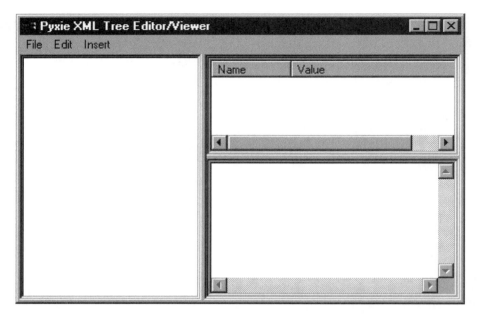

Figure 4–4   The c3 XML viewer application window.

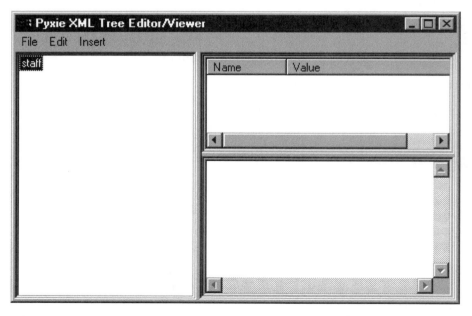

Figure 4–5   A collapsed XML file viewed with the C3 utility.

Figure 4–6 shows the `staff.xml` file with the first level of hierarchy expanded.

You can expand or collapse the levels at will by clicking the + or - box icons in the left-hand pane. See figure 4–7.

C3 can be used to edit as well as display XML. For full details of its capabilities, see chapter 17.

4.6 | In Conclusion

Parsing and basic processing of XML is like falling off a log once you have the `xmln` and `xmlv` to hand. As the book progresses, we will be developing many programs that work with the PYX notation that these utilities produce. In particular, the Pyxie library developed in chapter 12 is heavily based on the PYX notation.

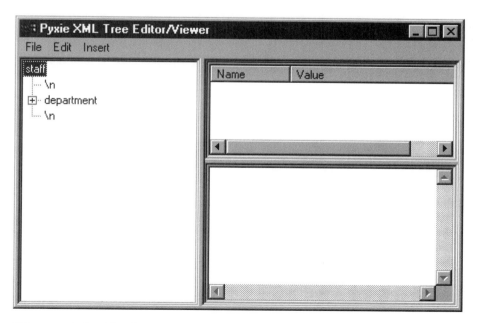

Figure 4–6   The first level of hierarchical detail in staff.xml.

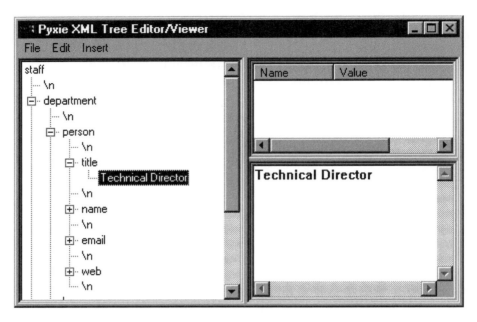

Figure 4–7   The staff.xml file viewed with the C3 XML viewer.

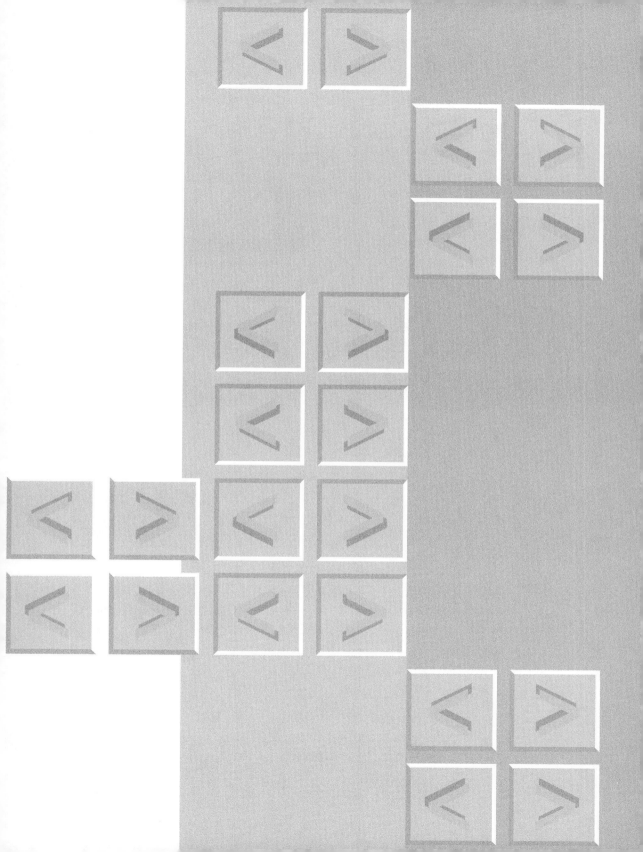

Just Enough Python

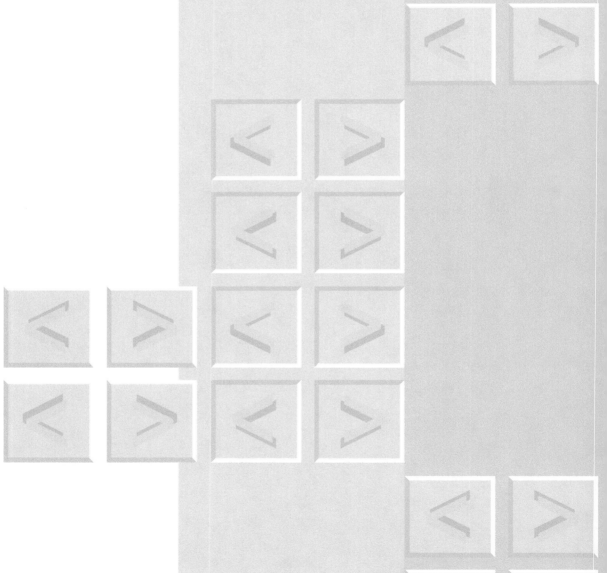

T his chapter provides an overview of the Python language, giving just enough detail to allow us to proceed into real-world XML processing with Python. Python is a multifaceted, general-purpose programming language with a particular affinity for text processing. Naturally, any high-level overview of such a versatile beast is doomed to be subjective. Therefore, be warned, this chapter is subjective! Here are my eight favorite bullet points about Python.

Python is:

- WYSIWYG
- Object oriented
- Cleanly designed
- Freely available
- Open
- XML friendly
- Interactive
- Interpreted

5.1 | Introduction

We start this chapter with a brief explanation of each of these bullet points and then proceed to a more thorough treatment that makes up the bulk of this chapter. By the time you have worked through this chapter, you should have a good "30,000 feet" overview of Python.

Obviously, full coverage of Python would take a lot more than the one chapter we are affording it here. I have omitted details that are not directly relevant to XML processing. Also, some difficult-to-classsify but important details have been relegated to chapter 6. I have also purposely left out some features that I know will crop up later on in the text, where they will be explained "on-the-fly."

Now, back to those eight bullet points . . .

5.1.1   *Python Is a WYSIWYG Language*

The term "WYSIWYG" may have caught you by surprise as it is not usually associated with programming languages. The term WYSI-WYG—What You See Is What You Get—is generally used to describe word processing and desktop publishing software where the on-screen representation of the printed page is very close to the final page output on paper.

Python is dubbed WYSIWYG for a different reason. Python uses the *indentation* of lines of code to work out how the lines should be grouped together for execution. This contrasts with most other languages, which use `begin`/`end` keywords or pairs of matching braces to represent code grouping.

The immediate consequence of Python's WYSIWYG approach is that simply glancing at how statements are indented relative to each other allows you to figure out how the statements are grouped together. The lack of block keywords or delimiters may shock you at first. I know it shocked me! However, once you see how it works, I promise you, you will be pleasantly surprised at how powerful and transparent this approach to statement grouping is.

5.1.2 *Python Is Object Oriented*

Python takes the ideas of object-oriented programming very seriously indeed. Pretty much everything in Python is an object. Although it is possible to write non-object-oriented software in Python, you will find that Python has a way of gently steering you toward an object-oriented programming style. If you are not familiar with the concepts of object-oriented programming, you might like to take a look at the tutorial available at `http://www.cyberdyne-object-sys.com/oofaq2/` before proceeding.

XML processing is well suited to an object-oriented programming style, and indeed some of the industry-standard XML APIs we will be discussing, such as SAX and DOM, have a strongly object-oriented flavor.

5.1.3 *Python Is Cleanly Designed*

In Python, a handful of core design ideas have been used and reused over and over again. The design is reminiscent of a well-designed mechanical device in that it has a minimal number of "moving parts." As a consequence, the language has very few "gotchas." In other words, there are very few occasions when some subtlety inherent in the Python programming language will cause you to scratch your head and wonder "what is going on?"

Moreover, the fact that a number of key design ideas are used and reused suggests that expertise acquired in one aspect of Python will most likely mean that other parts of Python make complete sense as a consequence.

5.1.4 *Python Is Freely Available*

Python is freely available in both source and executable form for every major computing platform on Earth. You are free to take the source code and do essentially anything you like with it—including incorporating it into commercial applications.

5.1.5   *Python Is Open*

The word "open" has a number of connotations in the Python world. First, Python is open in the sense that it assumes that the programmer knows what he or she is doing. Nothing about how Python proceeds about its business is hidden from the programmer. Even its internal operations are exposed in the sense that they can be overriden if the programmer so desires. This openness makes Python a fertile ground for innovation on the part of the programmer and makes for a very pleasant programming experience.

Python is also open in the sense of "Open Source." Programmers from all over the world, communicating over the Internet, are contributing to the continued development of Python and its ever-growing array of libraries and support tools.

5.1.6   *Python Is XML Friendly*

Python has a natural affinity for text processing in general. Its powerful built-in data structures and object orientation make it an excellent XML processing tool.

Interest in XML in the Python community is high, and the XML special interest group (XML-SIG) is busily working toward making Python the language of choice for XML processing.

5.1.7   *Python Is Interactive*

As we saw in chapter 2, Python can function interactively. In interactive mode, you can type Python code and have it executed exactly the way it would be executed if it were stored in a file.

For many Python users—myself included—Python is the default desk calculator for all sorts of "back of an envelope" calculations.

There is more to Python's interactivity than this, though. Interactive use is an excellent way to learn the language and familiarize yourself with new Python libraries. It is also a great debugging tool.

Python is easily embedded in other host applications written in Java, C, or C++. This makes it a compelling choice for large applications that need an interactive scripting environment.

5.1.8 *Python Is an Interpreted Language*

Python programs are executed directly from their textual form with no intermediate compilation/linking phase. Python variables automatically come into being when they are first used. They do not need to be declared beforehand, and they do not have any predefined *type*. That is, a variable x can be a string one minute, an integer the next, and a user-defined object the minute after that.

Python has a number of very powerful, very generic data structures built right into the language itself. Primary among these are strings, nested lists and dictionaries.[1]

The power of these three structures is such that an amazing amount can be achieved with very few lines of Python. The fact that small Python programs can be both very powerful and easy to read is one of the great engineering strengths of the language.

5.2 | Basic Control Structures

Python's WYSIWYG code layout philosophy is at the core of how Python programs are constructed. Control structures such as code repetition and code selection use indentation to express the grouping of code statements.

---

[1]Dictionaries are also known as "hashtables" or "associative arrays."

In this section, we talk a little about the philosophy behind this WYSIWYG approach and then look at the most important control structures provided by Python.

5.2.1   *Some WYSIWYG Code Layout Philosophy*

Here is a simple algorithm in the C programming language that uses braces to control statement grouping. Languages such as C++, Perl, and Java™ also take this general approach to statement grouping.

```
CD-ROM reference=5001.txt
while (alive) {
  if (hungry) {
    eat();
    if (thirsty) {
      drink();
    }
  }
  else {
    WriteSoftware();
  }
  alive = CheckPulse();
}
```

Here is the same algorithm as above, this time using begin/end keywords to control grouping. Languages such as Pascal/Delphi, Basic, and Modula take this approach.

```
CD-ROM reference=5002.txt
while (alive) BEGIN
  if (hungry) BEGIN
    eat();
    if (thirsty) BEGIN
      drink();
    END
  END
  else BEGIN
    WriteSoftware();
  END
  alive = CheckPulse();
END
```

In the above code snippets, the logical grouping of the code (as far as the programming language is concerned) is controlled by the block delimiters—the braces or BEGIN/END keyword pairs.

Note that the code has also been block-structured by means of *indentation* relative to the left margin of the page. It is important to remember that this indentation is *not* used by the programming language. It has been created by a human for human consumption. It is there to help human beings, as distinct from progamming language interpreters, to understand the structure of the code.

Indeed, the programming language interpreter typically does not "see" the indentation at all. It is preprocessed away early on in the analysis of the program text.

Most critically, the interpreter *does not* check that the indentation accurately reflecting the logical structure of the algorithm. To put it bluntly, indentation can tell lies!

For example, glance at the following code and then answer the question, "Is it possible to call drink() without first calling eat()?"

```
CD-ROM reference=5003.txt
while (alive) {
  if (hungry) {
    eat();
  if (thirsty) {
    drink();
    }
  }
  else {
    WriteSoftware();
    }
  }
  alive = CheckPulse()
}
```

The answer is NO, it is not possible to call drink() without first calling eat(), but thanks to the incorrect indentation, a quick glance at the source code could have left you with the impression that it is possible.

Here is the program reindented to properly match the logical structure created by the block delimiters.

```
CD-ROM reference=5004.txt
while (alive) {
  if (hungry) {
    eat();
    if (thirsty) {
      drink();
    }
  }
  else {
    WriteSoftware();
    }
  }
  alive = CheckPulse()
}
```

So, indentation can tell lies, but the problems do not end there. It is a fact of life that no two programmers can agree on how to indent code. Here is an indentation style I am strongly allergic to.

```
CD-ROM reference=5005.txt
while (alive) {
    if (hungry)
        {
            eat();
            if (thirsty)
                {
                    drink();
                }
        }
    else
        {
            WriteSoftware();
        }
    alive = CheckPulse();
}
```

The following style has an equally bad effect on me.

```
CD-ROM reference=5006.txt
while (alive) {
```

```
if (hungry) {eat();
      if (thirsty){drink();}
}
else {WriteSoftware();}
alive = CheckPulse();}
```

I find the former layout too wasteful of screen real estate, and I find the latter too crumpled up to be easily read either on paper or on a screen.

Fill a room with C/C++/Java/Perl/Pascal, or Smalltalk programmers and ask them to code up a simple algorithm like this and you will be guaranteed a hot debate about indentation and layout style!

It would be wrong to dismiss such debates as trivial. You only need to look at the pained expression on the face of a programmer reading an unfamiliar indentation style to see that there is more to it than that. The plain fact is that the physical layout of the code plays an important part in helping us to *understand* the code. Here is the algorithm of this section expressed in Python.

```
CD-ROM reference=5007.txt
# A simple Python Program
while alive:
  if hungry:
    eat()
    if thirsty:
      drink()
  else:
    WriteSoftware()
  alive = CheckPulse()
```

Note the complete lack of block delimiters such as braces or begin/end keywords. Python uses the indentation to block-structure the program. There is basically only one way to indent this algorithm!

Fill a room with Python programmers and ask them to implement this little algorithm and the solutions will all look essentially the same. The indentation of Python source code *never* lies. What You See Is What You Get!

On first sight, you might be (as I was) a little concerned about losing the right to indent your code as you wish. Python does indeed force you to lay out your code in a single, consistent, universal style. It forces all other Python programmers on the planet to do the same.

The result? No more misleading indentation, no more painful experiences reading other people's code. No more squabbles about the perfect way to lay out a nested `if` statement.

Ten minutes into using Python, all my fears about mandatory indentation style evaporated.

Yours will too.

5.2.2 *Control Structure Syntax*

Python has three main control structures: the `while` loop, the `for` loop, and the `if` statement.

They all look quite similar in that an expression occurs after the relevant keyword (`if`, `while`, or `for`). This is then followed by a ":" character. Statements to be executed are indented on the following lines. The general form of all three control stuctures is shown below.

```
CD-ROM reference=5008.txt
while <condition>:
       statements


if <condition>:
       statements


for <variable> in <sequence>:
       statements
```

5.2.3 *Truth and Falsehood*

The `while` and `if` statements conditionally execute code depending on the truth/falsehood of the condition. Truth/falsehood is determined according to the following simple rule: Every value is considered true except for the ones in table 5.1. (Do not worry about the exact meaning of the terms "list," "tuple," and "dictionary." We will return to them later on.)

Table 5.1	Values considered to be false
Value	*Description*
0	Numeric 0
None	A special built-in Python object denoting "no value"
""	The empty string
[]	The empty list
()	The empty tuple
{}	The empty dictionary

5.2.4   *Conditional Operators*

Python provides the normal assortment of conditional operators which are, for the most part, expressed in a C-style syntax. Conditions evaluate to one of two values. A 1 means that the condition is true. A 0 means that the condition is false. Here are some examples.

x < y	True if x is less than y
x > y	True if x is greater than y
x == y	True if x and y have equal values
x != y	True if x and y do not have the same value
x is y	True if x and y both reference the same object

5.2.5   *Boolean Operators*

Conditions can be combined by use of Boolean operators. The result of a Boolean condition is, again, 1 and 0 representing true and false, respectively. Here are some examples.

x and y	True if both x and y are true
x or y	True if either x or y is true
not x	True if x is false

Parentheses can be used to create arbitrarily complex Boolean expressions (table 5.3).

5.2.6   *The while Loop*

The `while` loop allows a group of Python statements to be executed an arbitrary number of times. Looping continues until the loop condition evaluates to false.

In this example, the contents of the `while` loop are executed exactly five times.

```
CD-ROM reference=5009.txt
x = 0
y = 5
while x < y:
      print x
      x = x + 1
```

To execute this code in interactive mode, we need to create the correct indentation for the statements in the body of the `while` loop. In interactive mode, the easiest indentation technique is to add a single

Table 5.3   Use of parentheses for complex expressions

Expression	*Evaluation*
x or (y and z)	True if x is true or if both y and z are true
not (a or b)	True if variables a and b are false
(a or (b and (c!=f))) and (not d)	The interpretation of this expression is left as an exercise to the reader

space for each level of nesting. For noninteractive work, I generally use one tab (set to be four spaces in my editor) for indentation.

Python does not care how many spaces you use for indentation as long as you are consistent. You can mix true tab characters (character 9 in ASCII) with spaces, but it is not a good idea. If you move code with mixed tab/spaces from one editing tool to another, the code indentation can be messed up because different editing tools use different tab settings.[2]

When you are creating an indented structure interactively, Python's prompt changes to "..." to indicate that it expects subsequent code to be indented.

```
CD-ROM reference=5010.txt
C>python

Python 1.5.2 (#0, Apr 13 1999, 10:51:12) [MSC 32 bit (Intel)]
on win32
Copyright 1991-1995 Stichting Mathematisch Centrum, Amsterdam
>>> x = 0
>>> y = 5
>>> while x < y:
...     print x
...     x = x + 1
...
0
1
2
3
4
>>>
```

If you type this code into Python's interactive mode, you will notice that Python continues to prompt with ... rather than >>> until you press Return on a blank line. The prompt then changes back to >>>.

while loops can occur within while loops. In this example, the print statement is executed nine times.

---

[2]The Python distribution comes with a utility, known as tabnanny.py and located in the Scripts subdirectory, that checks your use of tabs and spaces.

```
CD-ROM reference=5011.txt
>>> x = 0
>>> while x < 3:
...     y = 0
...     while y < 3:
...             y = y + 1
...             print x,y
...     x = x + 1
...
0 1
0 2
0 3
1 1
1 2
1 3
2 1
2 2
2 3
>>>
```

5.2.7   *The if Statement*

The if statement allows statements to be executed depending on the truth/falsehood of a condition. The simplest form is shown here.

```
CD-ROM reference=5012.txt
if x == 10:
    print "x is 10"

if name == "Sean":
    print "Name is Sean"

if x == 10 and name != "Sean":
    print "x is 10"
    print "and name is not Sean"
```

Note the use of double equal == throughout to indicate testing the value of two variables. In Python, a single equal sign indicates assignment.

```
CD-ROM reference=5013.txt
# if x is 10
```

```
if x == 10:
     # set x to 5
     x = 5
```

Unlike some languages, Python does not let you make the mistake of doing an assignment when you meant to test for equality.

```
CD-ROM reference=5014.txt
# Missing an equal sign here:
if x = 10:
     # set x to 5
     x = 5
```

Python reports this as a syntax error, like this.

```
CD-ROM reference=5015.txt
   if x = 10:
          ^
SyntaxError: invalid syntax
```

Statements to be executed if the condition is false can be entered after the `else` keyword.

```
CD-ROM reference=5016.txt
if x == 10:
     print "x is 10"
else:
     print "x is not 10"

if name == "Sean":
     print "Name is Sean"
else:
     print "name is not Sean"

if x == 10 and name != "Sean":
     print "x is 10"
     print "and name is not Sean"
else:
     print "Either"
     print "x is not 10"
     print "Or"
     print "name is not Sean"
```

Multiple routes through the `if` statement can be created with the `elif` keyword.

```
CD-ROM reference=5017.txt
if name == "Sean":
     print "Name is Sean"
elif name == "Noel":
     print "name is Noel"
else:
     print "Name is neither Sean nor Noel"
```

An `if` statement can contain nested `if` statements. Note that thanks to Python's WYSIWYG style, there is never any ambiguity about which `else` goes with which `if`.

```
CD-ROM reference=5018.txt
if name == "Sean":
     if x == 10:
          if z == 42:
               print "Sean,10,42"
          else:
               print "Sean,10,!42"
     else:
          print "x!=10"
else:
     print "Not Sean"
```

5.2.8   *The for Loop*

Python's `for` loop is very flexible: It allows a group of statements to be executed once for every member of a sequence of objects. We will see lots of examples later on. For now, we simply look at two simple sequences—a string and a simple list.

```
CD-ROM reference=5019.txt
>>> for x in "Sean":
...      print x
...
S
```

```
e
a
n
>>>
```

```
CD-ROM reference=5020.txt
>>> for x in (1,5,"Hello"):
...     print x
1
5
Hello
>>>
```

5.3 | Functions

A function is a named collection of Python statements. Functions can take any number of arguments. The general form of a function is:

```
CD-ROM reference=5021.txt
def <function name>(<arguments>):
<statements>
```

In the following example, a function `printHello` is declared and then executed interactively.

```
CD-ROM reference=5022.txt
>>> def printHello():
... print "Hello"
...
>>> printHello()
Hello
>>>
```

Note that the `print "Hello"` line is indented by one space relative to the `def printHello():` line. Python's interactive prompt changes to a ... when it is expecting to see indented lines. To stop entering indented lines, press RETURN on a blank line. Python's prompt then returns to >>>.

In the following example, a function `HoursFromDays` is declared. It takes a single parameter and returns the value of that parameter times 24. The function is then called with the parameter 10.

```
CD-ROM reference=5023.txt
>>> def HoursFromDays(d):
... return d * 24
...
>>> HoursFromDays(10)
240
>>>
```

5.4 | Modules

Python programs can consists of many files. Each file is known as a *module*. To gain access to the contents of a Python module, import the module by using the `import` keyword.

Python comes with a vast array of modules which, by default, live in the `python/lib` subdirectory.

The following example imports the `string` module and calls the `upper` function it provides. This function converts a string to all uppercase characters.

```
CD-ROM reference=5024.txt
>>> import string
>>> print string.upper ("Hello World")
HELLO WORLD
>>>
```

Python is case sensitive. This case sensitivity applies to keywords, variables, and modules.

The following statement fails because `Import` is not a keyword.

```
CD-ROM reference=5025.txt
>>> Import string
Syntax Error: invalid syntax
```

The following code illustrates how x and X are treated as two distinct variable names.

```
CD-ROM reference=5026.txt
>>># The variables "x" and "X" are two separate
   # variables.
>>> x = 1
>>> X = 2
>>> print x
1
>>> print X
2
```

The following code illustrates that module names are also case sensitive.

```
CD-ROM reference=5027.txt
>>># The following statement fails because "String" does
>>> not match the module name which is "string"
>>> import String
NameError: Case mismatch for module name String
(filename C:\Program Files\Python\Lib\string.py)
```

On Windows platforms, you can turn off the case sensitivity of module names by creating a PYTHONCASEOK environment variable. The value of the environment variables does not matter.

```
CD-ROM reference=5028.txt
C>set PYTHONCASEOK=1
C>python
>>> import String
>>> print String.upper ("Hello World")
HELLO WORLD
```

The string module has a global variable called hexdigits. The global variables in a module are available when a module is imported.

```
CD-ROM reference=5029.txt
>>> import string
>>> print string.hexdigits
0123456789abcdefABCDEF
```

When used in the above form, the name of the imported module can be used as a prefix to access the contents of the imported module. In the above example, the variable called `hexdigits` from the `string` module is accessed by prefixing its name with `string`.

The `import` statement can also be used like this.

```
CD-ROM reference=5030.txt
>>> from string import *
```

When used in the above form, the contents of the imported module can be accessed without any prefix.

```
CD-ROM reference=5031.txt
>>> from string import *
>>> print upper ("Hello World")
HELLO WORLD
>>> print hexdigits
0123456789abcdefABCDEF
```

There is a third variation in which named objects in a module are imported. It is possible to explicitly list the variables to be imported. In the example below, the variable `hexdigits` is imported from the `string` module.

```
CD-ROM reference=5032.txt
>>> from string import hexdigits
>>> print hexdigits
0123456789abcdefABCDEF
```

In the example below, the `hexdigits` variable and the `upper` function are imported from the `string` module.

```
CD-ROM reference=5033.txt
>>> from string import hexdigits,upper
>>> print hexdigits
0123456789abcdefABCDEF
>>> print upper ("Hello World")
HELLO WORLD
```

5.5 | Data Structures

One way to differentiate between high-level and low-level programming languages is by the richness of the data structures built into the language. Using this criterion as a measure, Python is definitely a high-level language.

Python directly supports the concepts of object-oriented programming such as classes, objects, and so on. It also provides a rich assortment of data structures "out of the box." The three that occur most frequently in XML processing are:

- Strings
- Nested lists
- Dictionaries

5.5.1 *Strings*

In Python, strings are ordered collections of characters that can shrink and grow to any size, with Python looking after all the details to do with allocating and deallocating memory for them.

```
CD-ROM reference=5034.txt
>>> x = "Hello World"
>>> print x
Hello World
>>> x = "Hello World twice over"
>>> print x
Hello World twice over
```

Strings can be delineated with double quotes or single quotes.

```
CD-ROM reference=5035.txt
>>> x = "Hello World"
>>> print x
Hello World

>>> x = 'Hello World'
```

```
>>> print x
Hello World
>>> x = "Hello 'World'"
>>> print x
Hello 'World'

>>> x = 'Hello "World"'
>>> print x
Hello "World"
```

Strings can also be delineated with triple quotes. Such strings can span multiple lines.

```
CD-ROM reference=5036.txt
>>> x = """Hello
... World"""
>>> print x
Hello
World
```

Multiline strings delineated by triple quotes are commonly used to create embedded Python documentation known as *docstrings*. We discuss docstrings in chapter 6.

Strings can be concatenated with the intuitive + operator.

```
CD-ROM reference=5037.txt
>>> x = "Hello"
>>> y = "World"
>>> print x + y
HelloWorld
>>> z = x + y
>>> print z
HelloWorld
```

5.5.1.1 String Slicing

The most compelling thing about strings in Python is the ease with which they can be chopped into pieces—a large part of day-to-day XML/text processing with Python revolves around this single feature.

Individual characters can be accessed with numeric offset surrounded by square brackets after the string variable name. The first character is at offset 0, the second character is at offset 1, and so on.

```
CD-ROM reference=5038.txt
>>> x = "Hello"
>>> print x[0]
H
>>> print x[2]
l
>>> print x[4]
o
>>> print x[14]
Traceback (innermost last):
  File "<stdin>", line 1, in ?
IndexError: string index out of range
```

In the final Python command above, we asked for the character at offset 14 in the string x. Since the string x is only 5 characters long, Python complains and generates an error. In particular, it generates what is known as a *traceback*. The purpose of a traceback is to provide details of what the program was doing when the error occurred.

Tracebacks are the result of Python raising an exception. Exceptions are an important part of Python and a key tool in making Python programs robust in the face of run-time error. Exceptions are closely linked with Python's object-oriented features. We will defer saying more until later on. For now, suffice it to say that in this case, Python has raised a class of exception known as an IndexError exception. When an exception is raised, the default behavior is for some details of the exception to be printed in a traceback and for the program to terminate.

Returning to the subject of string slicing: Offsets for accessing individual characters in strings can also be *negative*. Negative offsets are interpreted to mean "start counting from the end of the string, and work backwards." The following examples illustrate the idea.

```
CD-ROM reference=5039.txt
>>> x = "Hello"
>>> x[-1]
```

```
o
>>> x[-5]
H
>>> x[-14]
Traceback (innermost last):
  File "<stdin>", line 1, in ?
IndexError: string index out of range
```

As you can see, Python can be provoked into raising an exception when negative numbers go out of bounds, too.

Numbers can also be paired up—both positive and negative—to create *ranges*, also known as *slices*. The first number means "start here" and the second number means "stop just before here."

One good way to think of the numbers in a slice is as references to the circle points in figure 5–1.

The slice expression x:y then means "return all the elements between the two specified circles."

```
CD-ROM reference=5040.txt
>>> x = "Hello"
>>> print x[2:4]
ll
```

Omission of a number in a slice is interpreted to mean "from the beginning" or "until the end," depending on what side of the ":" the

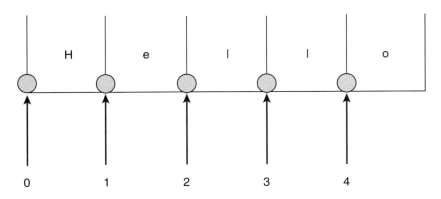

Figure 5–1   String slicing.

omission occurs on. The slice below means "from location 2 until the end of the string."

```
CD-ROM reference=5041.txt
>>> x[2:]
print llo
```

The slice below means "from the beginning until location 4."

```
CD-ROM reference=5042.txt
>>> print x[:4]
Hell
```

Slice numbers can also have a negative meaning: "start at the end and work backward."

```
CD-ROM reference=5043.txt
>>> print x[:-2]
Hel
```

Slices that go beyond the bounds of a string are cropped to the extremities of the string without causing an error.

```
CD-ROM reference=5044.txt
>>> x = "Hello"
>>> print x[2:400]
llo
```

I think you will agree that this string "slicing" syntax packs a lot of punch. It can also be used with Python lists, and indeed you can add slicing capability to your own Python data structures, as we will see later on.

5.5.1.2 String Interpolation

Python is written in C and has borrowed some naming conventions from it. Perhaps the most striking C-like syntax in Python is its string interpolation syntax, which is based on the time-honored `printf` function of C and C++. Python borrows this syntax but significantly extends the power of string interpolation by allowing it to happen essentially *anywhere* within a Python program.

The idea behind string interpolation is that *placeholders* in a string are constructed with various special characters preceded by a percent sign. The string itself is then followed by *another* percent sign and then the replacment objects.

The placeholder for a string is %s, as this example illustrates.

```
CD-ROM reference=5045.txt
>>> import string
>>> print "Hello %s" % "World"
Hello World
>>> print "Hello %s" % string.swapcase("World")
Hello wORLD
```

Note how the standard string module has been imported to provide access to the swapcase function.

The placeholder for an integer is %d.

```
CD-ROM reference=5046.txt
>>> print "Hello %d" % 43
Hello 43
>>> print "Hello %d" % 43*2
Hello 86
```

The %s and %d placeholders are easily the most common, but there are others. See the Python documentation Doc/lib/typesseq-strings.html for details.

Numerous interpolations can be performed at the same time by having multiple placeholders in the target string and multiple replacement objects surrounded by parentheses.

```
CD-ROM reference=5047.txt
>>> print "Hello %s %d" % ("World",42)
Hello World 42
>>> import string
>>> print "Hello %s %d" % (string.upper("World"),56/2)
Hello WORLD 28
```

A key facet of Python's string interpolation is that it can occur anywhere that a string can. For example, Python provides an `open` function that opens a file for reading or writing. The `open` function expects to be passed a string containing the filename and a string containing the permissions with which the file should be opened—"r" for read access, "w" for write access, and so on. In the following example, the file `SeanMcGrath.dat` is opened for reading and referenced by the variable `f`.

```
CD-ROM reference=5048.txt
>>> f = open ("SeanMcGrath.dat","r")
>>> print f
<open file 'SeanMcGrath.dat', mode 'r' at 7f6f10>
```

Note that the `print` statement was used to get some basic details back about the file object: the filename, the mode, and the address on the file object in memory.

The fact that when you print something, you get back something useful is common in Python. When you invent your own objects in Python, you have complete control over what will happen when Python tries to print them. More on this point later in this chapter.

Suppose that the filename needs to be constructed according to the following pattern:

```
CD-ROM reference=5049.txt
[name]-[shoe size]-[operating system].dat
```

Here is the Python code that will open a file that matches this pattern. This particular example was executed on Windows NT and so the `os.name` variable returns nt.

```
CD-ROM reference=5050.txt
>>> import os
>>> ShoeSize=13
>>> f = open ('SeanMcGrath-%d-%s.dat' % (ShoeSize,os.name))
>>> print f
<open file 'SeanMcGrath-13-nt.dat' mode r at 876410>
```

The key point here is that the `open` function knows *nothing* about string interpolation. The interpolation happens prior to the invocation of the `open` function, at which point the string placeholders have been completely resolved.

If you know C or C++, you might like to think about the extra code that would be needed to make this work in those languages.

5.5.2   *Lists*

Lists are implemented as objects in Python. This is our first serious encounter with objects in Python, and we need to tie down some terminology before proceeding.

An "Object" is a named collection of variables (known as *instance variables*) and functions (known as *methods*). Both instance variables and methods are accessed by a dot notation similar to that used with modules. So, for example, in the expression,

```
CD-ROM reference=5051.txt
x.y
```

x is the name of an object and y is the name of an instance variable or an instance method.

List objects can be created with square brackets, as follows:

```
CD-ROM reference=5052.txt
>>> x = [1,2,3]
```

The variable x is now a reference to a list object containing the three numbers 1, 2, and 3.

Lists have the following methods associated with them:

- **sort** – Sorts the elements

- **reverse** – Reverses the order of elements

- **remove** – Removes an element

- **pop** – Removes the last element

- **append** – Appends an object to the list

- **index** – Returns the index at which an object occurs in the list

- **extend** – Adds a specified list to the end of this list

- **insert** – Adds an element to a list before a specified index

- **count** – Counts the number of times an object occurs in the list

The sort method sorts the elements in a list. The list is changed in-place. That is, a new list is not returned; the items in the original list are rearranged.

```
CD-ROM reference=5053.txt
>>> x = [1,2,3,1]
>>> x.sort()
>>> print x
[1,1,2,3]
```

The reverse method reverses the elements in a list. Again, the list is changed in-place.

```
CD-ROM reference=5054.txt
>>> print x
[1,1,2,3]
>>> x.reverse()
>>> print x
[3,2,1,1]
```

The pop method is a convenient way of removing the last element in a list. The removed element is returned.

```
CD-ROM reference=5055.txt
>>> print x
[3,2,1,1]
>>> x.pop()
1
>>> print x
[3,2,1]
```

The append method adds new elements to the end of a list.

```
CD-ROM reference=5056.txt
>>> print x
[3,2,1]
>>> x.append(1)
>>> print x
[3,2,1,1]
```

The index method returns the index at which the specified object occurs in a list.

```
CD-ROM reference=5057.txt
>>> print x
[3,2,1,1]
>>> x.index(3)
0
>>> x.index(1)
2
```

If the object does not exist in the list, Python raises a ValueError exception.

```
CD-ROM reference=5058.txt
>>> print x
[3,2,1,1]
>>> x.index(42)
Traceback (innermost last):
  File "<stdin>", line 1, in ?
ValueError: list.index(x): x not in list
```

If the object occurs more than once in the list, the index method returns the index of the first occurrence.

You can test to see if an item is in a list by using the in operator.

```
CD-ROM reference=5059.txt
>>> print x
[3,2,1,1]
>>> 3 in x
1
>>> 42 in x
0
```

The `extend` method appends the contents of one list to another list.

```
CD-ROM reference=5060.txt
>>> print x
[3,2,1,1]
>>> x.extend ([5,6])
[3,2,1,1,5,6]
```

The `insert` method adds the specified object at the specified point in the list. In the example below, the number 42 is inserted at offset 2 in the list.

```
CD-ROM reference=5061.txt
>>> print x
[3,2,1,1]
>>> x.insert (2,42)
[3,2,42,1,1,5,6]
```

The `count` method counts the number of times a specified object occurs in the list.

```
CD-ROM reference=5062.txt
>>> print x
[3,2,42,1,1,5,6]
>>> x.count(1)
2
>>> x.count (42)
1
x.count(57)
0
```

Lists can contain any type of object, including other lists.

```
CD-ROM reference=5063.txt
>>> x = [ 1 , 2 , ["Hello","World"], 3]
>>> print x
[1, 2, ['Hello', 'World'], 3]
```

Here we have created a list that has four elements in it. The first two and the last one are the number objects 1 and 2 and 3 respectively. The second-last element is itself a list that consists of two string objects: "Hello" and "World," respectively.

Particular elements in lists can be referenced by specification of an offset from the beginning of the list in square brackets.

```
CD-ROM reference=5064.txt
>>> print x[2]
['Hello', 'World']
```

With nested lists, we can use multiple indexes to drill down to particular subelements.

```
CD-ROM reference=5065.txt
>>> x = [ 1 , 2 , ["Hello","World"], 3]
>>> print x[2][0]
Hello
>>> print x[2][1]
World
```

Just as with strings, offsets are allowed to be negative and mean "start at the end and work backwards."

```
CD-ROM reference=5066.txt
>>> print x[-2]
['Hello','World']
>>> print x[-3]
2
```

Positive and negative indexes can be mixed as required.

```
CD-ROM reference=5067.txt
>>> x = [ 1 , 2 , ["Hello","World"], 3]
>>> print x[2][-2]
Hello
>>> print x[-2][1]
World
>>> print x[-2][-2]
Hello
```

Remember the string slicing discussed earlier in this chapter? Remember how I said that you could use it with lists too? Here's how.

```
CD-ROM reference=5068.txt
>>> x = [ 1 , 2 , ["Hello" , "World"] , 3]
>>> x[2:4]
```

```
[['Hello', 'World'], 3]
>>> x[1:]
[2, ['Hello', 'World'], 3]
>>> x[:2]
[1, 2]
```

Note that when you slice a list you get a list back. Slice indexes can be positive or negative.

```
CD-ROM reference=5069.txt
>>> x = [ 1 , 2 , ["Hello" , "World"] , 3]
>>> x [1:2]
>>> x[-2:3]
['Hello','World']
```

Here is an example of some manipulation of a moderately complex list structure.

```
CD-ROM reference=5070.txt
x = [[1,2],"Hello",["X",["Y","X"]]]
>>> print x
[[1, 2], 'Hello', ['X', ['Y', 'X']]]
>>> print x[1]
Hello
>>> print x[2]
['X', ['Y', 'X']]
>>> print x[2][1]
['Y', 'X']
>>> x.reverse()
>>> print x
[['X', ['Y', 'X']], 'Hello', [1, 2]]
```

Let us take a step-by-step look at what has happened here. The statement print x[1] retrieved the second item in the list x—the string "Hello". The statement print x[2] retrieved the third item, which is another list ['X', ['Y', 'X']]. The statement print x[2][1] picks out the second item in this sublist, namely, ['Y', 'X']. Finally, the x.reverse() statement reverses the contents of the list x.

Nested lists come in very handy when processing XML. XML provides a notation for the representation of hierarchical data structures.

There is a clean fit between such hierarchical data structures and nested lists. To illustrate this fit, we will use the following simple XML file.

```
CD-ROM reference=5071.txt
C>type sample.xml

<Employee>
    <Name>
            <Given>Sean</Given>
            <Family>McGrath</Family>
    </Name>
    <Extension>
    1234
    </Extension>
</Employee>
```

Note how I have used white space to indent the document to give an impression of its hierarchical structure. A more graphical representation of the hierarchical structure is shown in figure 5–2.

The elliptical shapes in the diagram represent elements in the XML document and are known as *nodes* in computer science terms. Nodes in the tree structure can contain other nodes. The top-level node, Employee in this case, is known as the *root* node. The root node contains all the other nodes. The Employee node contains the Name node. The Name node contains the Given and Family nodes and so on.

By thinking of a node as a list, we can replicate this structure in Python with a nested list structure. Here is a simple Python list representation of the hierarchy in figure 5–2.

```
CD-ROM reference=5072.txt
['Element=Employee', ['Element=Name', ['Element=Given',
  ['Data=Sean']],
['Element=Family',
['Data=McGrath']]],['Element=Extension',['Data=1234']]]
```

This is not the most wonderful layout of this nested list from the point of view of *seeing* its structure. I have done it this way for a reason. It gives me an opportunity to introduce you to a very useful standard Python module known as pprint.

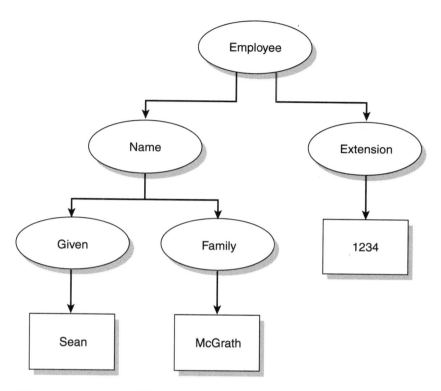

Figure 5–2 An XML file viewed as a hierarchical data structure.

The pprint module will "pretty-print" any Python data structure. Here is what happens when I pretty-print the above list structure.

```
CD-ROM reference=5073.txt
>>> import pprint
>>> x = ['Element=Employee', ['Element=Name',
  ['Element=Given',      ['Data=Sean']],
['Element=Family',
['Data=McGrath']]],['Element=Extension',['Data=1234']]]
>>> pprint.pprint(x)

['Element=Employee',
 ['Element=Name',
  ['Element=Given', ['Data=Sean']],
  ['Element=Family', ['Data=McGrath']]],
 ['Element=Extension', ['Data=1234']]]
```

Note how Python has added spaces on the left to line up the left brackets to show off the structure of the nested list. Note also that the output produced is itself in Python syntax. That is, you could use the output of `pprint` as a valid list in a Python program. This is quite common in Python. If at all possible, objects in Python provide a way of producing an executable presentation of themselves.

5.5.3 *Tuples*

A tuple is very much like a list except that it is delimited with parentheses rather than square brackets. The key difference between a list and a tuple is that a tuple is *immutable*—it cannot be modified once it has been created.

In the example below, a list is created containing the numbers 1, 2, and 3. The second item of the list is then changed to the string `"Hello"`.

```
CD-ROM reference=5074.txt
>>> x = [1,2,3]
>>> x[2] = "Hello"
>>> print x
[1,"Hello",2]
```

In this example, a tuple similar to the list is created. Note how the attempt to modify the tuple fails.

```
CD-ROM reference=5075.txt
>>> x = (1,2,3)
>>> x [2] = "Hello"
Traceback (innermost last):
  File "<stdin>", line 1, in ?
TypeError: object doesn't support item assignment
```

We have, in fact, already encountered tuples. The collection of values used in a string interpolation are housed in a tuple.

```
CD-ROM reference=5076.txt
>>> print "Hello %s %d" % ("World",42)
Hello World 42
```

Why does Python have tuples as well as lists? The answer lies in another powerful Python data structure called a *dictionary,* which we look at in the next section.

5.5.4 *Dictionaries*

We turn now to a third built-in data structure of great utility for XML processing—the dictionary. A dictionary is a data structure in which one object known as the *key* is associated with another object known as the *value.* A dictionary can have any number of keys and associated values. Values can be anything you like: numbers, strings, lists, user-defined objects, even dictionaries. Keys, too, can be pretty much anything; the only stipulation on keys is that they must be unchangeable or, in Python terminology, *immutable.* This restriction guarantees that the dictionary is always able to retrieve values correctly because nothing can change the value of a key after it has been used to add something to a dictionary. In practical terms, this means that most keys are either strings, integers, or Python tuples.

Like lists, dictionaries are implemented as objects in Python. Dictionaries are delineated by braces. Within the braces, keys and values are paired up, separated by a ":" character. The key/value pairs are separated by commas.

In the following code snippet, a dictionary object x is created in which the key 'Sean' is associated with the integer value 13 and the key string 'Paul' is associated with the integer value 10.

```
CD-ROM reference=5077.txt
>>> x = {'Sean':13,'Paul':10}
>>> print x
{'Paul': 10, 'Sean': 13}
```

Dictionaries support the following eight methods:

- **clear** – Removes all associations from the dictionary
- **copy** – Creates a second copy of the dictionary

- **get** – Retrieves the value associated with the specified key if it exists

- **has-key** – Returns true if the parameter is a key in the dictionary

- **items** – Returns a list of key, value tuples

- **keys** – Returns a list of keys in the dictionary

- **update** – Makes entries for all the key, value pairs in the specified dictionary

- **values** – Returns a list of values in the dictionary

Below we look at examples of the most frequently used methods. Values can be retrieved from dictionaries by indexing, using a key.

```
CD-ROM reference=5078.txt
>>> x = {'Sean':13,'Paul':10}
>>> x['Sean']
13
>>> x['Paul']
10
```

In the event that a key is provided for which the dictionary does not have an association, Python complains by raising an exception known as a KeyError.

```
CD-ROM reference=5079.txt
>>> x = {'Sean':13,'Paul':10}
>>> x['Harry']
Traceback (innermost last):
  File "<stdin>", line 1, in ?
KeyError: Harry
```

To determine whether a key has an associated value, use the has-key method. It returns either 1 or 0. A return value of 1 means the key exists, and a return value of 0 means the key does not exist.

```
CD-ROM reference=5080.txt
>>> x = {'Sean':13,'Paul':10}
```

```
>>> x.has-key('Sean')
1
>>> x.has-key('Harry')
0
```

The methods `keys`, `values`, and `items` are particularly useful. The `keys` method returns a list of keys occurring in a dictionary.

```
CD-ROM reference=5081.txt
>>> x = {'Sean':13,'Paul':10}
>>> x.keys()
['Paul', 'Sean']
```

Note that the order in which the keys appear in the list is essentially random. It has no relationship to the order in which the associations were added to the list.

The `values` method returns a list of values occurring in a dictionary.

```
CD-ROM reference=5082.txt
>>> x = {'Sean':13,'Paul':10}
>>> x.values()
[10, 13]
```

The `items` method returns a list of tuples—one for each (key,value) pair occurring in a dictionary.

```
CD-ROM reference=5083.txt
>>> x = {'Sean':13,'Paul':10}
>>> x.items()
[('Paul', 10), ('Sean', 13)]
```

In the above examples, the keys and values are very simple. Here are some examples with more complex objects used as both keys and values.

In this example, a key is created with a tuple. The tuple contains two items: a string and an integer. The key is associated with the string "Big feet".

```
CD-ROM reference=5084.txt
>>> x = {}
>>> # Using a tuple as a key. The tuple has two elements -
>>> # a string and a number.
>>> x [ ('Sean',13) ] = "Big feet"
```

In this example, a complex tuple is used as a key. This tuple contains other tuples nested within it.

```
CD-ROM reference=5085.txt
>>> # Using a deeply nested tuple as a key
>>> # The associated value is also a tuple.
>>> x [ ('X',(1,(2,3)))] =  (1234,"Foo")
```

The dictionary x now has two (key,value) pairs entered into it. If we ask Python to print the dictionary, we will get back a Python syntax representation of the dictionary.

```
CD-ROM reference=5086.txt
>>> print x
{('X', (1, (2, 3))): (1234, 'Foo'), ('Sean', 13): 'Big feet'}
```

We can print specific values from the dictionary by specifying a key.

```
CD-ROM reference=5087.txt
>>> print x[('Sean',13)]
Big feet
```

We can get a list of (key,value) pairs by calling the items method.

```
CD-ROM reference=5088.txt
>>> print x.items()
[(('X', (1, (2, 3))), (1234, 'Foo')), (('Sean', 13), 'Big
feet')]
```

The keys, values and items methods are commonly used with for loops.

In the example below, the list returned by the values method is iterated and each value in the dictionary is printed.

```
CD-ROM reference=5089.txt
>>> x = {'Sean':13,'Paul':10}
>>> for i in x.values():
...   print i
10
13
>>> for i in x.keys():
```

```
...     print i
Paul
Sean
```

In the `for` loops above, the loop variable `i` is set to successive list items each time around the loop. Python's `for` loop allows for multiple loop variables to be used at the same time. This feature is particularly useful with the `items` dictionary method, which returns a list of tuples, each consisting of a key and a value.

```
CD-ROM reference=5090.txt
>>> x = {'Sean':13,'Paul':10}
>>> for (k,v) in x.items():
...     print "Key is '%s'. Value is '%s'" % (k,v)

Key is 'Paul'. Value is '10'
Key is 'Sean'. Value is '13'
```

Dictionaries are so useful in Python that special support for them has been added to Python's string interpolation feature. Entering a key in parentheses in a string interpolation placeholder causes the corresponding value to automatically be looked up in the supplied dictionary:

```
CD-ROM reference=5091.txt
>>> x = {'Sean':13,'Paul':10}
>>> print "Sean wears size %(Sean)d shoes." % x
Sean wears size 13 shoes.
```

5.6 | Object Orientation

We have already encountered some of Python's object-orientation features in the discussion of the list and dictionary built-in classes.

In this section, we talk about declaring classes and creating objects. We also take a look at how inheritance works in Python.

Classes are created with the `class` keyword. The code below creates a trivial class `foo` that has a class variable x.

```
CD-ROM reference=5092.txt
>>> class foo:
... x = 1
>>> print foo.x
1
```

Objects can be created from the class `foo` in a syntax reminiscent of a function call:

```
CD-ROM reference=5093.txt
>>> class foo:
... x = 1
...
>>> f = foo()
>>> print f.x
1
```

Classes can contain methods. Methods are defined in a syntax similar to that for functions. The big difference is that methods always have an object as their first parameter. This is the object that was used to invoke the method. By convention, this first parameter is called `self`.

```
CD-ROM reference=5094.txt
>>> class foo:
... x = 1
... def Hello(self):
...   print "Hello World"
...
>>> f = foo()
>>> f.Hello()
Hello World
>>>
```

The class variable x above is shared by all objects derived from the `foo` class, as the example below illustrates.

```
CD-ROM reference=5095.txt

>>> #Create a simple class foo with a class variable x
```

```
>>> class foo:
...     x = 1
...
>>> #Create an object of class foo referenced by the
>>> #variable f
>>> f = foo()
>>>
>>> #Create an object of class foo referenced by the
>>> #variable g
>>> g = foo()
>>>
>>> # Print the x variable from both the f and g objects
>>> print f.x
1
>>> print g.x
1
>>> #Changing x, will affect both f and g objects
>>> foo.x = 42
>>>
>>> print f.x
42
>>> print g.x
42
```

Such class variables have their uses, but it is much more common for objects to have their own private storage space for variables. The most common place to create these instance variables is in a special method called the *constructor*. The constructor is called automatically whenever an object is created. The constructor has the special name __init__.

```
CD-ROM reference=5096.txt
>>> class foo:
...     def __init__(self):
...         print "In constructor"
...         self.a = 12
...
```

Note the two underscores before and after init. Names that start and end with two underscores are special in Python. There are many such names, and we will encounter most of them at some point in this book. The __init__ name is special because if a method with that name exists in a class, it is automatically called whenever an object of that class is created.

```
CD-ROM reference=5097.txt
>>> f = foo()
In constructor
>>> g = foo()
In constructor
```

Both f and g now have an instance variable called a.

```
CD-ROM reference=5098.txt
>>> f.a
12
>>> g.a
12
```

Each object has its own storage space for the variable a. Changing the a variable in one object has no effect on the variable a in any other object.

```
CD-ROM reference=5099.txt
>>> f.a = 42
>>> f.a
42
>>> g.a
12
```

Constructors can take parameters; this is a common way to initialize instance variables. In the example below, a value for the variable a is provided as a parameter to the constructor.

```
CD-ROM reference=5100.txt
>>> class foo:
...    def __init__(self,aValue):
...      self.a = aValue
...
```

Any attempt to create an object of class foo without supplying a value for a causes an error.

```
CD-ROM reference=5101.txt
>>> f = foo()
```

```
Traceback (innermost last):
  File "<stdin>", line 1, in ?
TypeError: not enough arguments; expected 2, got 1
```

In the code below, two objects `f` and `g` of class `foo` are created. Note how the value passed into the constructor is reflected in the value of the `a` instance variable.

```
CD-ROM reference=5102.txt
>>> f = foo(42)
>>> g = foo(99)
>>> f.a
42
>>> g.a
99
```

Let us move to a more realistic example of a class. Here is an example of an `Account` class implemented in Python. Each instance of `Account` will have associated with it two instance variables called `Balance` and `Name`.

```
CD-ROM reference=5103.txt
C>type accounts.py

# Simple bank Account Class
class Account:
      def __init__(self,balance,name):
              #Construct a bank account given an initial
              #balance and an account name

              print "In constructor for Account objects"
              self.Balance = balance
              self.Name = name

#Create an Account object referenced by the variable
#anAccount
anAccount = Account(0,"Sean McGrath")

C>python accounts.py

In constructor for Account objects
```

Let us add the ability to credit and debit `Account` objects. While we are at it, we will add a method to retrieve the balance of an `Ac-count` object. These methods are structured along the lines of the `__init__` method we have already seen.

```
CD-ROM reference=5104.txt
# Simple bank Accounts

class Account:
        def __init__(self,balance,name):
                # Construct a bank account given an initial
                # balance and an
                # account name.
                self.Balance = balance
                self.Name = name

        def Debit (self,amount):
                # Debit account by the specified amount if
                # sufficient funds are available.
                if self.Balance < amount:
                        print "Insufficient funds"
                        return
                self.Balance = self.Balance - amount

        def Credit (self,amount):
                # Credit account by the specified amount.
                self.Balance = self.Balance + amount

        def GetBalance (self):
                # Return balance on account.
                return self.Balance

# Main part of the program
# Create an Account object.
anAccount = Account(0,"Sean McGrath")

# Credit the account by 100 dollars.
anAccount.Credit (100)

# Debit the account by 40 dollars.
anAccount.Debit (40)
# Print the account balance.
```

```
print "Account balance is %d dollars." % anAccount
.GetBalance()
```

C>**python accounts.py**

```
Account balance is 60 dollars.
```

The three new methods are mostly self-explanatory. Note that they all have `self` as their first parameter—even `GetBalance`, which is called without any parameters. Remember, the first parameter to a method is *always* the object that is receiving the method call.

Imagine a situation in which we need to create a new variation on a bank account. This new account model will be very like the existing account model except that holders of these accounts will be able to debit their accounts up to some specified overdraft limit—accounts are allowed have negative balances as long as the negative balances do not exceed a specified number. Here is the code to implement this scenario, with some explanatory comments added.

```
CD-ROM reference=5105.txt
```

C>**type OverdraftAccount.py**

```
# import the existing Account class from the accounts module
from accounts import Account

import types

class OverdraftAccount(Account):
      # The OverdraftAccount class inherits from the
      # Account class.
      def __init__(self,balance,name,OverdraftLimit):
            # Initialize the Account superclass.
            Account.__init__(self,balance,name)

            # Create an instance variable and
            # initialize it to the specified
            # overdraft limit.
            self.OverdraftLimit = OverdraftLimit
```

```
        def Debit (self,amount):
            if self.Balance + self.OverdraftLimit < amount:
                print "Insufficient funds"
                return
            self.Balance = self.Balance - amount

# Main part of program
anOverdraftAccount = OverdraftAccount (0,"Sean McGrath",100)

# Credit the account by 50 dollars and print
# out the new balance.
anOverdraftAccount.Credit (50)
print "Balance is %d" % anOverdraftAccount.GetBalance()

# Debit the account by 100 dollars and print out
# the new balance.
anOverdraftAccount.Debit (100)
print "Balance is %d" % anOverdraftAccount.GetBalance()

C>python OverdraftAccount.py

In constructor for Account objects
Balance is 50
Balance is -50
```

The first thing that happens is that this Python module imports the `Account` class definition from the `accounts.py` module. The class declaration is similar to the earlier one except that this time, the class from which this class is derived is specified in parentheses.

This class specifies a constructor in which an extra variable for the overdraft limit is provided. Note how the constructor calls the constructor of its parent class (`Account`) with the statement `Account.__init__(self,balance,name)`.

There are no methods for `Credit` or `GetBalance` because these do not need to change for `OverDraftAccount`. They are thus simply *inherited* from the `Account` parent class. The `Debit` method does need to change to allow the account to go into the red as far as the overdraft limit, as shown.

5.7 | Design Principles

There is an old saying in computing that I heartily agree with: "If you have a lot of special cases, the design is wrong."

Apply this maxim to Python and the inescapable conclusion is that the design is pretty much right! Python has very few special cases, very few "gotchas," very few "deadly sins" to watch out for. A big part of Python's clean design is that a number of key ideas are applied *everywhere*. Among these principles are the following:

- Use lists as a general-purpose data structure.

- If you need to look something up, use a dictionary.

- Program the interface, not the implementation.

In the sections that follow, we look at each of these ideas in turn.

5.7.1 *Key Idea: Use Lists as a General-Purpose Data Structure*

As we have seen, lists are everywhere in Python and can contain pretty much anything—including other lists. As data structures go, lists are very general indeed, and the uses to which they can be put are endless.

The most straightforward use of lists in Python is as one-dimensional arrays. The items in one-dimensional lists are often tuples. For example, the `values()` method provided by dictionary objects returns a list of tuples.

Lists are everywhere to be found in Python's standard library. The `urllib` library, for example, makes good use of lists. This library provides facilities for manipulating and retrieving the contents of resources on the Internet identified by a URL.

As you may know, when a Web page is retrieved from a Web server, it is preceded by a variable number of headers for such things as date, server name, and so on. The `urllib` library uses a list to store these headers, as the following example illustrates.

```
CD-ROM reference=5106.txt
>>> import sys
>>> from urllib import urlopen
>>> f = urlopen("http://www.digitome.com/index.html")
>>> print f.info().headers

['Date: Thu, 01 Jul 1999 13:37:50 GMT',
 'Server: Apache/1.2.4 ( ntx enhanced server - referer/agent
1.0d6 )',
 'Last-Modified: Sun, 14 Mar 1999 13:08:03 GMT',
 'ETag: "1ef69a-211-36ebb4b3"',
 'Content-Length: 529',
 'Accept-Ranges: bytes',
 'Connection: close',
 'Content-Type: text/html']
```

The `string` module also uses lists. For example, it provides a function called `split` that splits a string into pieces separated by white space. The `split` function returns a list structure.

```
CD-ROM reference=5107.txt
>>> import string
>>> x = "Alpha Beta Gamma"
>>> string.split(x)
['Alpha', 'Beta', 'Gamma']
```

The `join` function performs the opposite transformation. Given a list of strings, `join` creates a single string by concatenating the elements in the list.

```
CD-ROM reference=5108.txt
>>>import string
>>>x = ['Alpha', 'Beta', 'Gamma']
>>>string.join (x)
>>>'Alpha Beta Gamma'
```

An optional, second parameter to `join` enables you to specify the separator, which defaults to a space.

```
CD-ROM reference=5109.txt
>>> x = ['Alpha', 'Beta', 'Gamma']
>>> string.join (x,"")
>>> 'AlphaBetaGamma'
>>> string.join(x,"!")
>>> 'Alpha!Beta!Gamma'
```

The os module provides a listdir function that returns all the files in a specified directory as a list structure. In the following example, listdir has been invoked on the current directory, which in this case is Python's lib directory (output of listdir abridged for legibility).

```
CD-ROM reference=5110.txt
>>> import os
>>> os.listdir(".")

['aifc.py', 'anydbm.py', 'asynchat.py', 'asyncore.py',
'audiodev.py', 'base64.py', 'BaseHTTPServer.py',
'Bastion.py', 'bdb.py',...]
```

The calendar module provides a method monthcalendar. Given a year and a month, it returns a nested list structure. Each entry in the list is itself a list of seven integers that represent a week. A 0 denotes that the day is not in the specified month. A 1 means first day of month, 2 means second day of month, and so on.

```
CD-ROM reference=5111.txt
>>> import calendar,pprint
>>> pprint.pprint (calendar.monthcalendar(2000,12))
[[0, 0, 0, 0, 1, 2, 3],
 [4, 5, 6, 7, 8, 9, 10],
 [11, 12, 13, 14, 15, 16, 17],
 [18, 19, 20, 21, 22, 23, 24],
 [25, 26, 27, 28, 29, 30, 31]]
```

As you can see, lists cover a lot of ground in the standard library. The fact that lists can contain anything—including other lists—makes them very useful for modelling many forms of data. They are even more appealing when you consider the rich functionality for manipulating lists that Python provides, such as facilities for sorting, slicing, extending, and reversing arbitrary list structures.

5.7.2 *Key Idea: If You Need to Look Something Up, Use a Dictionary*

We have already seen how dictionaries associate one object, called a *key*, with another object, called a *value*. Like lists, dictionaries are everywhere in Python. Indeed, the core Python language makes extensive use of dictionaries for its own lookup requirements. We will look at some of these internal dictionaries first.

We have seen how modules can contain things like functions, variables, and so on. Python uses a dictionary to keep track of all the objects in a module. When Python encounters a reference to an object in a module, it uses a dictionary lookup to find it. The dictionary Python uses for this purpose has a special name—`__dict__`.

In the example below, a partial listing of the dictionary associated with the `re` (regular expressions) module is pretty printed.

```
CD-ROM reference=5112.txt
>>> import re,pprint
>>> # Output abridged to reduce size
>>> pprint.pprint (re.__dict__)
{'ANCHORED': 4,
 '__builtins__':
     {
     'ArithmeticError': <class exceptions.ArithmeticError at
       41bbd0>,
     'AssertionError': <class exceptions.AssertionError at
       41bc90>,
     'AttributeError': <class exceptions.AttributeError at
       41b500>,
     }
 '__doc__'      : None,
 '__file__'     : 'C:\\Program Files\\Python\\Lib\\re.pyc',
 '__name__'     : 're',
 'search'       : <function search at 11b33d0>,
 'sys'          : <module 'sys' (built-in)>}

}
```

From this example, you can see that the `re` module has variables called ANCHORED, `__builtins__`, `__doc__` and so on. Note the `__builtins__` entry in the dictionary. Its value is *itself* a dictionary. Dictionaries can contain other dictionaries just as lists can contain other lists.

Python also associates a dictionary called `__dict__` with each object it creates. Whenever Python encounters a reference to a variable in an object, it uses this dictionary to look up the variable. In the example below, the instance variables associated with `input` objects from the `fileinput` class are printed, using its `__dict__` variable.

```
CD-ROM reference=5113.txt
>>> import pprint, fileinput
>>> f = fileinput.input()
>>> pprint.pprint(f.__dict__)
{'_backup'        : '',
 '_backupfilename': None,
 '_file'          : None,
 '_filelineno'    : 0,
 '_filename'      : None,
 '_files'         : ('a.txt', 'b.txt'),
 '_inplace'       : 0,
 '_isstdin'       : 0,
 '_lineno'        : 0,
 '_output'        : None,
 '_savestdout'    : None}
```

Notice that all the instance variables—the keys in the dictionary—start with a single underscore character. Starting a variable with an underscore signals to Python that the variable is intended for use internally in the object and should not be used directly by users of the object.

Two more internal dictionaries deserve a mention while we are on the subject. The functions `global()` and `local()` return the dictionaries Python uses to locate global and local variables, respectively.

```
CD-ROM reference=5114.txt
>>> globals()
```

```
{'__doc__': None,
 '__name__': '__main__',
 '__builtins__': <module '__builtin__' (built-in)>
}
>>> locals()
{'__doc__': None,
 '__name__': '__main__',
 '__builtins__': <module '__builtin__' (built-in)>}
```

Every time you create a global variable, Python adds it to the `globals` dictionary behind the scenes. Notice how after the assignment to x below, an entry `'x'` has been added to the `globals` dictionary.

```
CD-ROM reference=5115.txt
>>> x = 1
>>> globals()
{'__doc__': None,
 'x': 1,
 '__name__': '__main__',
 '__builtins__': <module '__bultin__' (built-in)>
}
```

To illustrate an addition to the `locals` dictionary, the following example creates a function called `AFunction` in which a local variable y is created. The function then prints out its local variables dictionary.

```
CD-ROM reference=5116.txt
>>> def AFunction():
...   y = 1
...   print locals()
>>> # Call AFunction
>>> AFunction()
{'y': 1}
```

Like lists, dictionaries are also to be found all over the standard Python library. The `rfc822` module contains a representative example of dictionary usage in Python. This module is responsible for parsing the headers of Internet e-mail messages. You provide it with an open file object, and it churns through it, returning a dictionary of the headers it finds.

We use the following e-mail message to illustrate `rfc822` in action.

```
CD-ROM reference=5117.txt
C>type email.txt

To: Duffy, Noel <noel@digitome.com>
From: Sean Mc Grath <sean@digitome.com>
Subject: The rfc822 library
Cc: neville@digitome.com

The rfc822 library sure takes the pain out of parsing e-mail
headers.

Sean
```

In the following code, the headers for the above e-mail are accessed as a dictionary by means of the `Message` object provided by the `rfc822` module.

```
CD-ROM reference=5118.txt
>>> import rfc822
>>> f = open ("email.txt","r")
>>> m = rfc822.Message(f)
>>> m.dict
{'subject': 'The rfc822 library',
 'from'   : 'Sean Mc Grath <sean@digitome.com>',
 'to'     : 'Duffy, Noel <noel@digitome.com>',
 'cc'     : 'neville@digitome.com'
}
```

5.7.3 Key Idea: Program the Interface, Not the Implementation

Side by side with Python's object-oriented features is the concept of object *typing*. This idea is not new to Python. It pops up in many programming languages under a variety of names.[3] In Java, it is

---

[3]See *Design Patterns Elements of Reusable Object-Oriented Software*, Erich Gamma, Richard Helm, Ralph Johnson, and John Vlissides, Addison Wesley, ISBN 0-201-63361-2, page 16.

known as an *interface*. In C++, it is called a *parametric type;* in Smalltalk, the effect is achieved through so-called *abstract classes.*

If you have been glancing through the Python documentation or reading the comp.lang.python newsgroup, you may have come across phrases like "sequence type," "file type," and "number type."

Essentially, a `type` is a name given to a set of operations that can be performed on an object. For example, objects that implement the type known as `number` provide operations for addition, subtraction, multiplication, and so on. Objects that implement the `sequence` type provide operations for retrieving items from the sequence based on their position, retrieving the number of items in the sequence, and so on.

If two objects implement the operations required for a particular type, then any code that relies solely on those operations can use either object *regardless* of the class of the object.

This is all a bit abstract, so let's take a concrete example. As we have already seen, the `rfc822` module can parse the headers of Internet e-mails from any given file object. What if you have an e-mail message sitting in a string that you want to parse? The string will not be acceptable to `rfc822` as shown here.

```
CD-ROM reference=5119.txt
>>> m = rfc822.Message ("To:
noel@digitome.com\nFrom:sean@digitome.com\n\nHello")
Traceback (innermost last):
  File "<interactive input>", line 1, in ?
  File "C:\Program Files\Python\Lib\rfc822.py", line 92, in
    __init__self.readheaders()
  File "C:\Program Files\Python\Lib\rfc822.py", line 136, in
    readheadersline = self.fp.readline()
AttributeError: 'string' object has no attribute 'readline'
```

The important line to look at in the trackback is the last one: `AttributeError: 'string' object has no attribute 'readline'`. If you read the documentation for the `rfc822` module, you will see that it has been written to work with any object that implements at least a subset of the operations for a `file` type object. In total, the `file` type comprises 12 operations—`read()`, `seek()`, `tell()`, etc. Of these, only `readline()` is required by `rfc822`.

If we had a way to make a string masquerade as a file, that is, a way to make a string implement the operations associated with the `file` type, the `rfc822` module would be happy to work with our string.

Enter the standard module `StringIO`. Its purpose in life is to make a string object look like a file object by providing implementations of the operations required by the `file` type.

```
CD-ROM reference=5120.txt
>>> from StringIO import StringIO
>>> m = rfc822.Message (
        StringIO("To: noel@digitome.com\nFrom:sean@digitome
        .com\n\nHello")
            )
>>> m.headers
['To: noel@digitome.com', 'From:sean@digitome.com']
>>>
```

Let us replay that in slow motion so that you can see what happened. The `StringIO` module provides a class of the same name. This is imported with the line:

```
CD-ROM reference=5121.txt
>>> from StringIO import StringIO
```

Let's create a string variable for the e-mail message.

```
CD-ROM reference=5122.txt
>>> message = "To: noel@digitome.com\nFrom:sean@digitome
    .com\n\nHello"
```

Now we create a new `StringIO` object passing in this string.

```
CD-ROM reference=5123.txt
>>> s = StringIO(message)
```

The object is not a file and it is not a string. It is an instance of the `StringIO` class. The class of an object can be retrieved from the special `__class__` variable.

```
CD-ROM reference=5124.txt
>>> s.__class__
<class StringIO.StringIO at 11bb0d0>
```

The critical thing from the point of view of the rfc822 module is that it has a readline method.

```
CD-ROM reference=5125.txt
>>> s.readline()
'To: noel@digitome.com\012'
>>> s.readline()
'From:sean@digitome.com\012'
```

The main point here is that the rfc822 module has been written to an interface, not an implementation. It works with objects that implement operations of the file type regardless of what class they are created from.

This concept is pervasive in Python—not just in Python's standard library, but in the very heart of the language. For example, Python's for loop will work with *any* object that implements a method called __getitem__. Such objects are collectively referred to as sequence type objects. The native sequence type objects in Python are strings, lists, and tuples. We can implement our own by simply implementing the __getitem__ method in our own classes. In the example below, we implement a class called MyList. It has a __getitem__ method and so can then be used in a Python for loop. The presence of a __getitem__ method also enables us to index into a object by using positive or negative indexes, as the example below illustrates.

```
CD-ROM reference=5126.txt

C>type sequence.py

# A list object suitable for use with for loops.

# Create a class called MyList.
class MyList:
    def __init__(self,L):
            # The constructor for the class takes 1 parameter
            which
```

```
            # is a list.
            # A reference to this list is stored in the _list
            # instance variable
            self._list = L

        # Implement __getitem__ so that objects of this class can
        # be used in for loops and other sequence type
          operations.
        def __getitem__(self,n):
            # Parameter n is the offset of the item to return.
            if n < len(self._list):
                    # Index requested is less than size of list.
                    # Return item at that index.
                    return self._list[n]
            else:
                    # index out of range - raise an IndexError.
                    raise IndexError

# Create a list object to play with.
m = [1, 2, 3, 4, 5, 6]

# Loop over the elements in the list with a for loop.
print "\nFor loop on a standard list object"
for e in m:
        # Print out each item. The trailing "," tells Python not
        # to output a line end character after the print.
        print e,

# Create an object of class MyList.
MyListObject = MyList(m)

# Using a for loop, print out each item in MyListObject.
print "\nFor loop on a MyList object"
for e in MyListObject:
        # Print out each item. The trailing "," tells Python not
        # to output a line end character after the print.
        print e,

print "Third item in MyListObject is",MyListObject[3]
print "Second last item in MyListObject is",MyListObject[-2]
```

C>**python sequence.py**

```
For loop on a standard list object
1 2 3 4 5 6
```

```
For loop on a MyList object
1 2 3 4 5 6
Third item in MyListObject is 4
Second last item in MyListObject is 5
```

So far, so good. This time, we will do something more useful than MyList. ReverseList is a class that can be used in a for loop that feeds its elements out backwards.

```
CD-ROM reference=5127.txt
C>type ReverseList.py

#A class that implements basic sequence type. Feeds elements out
#of sequence backwards.

class ReverseList:
    def __init__(self,l):
        self.-list = l
        self.offset = len(l)-1

    def __getitem__(self,n):
        if n < len(self._list):
            return self._list[self.offset - n]
        else:
            raise IndexError

print "\nIterate a list backwards using ReverseList object"
m = [1, 2, 3, 4, 5, 6]
for e in ReverseList(m):
    print e,
```

```
C>python reverselist.py

Iterate a list backwards using ReverseList object
6 5 4 3 2 1
```

Here is another example; this class can be used to retrieve every second object from a sequence.

```
CD-ROM reference=5128.txt
C>type EverySecondOne.py

# A class that implements basic sequence type. Feeds elements out
# of sequence, skipping every second one.
class EverySecondItem:
```

```
    def __init__(self,l):
        self._list = l

def __getitem__(self,n):
        if (2 * n) < len(self._list):
            return self._list[2 * n]
        else:
            raise IndexError
m = [1, 2, 3, 4, 5, 6]
for e in EverySecondItem(m):
    print e,
```

C>**python EverySecondOne.py**

1 3 5

One more thing before we leave this subject. It is occasionally useful to have a `for` loop that iterates exactly N times. The easiest way to do this in Python is to use the built-in `range()` function. This function creates a tuple with consecutive numbers from 0 to N-1, as shown below.

```
CD-ROM reference=5129.txt
>>> m = range(6)
>>> print m
[0, 1, 2, 3, 4, 5]
```

We can use this to do bigger tests of the reverse list class:

```
CD-ROM reference=5130.txt
>>> from ReverseList import ReverseList
>>> m = range(100)
>>> for n in ReverseList(m):
...   print n,

99 98 97 96 ... 0
```

What happens if we try to *set* a value in the `ReverseList` object?

```
CD-ROM reference=5131.txt
>>> from sequence import ReverseList
>>> r = ReverseList ([1,2,3])
>>> print r[0]
3
```

```
>>> r[0] = 99
Traceback (innermost last):
  File "<interactive input>", line 1, in ?
AttributeError: __setitem__
>>>
```

To support setting elements, the ReverseList class would have to implement another special method:__setitem__. How about slicing?

```
CD-ROM reference=5132.txt
>>> print r[1:3]
Traceback (innermost last):
  File "<interactive input>", line 1, in ?
AttributeError: __getslice__
>>>
```

To support slices, the ReverseList class would have to implement the special method:__getslice__. Do you see a pattern emerging here? Basically, for every operation that Python performs on lists, there is a corresponding "magic method" with a name like __getslice__ or __getitem__. By implementing these methods in your own classes, you can make core Python language features such as for loops, slicing, and so on, work directly with your data structures as if they were part of the core language!

Two more magic methods are sufficiently common to merit attention here. The __str__ method controls what happens when Python tries to get a string representation of an object. This happens, for example, any time Python tries to print something with the print statement. The __repr__ method is similar except that Python expects it to return a string which, if executed, would re-create the object. Here is the __str__ method implemented for the Account class.

```
CD-ROM reference=5133.txt
C>type accounts.py
class Account:
    ...

    def __str__ (self):
```

```
                # Return string representation of this object.
                # Include details of account balance and account name.
                res = "Account Object:"
                res = res + " Balance is '%d'. Account Name is
                  '%s'" % (
                        self.Balance, self.Name
                        )

# Create an Account object.
anAccount = Account(0,"Sean McGrath")
# Ask Python to print it
print anAccount
```

```
C>python accounts.py
```

```
Account Object: Balance is '0'. Account Name is 'Sean Mc-
Grath'
```

Where possible, the __repr__ method should return an executable representation of the object. Here it is for the Account class.

```
CD-ROM reference=5134.txt
C>type accounts.py

class Account:
    ...

    def __repr__(self):
            # Return executable representation
            return 'Account (%d,"%s")' % (self.Balance,
                self.Name)
```

You can ask for the executable representation of an object in two ways. First, you can surround the object name with back-ticks (`), like this:

```
CD-ROM reference=5135.txt
>>> from accounts import Account
>>> anAccount = Account(0,"Sean McGrath")
>>> print `anAccount`
Account (0,"Sean McGrath")
```

Second, you can use the built-in repr function, like this:

```
CD-ROM reference=5136.txt
>>> from accounts import Account
>>> anAccount = Account(0,"Sean McGrath")
>>> print repr(anAccount)
Account (0,"Sean McGrath")
```

The string returned by __repr__ can be executed with the built-in eval method. In the example below, an Account object a is created. The executable representation of a is stored in the s variable, which is a String. This string is then passed into the eval function, which creates a second Account object referenced by variable b.

```
CD-ROM reference=5137.txt
>>> from accounts import Account
>>> a = Account (100,"Sean")
>>> print a
Account Object: Balance is '100'. Account Name is 'Sean'
>>> s = repr(a)
>>> print s
Account (0,"Sean")
>>> b = eval (s)
>>> print b
Account Object: Balance is '100'. Account Name is 'Sean'
```

5.8 | In Conclusion

Well, that is the bulk of it! You may need to run through the contents of this chapter more than once for everything to sink in. Executing and playing with the code samples are strongly recommended. With Python, an ounce of practice is worth ten tons of theory.

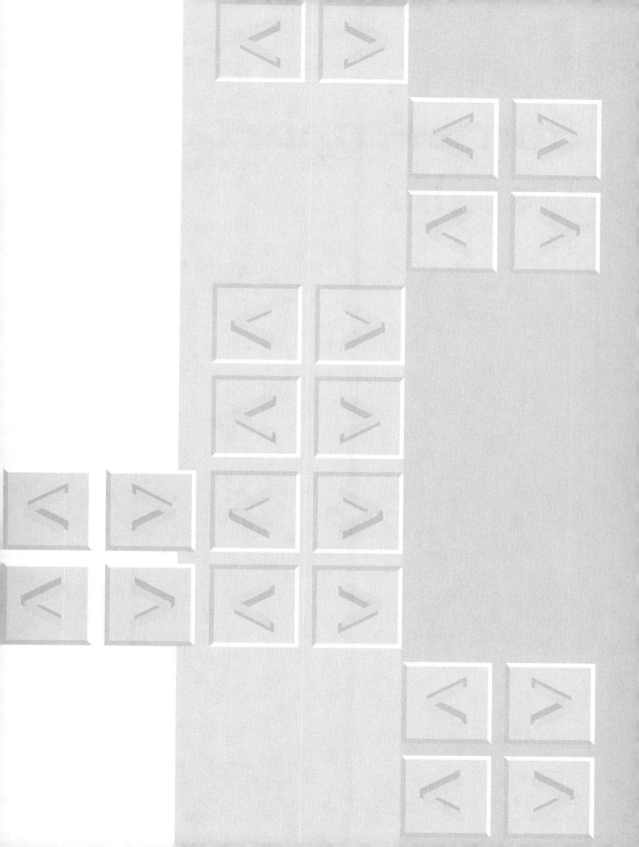

Some Important Details

6.1 | Dealing with Long Lines

As you know, Python uses indentation to control the grouping of statements for execution. Depending on personal taste or editing environment restrictions, this indentation can cause problems. The program below is not syntactically correct because the assignment to the variable with the very long name has wrapped around to two lines.

```
CD-ROM reference=6001.txt
if x:
        if y:
            if z:
                if a:
                    if b:
                        while x:
                            for n in foo:
SomeVeryLongVariableNameGoshWouldAnyoneReallyHave
  OneOfThese =
SomeVeryLongVariableNameGoshWouldAnyoneReallyHave
  OneOfThese + 1
```

The first thing to say about a long line is that it occurs very infrequently in practice! If it does occur, there are a number of ways to deal with it. First, terminating a line with a "\" character tells Python that the next line is actually a continuation of the current line.

```
CD-ROM reference=6002.txt
if x:
    if y:
        if z:
            if a:
                if b:
                    while x:
                        for n in foo:
    SomeVeryLongVariableNameGoshWouldAnyoneReally
      HaveOneOfThese =\
    SomeVeryLongVariableNameGoshWouldAnyoneReally
      HaveOneOfThese + 1
```

Second, expressions involving parentheses, brackets, or braces can split over multiple lines. We can take advantage of that behavior in this case by introducing parentheses in the assignment.

```
CD-ROM reference=6003.txt
if x:
    if y:
        if z:
            if a:
                if b:
                    while x:
                        for n in foo:
    SomeVeryLongVariableNameGoshWouldAnyoneReally
      HaveOneOfThese = (
    SomeVeryLongVariableNameGoshWouldAnyoneReally
      HaveOneOfThese + 1)
```

The parentheses solution is very useful for function or method calls with lots of parameters.

```
CD-ROM reference=6004.txt
if x:
    if y:
        if z:
```

```
        if a:
            if b:
                while x:
                    for n in foo:
                        AMethodWithALongName(
                            "long paremeters",
                        31415926535927182818282846,
                            AnotherVeryLong
                                VariableName
                            )
```

Line length can occasionally be an issue with single-line strings. If two literal strings occur side-by-side, separated only by white space, Python treats them as parts of one string.

```
CD-ROM reference=6005.txt
if x:
    if y:
        if z:
            if a:
                if b:
                    while x:
                        for n in foo:
                            AMethodWithALongName(
                            "Although this string "
                            "might look like it "
                            "has more"
                            "than one line in it, "
                            "it is in fact"
                            "a single line string "
                            "as Python automati
                              cally"
                            "joins the pieces "
                            "together when it"
                            "analyses the "
                            "program text.")
```

6.2 | Using the dir Function

The `dir` function is one of the most useful functions in Python when it comes to digging around in Python's interactive mode. You provide it with the name of a module or object, and it returns lots of useful information about the contents of that module or object. In the example below, the dir command is used to list the variables and functions provided by the sys module.

```
CD-ROM reference=6006.txt
>>> import sys
>>> dir(sys)
['__doc__', '__name__', '__stderr__', '__stdin__', '__stdout__',
'argv', 'builtin-module-names', 'copyright', 'dllhandle',
  'exc-info',
'exc-type', 'exec-prefix', 'executable', 'exit', 'getrefcount',
'hexversion', 'last-traceback', 'last-type', 'last-value',
'maxint', 'modules', 'path', 'platform', 'prefix', 'ps1', 'ps2',
'setcheckinterval', 'setprofile', 'settrace', 'stderr',
  'stdin',
'stdout', 'version', 'winver']
>>> print sys.version
1.5.2 (#0, Apr 13 1999, 10:51:12) [MSC 32 bit (Intel)]
```

The dir command is equally at home when supplied with the name of an object. Here is the output of the dir command when applied to a list object.

```
CD-ROM reference=6007.txt
>>> x = [1,2,3]
>>> dir(x)
['append', 'count', 'extend', 'index', 'insert', 'pop', 'remove',
'reverse', 'sort']
```

The variable x references a list object and, as a result, has been anointed with all the capabilities bestowed on it by membership in the list class. These include methods for appending, counting, etc., as you can see from the list above.

You can often deduce what each of these list methods does just from its name. Of course, if you want to be sure, you can consult the embedded documentation.

```
CD-ROM reference=6008.txt
>>> print x.count.__doc__
L.count(value) -> integer – return number of occurrences of value
```

```
>>> print x.extend.__doc__
L.extend(list) - extend list by appending list elements
>>>
```

You may have guessed that the dir function does its job by simply printing out the keys from __dict__ dictionaries. Here is a variation on the above example, using both direct access to the __dict__ dictionary and the dir function to print out the keys.

```
CD-ROM reference=6009.txt
>>> import pprint, fileinput
>>> f = fileinput.input()
>>> dir(f)
['_backup', '_backupfilename', '_file',
'_filelineno', '_filename', '_files',
'_inplace', '_isstdin', '_lineno', '_output',
'_savestdout']
>>> print f.__dict__.keys()
['_isstdin', '_files', '_backup',
'_file', '_inplace', '_savestdout',
'_filename', '_lineno', '_filelineno',
'_output', '_backupfilename']
```

The lists have the same elements but occur in different orders because the order in which keys occur in a dictionary is irrelevant and essentially random. To see more clearly that the lists have the same entries, we can sort the list returned by the keys() method. There is no need to sort the list returned by dir because it is already sorted.

```
CD-ROM reference=6010.txt
>>> a = f.__dict__.keys()
>>> b = dir(f)
>>> b.sort()
>>> a
['_backup', '_backupfilename', '_file', '_filelineno',
  '_filename',
'_files', '_inplace', '_isstdin', '_lineno', '_output',
  '_savestdout']
>>> b
['_backup', '_backupfilename', '_file', '_filelineno',
  '_filename',
'_files', '_inplace', '_isstdin', '_lineno', '_output',
  '_savestdout']
```

The `dir` function can also be used without any parameter, in which case it returns the variables known to Python at the point where the `dir` function was called.

```
CD-ROM reference=6011.txt
>>> dir()
['__builtins__', '__doc__', '__name__']
>>> import string
>>> dir()
['__builtins__', '__doc__', '__name__', 'string']
>>> import sys
>>> dir()
['__builtins__', '__doc__', '__name__', 'string', 'sys']
```

In the above interactive session, the modules `string` and `sys` are added, showing how each import adds an entry to the list of known variables at Python's disposal.

6.3 | Working with Docstrings

Every Python module has a variable called `__doc__` associated with it. This variable holds any embedded documentation created by the programmer for the module. You can create documentation for a module by entering a string at the very top of the module file.

Moreover, if the first thing you type into a class/method/function or module is a string, it will become the documentation string associated with that class/method/function or module. Here is a `SimpleInterest` calculator with embedded documentation.

```
CD-ROM reference=6012.txt
>>> def SimpleInterest(p,t,r):
...    "Simple Interest Rate Calculator"
...    return (p * t * r)/100
```

We can interrogate the `SimpleInterest` function with our trusty `dir` command.

```
CD-ROM reference=6013.txt
>>> dir (SimpleInterest)
['__doc__', '__name__', 'func_code', 'func_defaults',
'func_doc',
'func_globals'
, 'func-name']
```

Note that __doc__ is in the list returned by the `dir` command. We can print it by using the `print` statement.

```
CD-ROM reference=6014.txt
>>> print SimpleInterest.__doc__
Simple Interest Rate Calculator
```

Note how the documentation string for `SimpleInterest` is carried around by Python along with the function. This behavior contrasts dramatically with most programming languages that throw such documentation away early on in the parsing process. I think you will agree that conscientious use of *docstrings*, as they are called, can be a great boon to the Python programmer on a learning curve.

In the last chapter we created a two-line Python program. Here it is again with a docstring added at the top of the file.

```
CD-ROM reference=6015.txt
C>type foo.py

"This is the documentation for the foo module. Pretty useful, huh?"
print 1+2
print "Hello World"
```

We can execute this just as in the previous chapter, and we will get the same result as before. The docstring has not affected it in any way:

```
CD-ROM reference=6016.txt
C>Python foo.py
3
Hello World
```

We can also import this module into Python interactively. When modules are imported, any executable statements (such as the `print` statements in this case) are executed automatically.

```
CD-ROM reference=6017.txt
>>> import foo
3
Hello World
```

We can now interrogate the foo module by using the dir command.

```
CD-ROM reference=6018.txt
>>> dir(foo)
['__builtins__', '__doc__', '__file__', '__name__']
```

Note the presence of the __doc__ variable. Let's print it.

```
CD-ROM reference=6019.txt
>>> print foo.__doc__
This is the documentation for the foo module. Pretty
  useful huh?
```

As you can see, the first string entered into the file foo.py has found its way into the foo module as the __doc__ variable.

Docstrings regularly need to be longer than a single line and so the triple-quoted form of Python strings is regularly used.

```
CD-ROM reference=6020.txt
"""
This is the documentation for the foo module.
It is not more useful than it was before but it does illus-
trate how docstrings contained in triple quotes can extend
over
multiple lines.
"""
print 1+2
print "Hello World"
```

Python does not force you to add docstrings, but it is part of the "Python way" to make judicious use of them both for your own benefit and the benefit of others using your code!

6.4 | Importing Modules

Python does a lot of work to guess where to look for the modules it needs to import. You can see the fruit of its labors by looking at the path variable of the sys module. Each directory listed in this path will be searched for modules when an import statement is executed. You can add directories to this list if you need to by means of an environment variable called PYTHONPATH.

Here is my path on Windows NT:

```
CD-ROM reference=6021.txt
>>> import sys
>>> print sys.path
['', 'c:\\',
C:\\PROGRA~1\\PYTHON',
'C:\\Program Files\\Python\\Lib\\plat-win',
'C:\\Program Files\\Python\\Lib',
'C:\\Program Files\\Python\\DLLs',
'C:\\Program Files\\Python\\Lib\\lib-tk',
'c:\\program files\\python\\DLLs',
'c:\\program files\\python\\lib',
'c:\\program files\\python\\lib\\plat-win',
'c:\\program files\\python\\lib\\lib-tk',
'c:\\program files\\python']
```

Windows

Here is my path on Linux:

```
CD-ROM reference=6022.txt
>>> import sys
>>> print sys.path
['', '/usr/lib/python1.5/',
'/usr/lib/python1.5/lib-old',
'/usr/lib/python1.5/plat-linux2',
'/usr/lib/python1.5/lib-tk',
'/usr/lib/python1.5/lib-dynload',
'/usr/lib/python1.5/site-packages',
'/usr/lib/site-python']
```

Linux

If you are having trouble with an `import` statement not finding a module, your first port of call should be the `sys.path` variable to see if Python has been told where to find the module.

6.5 | Executing Python Programs

As you know, Python programs are executed directly from their textual form rather than compiled. Behind the scenes, Python does a certain amount of compilation on source files. They are compiled into into an intermediate representation known as Python bytecode. The bytecode is an intermediate representation of your program suitable for execution on the *Python Virtual Machine*. Python is similar to Java, Visual Basic, and Smalltalk in this regard. This bytecode is written to disk as a file with the same base name as the `.py` file but with a `.pyc` extension. Python uses timestamp logic to decide if it needs to regenerate the `.pyc` files from `.py` files. That is, it checks the modification time of the `.py` file against the modification time of the corresponding .pyc file. If the `.py` file is more up-to-date, it is recompiled and a new `.pyc` file is generated.

In the example below, a Python module is created and imported. As a consequence of the `import` statement, a compiled version of the module is created behind the scenes.

```
CD-ROM reference=6023.txt
C>type hello.py
def Hello():
x = 1
y = 2
if x < y:
print "Hello"

C>python
>>> import hello
>>> ^C
```

The `import` statement above causes Python to search for the `hello.py` module. It then creates a compiled version of it in the file `hello.pyc`. Here is a hex dump of the first few bytes of `hello.pyc`.

```
CD-ROM reference=6024.txt
C>debug hello.pyc

C:\>debug hello.pyc
-d
0C9A:0100  99 4E 0D 0A E4 02 DD 37-63 00 00 00 00 01 00 00
           .N.....7c.......
0C9A:0110  00 73 13 00 00 00 7F 00-00 7F 01 00 64 00 00 84
           .s..........d...
0C9A:0120  00 00 5A 00 00 64 01 00-53 28 02 00 00 00 63 00
           ..Z..d..S(....c.
0C9A:0130  00 02 00 02 00 03 00 73-35 00 00 00 7F 01 00 7F
           .......s5.......
```

You can ship an application with just the `.pyc` files if you want to prevent users from having access to the source code. The bytecode is also completely portable; a `.pyc` file created on a Sun® Solaris™ machine will run quite happily on a Windows PC.

If you are curious as to what the bytecode actually means, you can disassemble it with the standard `dis` module. If you have ever worked at the assembly language level, you should be able to work out what most of the instructions below are doing.

```
CD-ROM reference=6025.txt
>>> import hello
>>> from dis import dis
>>> dis(hello)
Disassembly of Hello:
          0 SET-LINENO          1

          3 SET-LINENO          2
          6 LOAD-CONST          1 (1)
          9 STORE-FAST          0 (x)

         12 SET-LINENO          3
         15 LOAD-CONST          2 (2)
```

```
        18  STORE-FAST            1 (y)

        21  SET-LINENO            4
        24  LOAD-FAST             0 (x)
        27  LOAD-FAST             1 (y)
        30  COMPARE-OP            0 (<)
        33  JUMP-IF-FALSE        12 (to 48)
        36  POP-TOP

        37  SET-LINENO            5
        40  LOAD-CONST            3 ('Hello')
        43  PRINT-ITEM
        44  PRINT-NEWLINE
        45  JUMP-FORWARD          1 (to 49)
   >>   48  POP-TOP
   >>   49  LOAD-CONST            0 (None)
        52  RETURN-VALUE
```

6.6 | Using the Special Object None

None is a special object in Python used to signify the *absence* of a value. It pops up all over the place in Python. It is the value automatically returned by a function or method unless you specify otherwise. The existence of None gets nicely around an ambiguity found in languages with no such concept. This is best illustrated by example.

In the following code snippet, the empty string and the number 0 are used to mean "Surname does not exist" and "No such account holder," respectively.

```
CD-ROM reference=6026.txt
x = getSurname("Sean")
if x == "":
      print "Surname does not exist"
      balance = getBalance("Sean")
      if balance == 0:
            print "No such account holder"
```

In the getSurname case, the use of an empty string to indicate failure looks okay because a blank surname is presumably illegal. In the `getBalance()` case, the use of the integer 0 to mean failure creates an ambiguity. Does it mean "No such account holder" or does it mean "Account exists with balance 0"?

The object known as `None` gets around this issue cleanly.

```
CD-ROM reference=6027.txt
x = getSurname("Sean")
if x == None:
    print "Surname does not exist"

balance = getBalance("Sean")
if balance == None:
    print "No such account holder"
```

6.7 | Memory Management

Python uses a memory management scheme known as *reference counting*. For each object in the system, Python keeps track of how many variables reference that object. When the number of references to an object shrinks to zero, the memory used by the object is reclaimed or *garbage collected*.

The fact that variables are nothing more than references to objects is a very important one. Consider the following interactive Python session.

```
CD-ROM reference=6028.txt
>>> x = [1,2,3]
>>> print x
[1,2,3]
>>> y = x
>>> print y
[1, 2, 3]
```

The point here is that although both x and y will print the list [1,2,3], there is only *one* list. The variables x and y reference the same object. A diagram will help illustrate what is going on here. See figure 6–1.

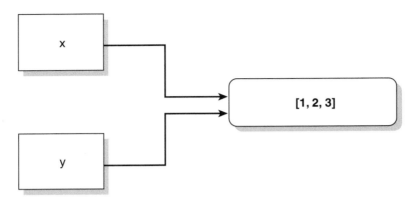

Figure 6–1 Two variables assigned to the same Python list object.

The variables x and y point to the same list object. Either variable can be used to change the list.

```
CD-ROM reference=6029.txt
>>> x = [1,2,3]
>>> print x
[1, 2, 3]
>>> y = x
>>> print y
[1, 2, 3]
>>> y[1] = "Hello"
>>> print y
[1, 'Hello', 3]
>>> print x
[1, 'Hello', 3]
```

This behavior applies to all objects in Python. It even applies to numbers. In fact, the number 1 is simply a predefined Python object. So, when you say x = 1, the variable x is made to point to an existing object known as 1.[1]

In fact, the last diagram would be a more accurate reflection of Python's internal storage of the list [1,2,3] and the two variables x and y if it looked like figure 6–2.

---

[1]Because the number 1 is predefined, it always has at least one reference to it. Thus, the number 1 cannot be garbage collected.

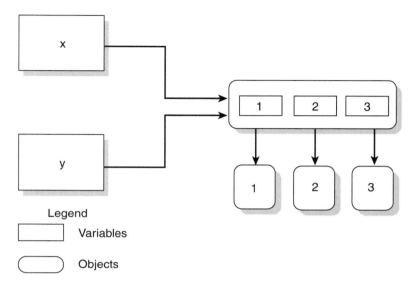

Figure 6–2 Basic numbers are also objects in Python.

Here is another example, this time using the Account class developed earlier:

```
CD-ROM reference=6030.txt
>>> from accounts import Account
>>> a = Account (10,"Sean")
>>> b = Account (20,"Paul")
>>> x = a
>>> for i in (a,b,x):
...    print i
...
Account Object: Balance is '10'. Account Name is 'Sean'
Account Object: Balance is '20'. Account Name is 'Paul'
Account Object: Balance is '10'. Account Name is 'Sean'
```

In the above code fragment there are three variables called x, a and b, but there are only two Account objects. Both x and a refer to the same Account object.

If you need to make a true copy of an object rather than create another reference to it, you can use the standard copy module.

```
CD-ROM reference=6031.txt
>>> import copy
>>> x = [1,2,3]
>>> y = copy.copy(x)
```

In the above example, the object referenced by x is cloned by the copy function and assigned to the variable y. There are now two separate lists of the form [1,2,3], as shown in figure 6–3.

Now that x and y reference separate objects, changes to the variable y have no effect on the variable x.

```
CD-ROM reference=6032.txt
>>> y[1] = "Hello"
>>> print y
[1, 'Hello', 3]
>>> print x
[1, 2, 3]
```

If the objects to be copied are complex objects, that is, objects that themselves contain objects, you may need to use the deepcopy method to get a true second copy.

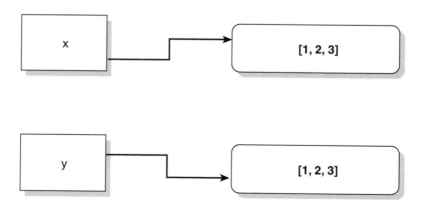

Figure 6–3   A second list created by the copy function.

6.8 | Copying Objects

As we saw in the last section, the default behavior of assignment operations in Python is to make references to objects rather than to create
duplicate copies of objects.

So, what if you really do need to make a copy of a list, for example?
Python provides a module, known as `copy`, that can copy arbitrary
data structures.

```
CD-ROM reference=6033.txt
>>> import copy
>>> x = [1,2,3]
>>> print x
[1, 2, 3]
>>> y = copy.copy(x)
>>> print y
[1, 2, 3]
>>> print id(x)
8376864
>>> print id(y)
8378848
>>> x is y
0
```

The `copy` module can also deal with nested list structures. It provides a `deepcopy` method that recursively handles objects contained
within other objects.

```
CD-ROM reference=6034.txt
>>> import copy
>>> x = [1,2,["Button my shoe",[3,[4,["close the door"]]]]]
>>> y = copy.deepcopy(x)
>>> print y
[1, 2, ['Button my shoe', [3, [4, ['close the door']]]]]
>>> print y[2][1][1][1]
'close the door'
>>> y[2][1][1][1] = "close the window"
>>> print x
[1, 2, ['Button my shoe', [3, [4, ['close the door']]]]]
>>> print y
[1, 2, ['Button my shoe', [3, [4, ['close the window']]]]]
```

Note how the change to a deeply nested string in y does not affect the string at the same location in x.

A quick and easy alternative to using the copy module can be used with lists. Remember the list-slicing syntax discussed in chapter 5? Slicing makes a copy of the sliced portion of the list. In this example, the variable y references a new list object created by shaving off the first element of x.

```
CD-ROM reference=6035.txt
>>> x = [1,2,3]
>>> y = x[1:]
>>> y
[2, 3]
>>> id(y)
18599072
>>> id(x)
18602896
```

If both indexes in the slice are left blank, it means "slice the whole list." This has the effect of making a complete copy as shown here.

```
CD-ROM reference=6036.txt
>>> x = [1,2,3]
>>> y = x[:]
>>> y
[1, 2, 3]
>>> id(y)
18603008
>>> id(x)
18602128
```

6.9 | Determining Object Identity

It can be very useful to quickly determine if two objects are the same object. There are a number of ways to determine this.

First, Python provides the operator is for this purpose. The expression x is y returns 1 (i.e., true) if x and y are the same object and 0 (false) otherwise.

```
CD-ROM reference=6037.txt
>>> x = [1,2,3]
>>> y = x
>>> print x
[1, 2, 3]
>>> print y
[1, 2, 3]
>>> x is y
1
>>> z = [1,2,3]
>>> x is z
0
```

An alternative method of checking for sameness is to use the built-in `id` function. Given a variable name, the `id` function returns the memory address of the object referenced by the variable. If two objects have the same address in memory, they are the same object.

```
CD-ROM reference=6038.txt
>>> x = [1,2,3]
>>> y = x
>>> x
[1, 2, 3]
>>> y
[1, 2, 3]
```

By calling the `id` function, we can see that both x and y refer to the same object at this point. The object lives at memory location 8349408.

```
CD-ROM reference=6039.txt
>>> x = [1,2,3]
>>> print id(x)
8349408
>>> y = x
>>> print id(y)
8349408
>>> z = [1,2,3]
>>> print id(z)
8352384
```

6.10 | Handling Errors

The problem of dealing with error conditions is as old as programming itself. Historically, dealing with errors was left to the programmer to worry about. That is, programming languages did not provide any special functionality for dealing with the error-handling problem. The time-honored way to deal with errors involves two things:

- Testing to see if an error has occurred.

- Having decided that something has gone wrong, either (a) deal with it, or (b) return some signal to indicate that something has gone wrong.

Returning some form of error code gives other parts of the software a chance to deal with the error. This approach results in the following code pattern.

```
CD-ROM reference=6040.txt
def DoSomeThingClever:
    . . .
    if x < y:
        # Return magic value indicating error.
        return -1
    result = DoSomeThingReallyClever()
    if result == 0:
        # Return magic value indicating error
        return -1
    . . .

# Main Program Starts Here
res = DoSomeThingClever()
if res == -1:
    exit ("Bad Karma")
. . .
res = DoSomeThingReallyClever()
if res == 0:
    # Check for magic value indicating error.
    exit ("Bad Karma")
```

Note that the function DoSomeThingClever uses the value -1 as a "magic value" to indicate an error condition. Parts of the code that call this function need error-detecting code to monitor the value returned. Note also that the other function DoSomeThingReally-Clever uses 0 as its magic value.

This style of coding has a number of problems:

■ Programmers must invent "magic values" to indicate error conditions. Some programmers will use 0 in one context and -1 in another to mean "error." Sometimes they will use both within the same library! Of course, if you are using Python, you can use the special variable None to get around this problem.

■ Programmers need to be methodical about checking for error conditions every step of the way. This can add up to a lot of code. Incorporating this error-catching code is an error-prone task and makes the code harder to read.

Modern object-oriented languages have to take a different approach and provide support for error handling directly within the language itself. This facility is generally referred to as "exception handling." Here is a Python snippet that illustrates exceptions.

```
CD-ROM reference=6041.txt
C>type karma.py

from exceptions import Exception
x = 0
y = 1
class KarmaException (Exception):
      def __init__(self,s=""):
            self.problem = s

def DoSomethingClever():
      if x < y:
            raise KarmaException("Expected x > y")

try:
```

```
    DoSomethingClever()
except KarmaException,e:
    print e.problem
```

```
C>python karma.py
```

```
Expected x > y
```

What happens is this. The programmer adds code so that when an error occurs, the program raises an exception. When calling routines that may raise exceptions, the programmer adds "catch code" to be executed when the exception is raised.

If an error condition occurs when the program is running, normal execution of the routine that caused the exception is ended. The program then looks around to find catch code for the exception that has been raised. If it finds such code within the current subroutine, great, the catch code is executed.

If catch code is not found, the program looks for it in the routine that called this one. Again, if it is found, it is executed. If not, the routine that called the routine that called this one is tried . . . and so on.

If the search for suitable catch code fails (by reaching the very top of the program), then a default exception handler is executed and the program terminates.

This style of coding has a number of benefits:

■ Programmers can explicitly state what errors their program detects and raises exceptions for. Programming language compilers or interpreters can then perform checks to make sure that there is a proper match between exceptions thrown and exceptions caught.

■ Programmers have the freedom to put a group of statements together into a single block of statements without worrying about handling error conditions every step of the way.

■ Having caught an exception, if programmers decide they cannot deal with it, they can raise it again to allow other error handling code to deal with it.

6.11 | The Dynamic Nature of Python

Python is what is known as a *dynamically typed* language. That is, its variables are not restricted to referencing objects of any particular type by the language. In Python, variables spring into existence as required. They do not need to be declared beforehand. Moreover, a variable x can be an integer one minute, a string the next, and an user-defined object the next. This is a very flexible way of doing things and can be a great boon for certain types of programming tasks. However, it does mean you have to be careful, as the example below will illustrates.

```
CD-ROM reference=6042.txt
>>> def DaysFromHours(h):
...return h / 24
...
>>> DaysFromHours(240)
10
>>> DaysFromHours("Hello World")
Traceback (innermost last):
  File "<stdin>", line 1, in ?
  File "<stdin>", line 2, in DaysFromHours
TypeError: bad operand type(s) for /
```

The first thing to note is that this error message is not the result of the Python language interpreter analyzing the code and finding a problem. In other words, it is not a *compile-time* error. The error message is a *run-time* error—a problem that occurs when Python is executing a syntactically correct program.

The root of the problem is that the DaysFromHours function has attempted to divide a string "Hello World" by 24 and has quite understandably failed. Clearly, the `DaysFromHours` method will not function without having a number as its parameter.

We cannot *guarantee* that the function will always be passed a number because, as already mentioned, Python variables are not restricted to particular types. What we can do is add logic to the program to deal with this eventuality. We could, for example, write an error to a log file and carry on without changing the balance. We could also take the view that passing a string where an integer is required is something that should never happen and treat it as a logical error in the way the program was coded.

To help find logical coding errors, Python provides a built-in function known as `assert`. Given an expression, the `assert` function raises an exception if the expression is false. It is often used in conjunction with another built-in function, called `type`. Given a variable as a parameter, the `type` function returns a value indicating the type of that variable. All the possible return values from the `type` function are in the standard module called `types`.

In the code below, a combination of the `type` and `assert` functions is used to catch the logical error created if the `HoursFromDays` function is called with anything other than an integer parameter.

```
CD-ROM reference=6043.txt
import types
...
def DaysFromHours(d):
    assert(type(d) == types.IntType)
    return d / 14
```

This time when we call `HoursFromDays` with a string parameter, we get an exact indication of the root cause of the problem.

```
CD-ROM reference=6044.txt
>>> DaysFromHours("Hello World")
Traceback
    DaysFromHours("Hello World")
    assert(type(d) == types.IntType)
AssertionError
```

Assertions are very useful during program development. When you are confident that your software works as it should, you can disable the checking of assertions by means of the -o switch to the Python interpreter. This switch turns on various optimizations, one of which is the disabling of assertions.

6.12 | Named Parameters

Python allows you to add the names of parameters to function and method calls. This naming can help make the code easier to read, especially when there are lots of parameters.

```
CD-ROM reference=6045.txt
class Account:
    ...
    def __repr__(self):
        """
        Return executable form
        """
        return 'Account (balance=%d,name="%s")' %
(self.Balance,self.Name)

>>> from accounts import Account
>>> a = Account (100,"Sean")
>>> print a
Account Object: Balance is '100'. Account Name is 'Sean'
>>> s = repr(a)
>>> print s
Account (balance=100,name="Sean")
>>> b = eval (s)
>>> print b
Account Object: Balance is '100'. Account Name is 'Sean'
```

6.13 | The Pass Statement

The pass statement provides a way of saying "do nothing" that can be very useful during program development. For example, you want to lay out an `if` statement in which you have not yet filled in one of the branches but you want to be able to execute the program:

```
CD-ROM reference=6046.txt
if x > y:
    x = x - 1
elif x == y:
    # XXX deal with this case later.
    pass
else:
    print "Hello World"
```

The `pass` statement is also used with methods as a way of indicating that the method should be overridden by a subclass to do something useful. This idea is used heavily in the SAX API, which we discuss in chapter 10.

```
CD-ROM reference=6047.txt
class DocumentHandler:
    def characters(str):
    # Override this method to do something useful.
    pass
```

6.14 | Packages

In chapter 3, when we proved the existence of the XML package, we executed a program called `testpyexpat.py`. If you looked inside this program, you will have seen that the first executable line looks like this:

```
CD-ROM reference=6048.txt
from xml.parsers import pyexpat
```

This is another variation on the syntax of an `import` statement. A collection of modules can be organized into a hierarchical collection of submodules. Any dots in a module name are interpreted as separating the overall module collection (or package) into submodules.

Typically, the dotted module names will map onto directory hierachies. So, for example, we can tell by looking at the above `import` statement that there is a subdirectory called `parsers` in the XML package directory.

Clearly, there could be many submodules in a package and thus many subdirectories. In the case of the XML package, these subpackages are called `arch`, `dom`, `parsers` and `sax` and `unicode`. There will be times when you simply want to import everything like this.

```
CD-ROM reference=6049.txt
from xml import *
```

In an ideal world, this statement would work by listing the contents of the `xml` directory, detecting the subdirectories, and importing them all. Unfortunately, it is not possible to do that in a platform-independent way.

Instead, Python looks for a special Python file named `__init__.py`. In it, Python expects to find a list named `__all__` that explicitly lists the subdirectories containing modules. Here is the `__init__.py` file from the `xml` directory.

```
CD-ROM reference=6050.txt
__all__ = ['arch', 'dom', 'parsers', 'sax', 'unicode']
```

The effect of the presence of the `__init__.py` file is shown below:

```
CD-ROM reference=6051.txt
>>> dir()
['__builtins__', '__doc__', '__name__']
>>> from xml import *
>>> dir()
['__builtins__', '__doc__', '__name__', 'arch', 'dom',
'parsers', 'sax', 'unicode']
>>>
```

We will make extensive use of the package facility in this book—especially in the discussions about Python's SAX and DOM implementations. For a full discussion of the package facility, see `http://www.python.org/doc/essays/packages.html`.

Processing XML with Regular Expressions

Regular expressions arose in the mathematical community in the fifties and came to prominence in the software development world with the Unix operating system in the seventies. When we think of regular expressions for text processing, especially in the context of Unix, the Perl programming language naturally springs to mind. Perl is rightly acknowledged as having wonderfully powerful regular expression capabilities. Python's regular expression support has been highly influenced by Perl; in particular, Perl 5.

In this chapter, we explore Python's regular expression support. On the way, we will build a useful utility program, xgrep.py, that can be used to find patterns in text files by using regular expressions. It will be analogous in functionality to the time-honored grep utility except that it will use Python-style regular expressions.

Why is it called xgrep? It is called xgrep because we will be making it XML-aware over the course of the next two chapters. In this chapter, we concentrate on making xgrep work with plain text files and illustrate how, with due care, XML can usefully be processed as a plain text notation.

On the way through this chapter, we will encounter a number of useful Python modules that make writing `xgrep` significantly easier. We will see how the `sys` module provides access to command-line parameters. We will use the `getopt` module for command-line parameter parsing and the `glob` module for filename wildcard expansion. We also introduce the concept of a Python *module test harness*.

7.1 | Command-Line Arguments

We already encountered the `sys` module when we printed out the `path` variable as part of the Python existence proof in chapter 2. The `sys` module provides the variable `argv` for accessing command-line arguments. The `argv` variable is an example of a Python *list*. A list is simply an ordered collection of objects. Lists are delimited by square brackets, and items in a list are separated by a ",". Here is a list consisting of integers 1, 2, and 3.

```
CD-ROM reference=7001.txt
[1,2,3]
```

Here is a list consisting of the string `"Hello"`, the floating point number `3.14`, and the integer `1`.

```
CD-ROM reference=7002.txt
["Hello",3.14,1]
```

The `argv` variable is a list of strings—one for each command-line argument. When Python is executed interactively, there are no command-line arguments, so the list is empty, as illustrated below.

```
CD-ROM reference=7003.txt
>>> import sys
>>> print sys.argv
['']
```

Here is a small Python program file `args.py` that illustrates access to command-line arguments.

```
CD-ROM reference=7004.txt
C>type args.py

# Import the sys module
import sys

# The sys.argv is a list of command-line arguments
# Use the built-in len() function to find out how long the
# list is
print "There are", len(sys.argv), "command-line parameter(s)"

# Print the list
print sys.argv
```

The code is straightforward. First, the `sys` module is imported and then Python's multitalented `print` statement is used to print out information about the number of command-line arguments (provided by the `len` function; use this function to get the length of any list). The list itself is then printed. Here are some sample runs of the `args.py` program.

```
CD-ROM reference=7005.txt
C>Python args.py

There are 1 command-line parameter(s)
['args.py']

C>Python args.py a.txt

There are 2 command-line parameter(s)
['args.py', 'a.txt']

C>Python args.py a.txt b.txt

There are 3 command-line parameter(s)
['args.py', 'a.txt', 'b.txt']
```

Note that the first command-line argument is always the name of the program. Python—like C and C++ before it—expects the first command-line argument to be the name of the invoking program.

7.2 | A Module Test Harness for xgrep

Python actively encourages programmers to split programs into *modules*. A Python program typically imports all or part of many other modules. These can be a mixture of standard modules, user-defined modules, or third-party modules.[1]

Frequently, a Python module that can be imported into another program is also a useful standalone application. The xgrep utility, for example, will obviously have a useful life as a command-line tool as well as being a candidate module for inclusion in larger programs.

Imagine for a moment that the main entry point to xgrep is the function XMLGrep. In the example below, a larger program called My-CGIScript imports the XMLGrep function from the xgrep module and calls it, passing it a pattern to search for and a filename.

```
CD-ROM reference=7006.txt
C>type MyCGIScript.py

from xgrep import XMLGrep
...
# Use the imported XMLGrep routine to search for "Sean" in
# the file "staff.xml"
XMLGrep ("Sean","staff.xml")
```

In the example below, the xgrep module is invoked directly from the command line.

```
CD-ROM reference=7007.txt
C>python xgrep.py staff.xml
```

There is a standard way to structure a Python program so that it can be both a module of a larger program and a standalone program as illustrated with xgrep above. Here is how it is done.

---

[1]There are a great many of these modules. See http://www.python.org /download/Contributed.html.

```
CD-ROM reference=7008.txt
C>type xgrep.py

# define the XMLGrep function. It takes two parameters:
# pattern  = the pattern to search for
# filename = the text file to search in

def XMLGrep(pattern, filename):
    print "XMLGrep will search the file '%s' for the pattern
      '%s'" %(filename,pattern)

# Check to see if this script is executing as the main
# program.
if __name__ == "__main__":
    # Import sys module, which gives us access to the command-
    # line parameters via the argv variable.
    import sys
    # Call the XMLGrep function. The first parameter will be
    # the first command-line argument.
    XMLGrep (sys.argv[1],"Sean")
```

The line to focus on above is if __name__ == "__main__":.
Every Python module has an associated __name__ variable. The variable takes one of two values depending on whether the module is being executed from the command line or imported into a larger program.

If a Python module is being executed directly, then its __name__ variable will be set to "__main__". If it is being imported into a larger program, the __name__ variable will be set to the name of the Python file without the .py extension.

Here is a Python program that prints outs its __name__ variable.

```
CD-ROM reference=7009.txt
C> type foo.py

print "Hello. I am a module. My name is",__name__
```

An interactive import of the module is shown below.

```
CD-ROM reference=7010.txt
>>> import foo
Hello. I am a module. My name is foo
```

As you can see, the __name__ variable is set to "foo". Now let's execute the program from the command line.

```
CD-ROM reference=7011.txt
C>python foo.py

Hello. I am a module. My name is __main__
```

The __name__ variable has changed to "__main__", reflecting the fact that the module has been executed as a standalone program rather than imported into another program.

Armed with this information about how the __name__ variable works, the module harness for xgrep should now make sense. Here it is again for ease of reference.

```
CD-ROM reference=7012.txt
if __name__ == "__main__":
    import sys
    XMLGrep (sys.argv[1],"Sean")
```

A plain English reading of the if statement goes something like this:

"If I am being executed as the main program, import the sys module and then call the XMLGrep function; otherwise, do nothing."

Thus, we have a mechanism for executing code when the module is a standalone program and skipping the code when it has been imported into a larger program. The two modes of invoking xgrep are shown below.

```
CD-ROM reference=7013.txt
C>python xgrep.py staff.xml

XMLGrep will process the file 'staff.xml' for the pattern
  'Sean'

>>> import xgrep
>>> xgrep.XMLGrep("staff.xml","Paul")
XMLGrep will process the file 'staff.xml' for the pattern
  'Paul'
```

7.3 | What If There Are No Command-Line Parameters?

A weakness in the current module harness is shown up when `xgrep` is invoked without any command-line parameters.

```
CD-ROM reference=7014.txt
C>python xgrep.py

Traceback (innermost last):
  File "xgrep.py", line 8, in ?
    XMLGrep (sys.argv[1])
IndexError: list index out of range
```

The program has trouble accessing the first command-line parameter, which should be at index 1 in the `argv` list. However, we have not typed in any command-line parameters and therefore there is no entry at offset 1 in the `argv` list. Python's reaction to this is to raise an exception known as `IndexError`, and the program terminates.

We will show two ways of gracefully handling this situation.

First, we can check the length of the `argv` array and generate an error message if it is equal to 1 (the name of the program is always in the `argv` list at offset 0; therefore, a length of 1 indicates no parameters were passed).

```
CD-ROM reference=7015.txt
C>type xgrep.py

def XMLGrep(filename,pattern):
    print "XMLGrep will search the file '%s' for the
     pattern '%s'" %(filename,pattern)

if __name__ == "__main__":
    import sys
    if len(sys.argv)==1:
        #No command line parameters supplied
        #write an error message to standard error
```

```
        sys.stderr.write ("Usage: xgrep.py <filename>")
        #Terminate the program
        sys.exit()
else:
        XMLGrep (sys.argv[1],"Sean")
```

Notice the `sys.stderr.write` statement that is used to write a string to standard error. The `sys` module provides the usual three streams known as `stdin` (standard input), `stdout` (standard output), and `stderr` (standard error). Note also the use of the `exit()` function from the `sys` module to cleanly exit the program.

Invoking the program with no arguments now produces a sensible error message.

```
CD-ROM reference=7016.txt
C>python xgrep.py

Usage: xgrep.py <filename>
```

One small improvement to the above code is worth making at this point. At the moment, the program *hardwires* the name of the program `xgrep` into the error message. What happens if we rename the file to, say, `xgrep1.py`?

```
CD-ROM reference=7017.txt
C>python xgrep1.py

Usage: xgrep.py <filename>
```

The error message still refers to `xgrep.py`, but the Python file has been renamed to `xgrep1.py`. The error message no longer correctly reflects the name of the program. This is easily fixed by changing the line

```
CD-ROM reference=7018.txt
sys.stderr.write ("Usage: xgrep.py <filename>")
```

to

```
CD-ROM reference=7019.txt
sys.stderr.write ("Usage: %s <filename>" % sys.argv[0] )
```

We have used the fact that the name of the program is always available to us as sys.argv[0] to make the error message independent of the filename it is housed in. Now the error message will always reflect the correct filename.

```
CD-ROM reference=7020.txt
C>python xgrep1.py

Usage: xgrep1 <filename>
```

Checking the length of the sys.argv list is perhaps the most common way of checking for the existence of command-line parameters. We saw a hint at the second, alternative way by the fact that Python raises an IndexError exception if it finds that sys.argv[1] does not exist. We can instruct Python to watch out for such IndexError exceptions and then "catch" them to take remedial action. Take a look at the modified code below.

```
CD-ROM reference=7021.txt
def XMLGrep(pattern, filename):
     print "XMLGrep will search the file '%s' " % filename
     print "for the pattern '%s'" % pattern

if __name__ == "__main__":
     import sys
     try:
          filename = sys.argv[1]
     except IndexError:
          # IndexError raised -> no command line parameters
          sys.stderr.write ("Usage: %s <filename>" %
            sys.argv[0] )
          sys.exit()

     XMLGrep (filename,"Sean")
```

Note the try and except keywords. The use of try informs Python that exceptions raised in the following block of code might be caught in the corresponding except block below it. When an exception is raised, Python checks to see if the except block handles the type of exception raised; if it does, then the except block is executed. In the example above, the program catches the IndexError exception, prints a sensible message, and then exits.

Sometimes the most sensible thing to do, having caught an exception, is to clean up and then exit. However, it is often entirely sensible to fix things up somehow and continue execution. One reasonable course of action for xgrep might be to default to a file test.xml in the event that no command-line parameters have been provided.[2] The changed part of the code is shown below.

```
CD-ROM reference=7022.txt
...
      except IndexError:
          # IndexError raised -> default to test.xml
          sys.stderr.write (
              "No filename specified. "
              "Defaulting to test.xml\n")
          XMLGrep ("test.xml","Sean")
```

An invocation of the modified program without command-line parameters is shown below.

```
CD-ROM reference=7023.txt
C>python xgrep.py

No filename specified. Defaulting to test.xml
XMLGrep will process the file 'test.xml' for the pattern 'Sean'
```

7.4 | Adding Support for Wildcards

We now have a robust test harness for the xgrep module. It can be used both as a module in a larger program and as a standalone program. It gracefully handles the case where it has been invoked directly

---

[2]An even better course of action would be to have xgrep read from standard input when invoked with no parameters. We will see examples of how this is done later on in the book.

without any command-line parameters. The warning message it generates is sensible, even if the module filename is changed from xgrep.py to something else.

The next improvement we make will allow xgrep to process any number of command-line parameters—including command-line parameters that contain wildcards. If your computing platform is exclusively Unix, you may be wondering why this is necessary, given that the shell expands wildcards on behalf of the programs it executes. Well, although this is true on Unix, it is not true on Windows. The good news is that adding support for wildcard expansion (commonly known as *globbing*) will allow your scripts to work on Windows without adversely affecting their ability to run on Unix.

First, let's make xgrep capable of handling multiple command-line arguments. The changed part of the code is shown below.

```
CD-ROM reference=7024.txt
...
    try:
        for a in sys.argv[1:]:
            # Process each parameter in turn
            XMLGrep (a,"Sean")
    except IndexError:
```

Instead of simply accessing sys.argv[1], the program takes a slice of the command-line parameters starting at offset 1. This list is then iterated by a for loop. Each time around the loop, the a variable is set to the next item in the sys.argv array—that is, the next command-line parameter—until the list is exhausted. For each a, the XMLGrep function is called. A sample invocation is shown below.

```
CD-ROM reference=7025.txt
C>python xgrep.py test.xml staff.xml
XMLGrep will process the file 'test.xml' for the pattern 'Sean'
XMLGrep will process the file 'staff.xml' for the pattern 'Sean'
```

The program can now handle any number of command-line parameters, but it still does not know what to do with wildcards on Windows, as the following example illustrates.

```
CD-ROM reference=7026.txt
C>python test.xml s*.xml

XMLGrep will process the file 'test.xml' for the pattern
  'Sean'
XMLGrep will process the file 's*.xml' for the pattern 'Sean'
```

Adding support for wildcards is as simple as adding one line and modifying one other line. We simply need to

- Import Python's standard `glob` module
- Call the `glob` method from the `glob` module to get back a list of filenames for each filename that might contain wildcards

The modified part of the program is shown below.

```
CD-ROM reference=7027.txt
    ...
    try:
        for a in sys.argv[1:]:
            for g in glob.glob(a):
                # Process each parameter in turn
                XMLGrep (g,"Sean")
    ...
```

Some sample invocations in a directory that contains the files `test.xml`, `staff.xml`, and `staff1.xml` are shown here.

```
CD-ROM reference=7028.txt
C>python xgrep.py t*.xml

XMLGrep will process the file 'test.xml' for the pattern 'Sean'

C>python xgrep.py t*.xml staf?.xml

XMLGrep will process the file 'test.xml' for the pattern 'Sean'
XMLGrep will process the file 'staff.xml' for the pattern 'Sean'
XMLGrep will process the file 'staff1.xml' for the pattern 'Sean'
```

7.5 | Parsing Command-Line Options

The time has come to start thinking about how we will pass the pattern we are searching for into xgrep to replace the dummy pattern "Sean" we have been carrying around to date.

One reasonable approach would be to add a -p option. The overall command syntax looks like this:

```
CD-ROM reference=7029.txt
xgrep.py -p pattern <file>...<file>
```

Python provides a module known as getopt for handling command-line options that begin with a minus sign. This module contains a function also known as getopt that generally takes two parameters. The first parameter specifies the argument list to be processed—typically, sys.argv[1:]. The second parameter is a string specifying the option names you wish to parse for. A colon character ":" after an option signifies that the option be followed by a value that is to be associated with that option.

As always when a new Python module is tackled, a few minutes spent playing with it interactively pays dividends. Here is an abridged transcript of my own doodles as I wrote this section of the book.

```
CD-ROM reference=7030.txt
>>> import getopt
```

Have a look at what functions, variables, etc., the module contains.

```
CD-ROM reference=7031.txt
>>> dir (getopt)
['__builtins__', '__doc__', '__file__', '__name__', 'do-
  longs',
'do-shorts',
'error', 'getopt', 'long-has-args', 'short-has-arg',
  'string']
```

Print the top-level embedded documentation.

```
CD-ROM reference=7032.txt
>>> print getopt.__doc__

Module getopt -- Parser for command line options.

This module helps scripts to parse the command-line arguments in
sys.argv.  It supports the same conventions as the Unix getopt()
function (including the special meanings of arguments of the
form '-' and '--')
...

getopt() -- Parse command line options
error    -- Exception (string) raised when bad options are
   found
```

Print documentation for the getopt function.

```
CD-ROM reference=7033.txt
>>> print getopt.getopt.__doc__

getopt(args, options[, long-options]) -> opts, args

    Parses command-line options and parameter list.  args is the
    argument list to be parsed, without the leading reference to the
    running program.  Typically, this means "sys.argv[1:]".
    shortopts is the string of option letters that the script
    wants to recognize, with options that require an argument
    followed by a colon (i.e., the same format that Unix
    getopt() uses).
...
```

Set up a list to test the getopt function. The list will contain four
strings corresponding to four command-line parameters.

```
CD-ROM reference=7034.txt
>>> x = ["-p","pattern","staff.xml","test.xml"]
```

Parse this list with getopt. Tell getopt to look for a -p option
that should have a value associated with it.

```
CD-ROM reference=7035.txt
>>> res = getopt.getopt (x,"p:")
```

Inspect the result.

```
CD-ROM reference=7036.txt
>>> print res
([('-p', 'pattern')], ['staff.xml', 'test.xml'])
```

The result is a tuple with two lists in it. The first list is the options found; the second list is the remainder of the command line. Split the parsed options from the rest of the command line.

```
CD-ROM reference=7037.txt
>>> (options,remainder) = getopt.getopt (x,"p:")
```

Inspect the `options` variable, which will contain the command options spotted by `getopt`.

```
CD-ROM reference=7038.txt
>>> print options

[('-p', 'pattern')]
```

Inspect the `remainder` variable, which will contain the parts of the list not consumed by `getopt` processing:

```
CD-ROM reference=7039.txt
>>> print remainder

['staff.xml', 'test.xml']
```

The code below is the `xgrep` harness modified to collect a value for the `-p` command-line option.

```
CD-ROM reference=7040.txt
def XMLGrep(filename,pattern):
    print "XMLGrep will process the file '%s' for the pattern
'%s'" %(filename,pattern)

if __name__ == "__main__":
        import sys,glob,getopt

        # Use getopt to parse the -p option.
```

```
# getopt returns a list with two items. The first is a
# tuple of the options processed. The second is what
# is left of the command- line parameters after any
# options have been processed.
(options,remainder) = getopt.getopt (sys.argv[1:],"p:")
pattern = None
for (option,value) in options:
        if option == '-p':
                pattern = value
        else:
                sys.stderr.write ("Unknown option '%s'" %
                    option)
if pattern == None:
        # No -p option specified.
        sys.stderr.write (
                "Usage: %s -p pattern " % sys.argv[0]
                "[filename]...[filename]"
        )
        sys.exit()
if len(remainder)==0:
        # No filenames after options have been
        # processed out of sys.argv.
        sys.stderr.write (
                "No filename specified. "
                "Defaulting to test.xml\n")
        XMLGrep ("test.xml",pattern)
else:
        # Filenames present on command line. Glob each of
        # them in turn
        for a in remainder:
                for g in glob.glob(a):
                        # Process each parameter in turn
                        XMLGrep (g,pattern)
```

A number of sample invocations of the new xgrep are shown below.

```
CD-ROM reference=7041.txt
C>python xgrep.py
Usage: xgrep.py -p pattern [filename]...[filename]
C>python xgrep.py test.xml

Usage: xgrep.py -p pattern [filename]...[filename]
C>python xgrep.py -p sean

No filename specified. Defaulting to test.xml
```

XMLGrep will process the file 'test.xml' for the pattern
  'sean'
C>**python xgrep.py -p sean test.xml**

XMLGrep will process the file 'test.xml' for the pattern 'sean'
C>**python xgrep.py -p sean st*.xml**

XMLGrep will process the file 'staff.xml' for the pattern 'sean'
XMLGrep will process the file 'staff1.xml' for the pattern 'sean'

7.6 | A Pattern-Matching Dry Run

Before we delve into regular expressions, it would be useful to have a functioning xgrep that can search for plain vanilla strings in the files specified on the command line. Doing this much enables us test the end-to-end operation of xgrep. We are nearly there; all we need is to beef up the XMLGrep function a little bit. The modified XMLGrep function is shown below.

```
CD-ROM reference=7042.txt

import string

def XMLGrep(filename,pattern):
     # for the moment, search the specified file, treating
     # the pattern argument as a
     # straight string i.e., not as a regular expression
     f = open (filename,"r")
     for l in f.readlines():
          pos = string.find (l,pattern)
          if pos != -1:
               # print out the match, using square
               # brackets to show the "hit"
               print "%s:%s[%s]%s" % (
                    filename,
                    l[:pos],
                    pattern,
                    l[pos+len(pattern):])
```

The `string` module provides a useful `find` function that searches one string for occurrences of another string. If the searched-for string is present, the offset at which it occurred is found. If it is not found, `-1` is returned.

We will use the `staff.xml` file again for ease of reference in the examples that follow.

```
CD-ROM reference=7043.txt
C>type staff.xml

<staff>
<department name="Technical">
<person>
<title>Technical Director</title>
<name>
<given>Sean</given>
<family>Mc Grath</family>
</name>
<email>sean@digitome.com</email>
<web>http://www.digitome.com/sean.html</web>
</person>
...
```

A sample invocation of the new `xgrep` is shown below.

```
CD-ROM reference=7044.txt
C>python xgrep.py -p sean staff.xml

staff.xml:<email>[sean]@digitome.com</;email>

staff.xml:<web>http://www.digitome.com/[sean].html</web>
```

Note how the text that caused a match appears in square brackets in the output. Explicitly marking the hits like this can be useful but can also be a problem if, for example, the output of `xgrep` is intended to go through some further process. Better to make marking of hits an option to `xgrep`. We introduce the `-m` switch to do this. The modified code is shown below, with the main changes in bold.

```
CD-ROM reference=7045.txt
import string
```

```
#The parameter MarkHits will default to 0 if not specified
def XMLGrep(filename,pattern,MarkHits=0):
        # for the moment, search the specified file, treating
        # the pattern argument as a
        # straight string i.e., not as a regular expression

        # The variable MarkHits controls whether or not hits
        # should be marked in the output of xgrep. If MarkHits
        # is not specified in the call to XMLGrep it defaults
        # to zero
        if MarkHits == 0:
                # Do not mark hits, make hit delimiters blank
                # strings
                StartOfHit = ""
                EndOfHit = ""
        else:
                # Mark hits, make hit delimiters matching square
                # brackets
                StartOfHit = "["
                EndOfHit = "]"
        f = open (filename,"r")
        for L in f.readlines():
                pos = string.find (l,pattern)
                if pos != -1:
                        # print out the match, using match
                        # delimiters to show the "hit"
                        print "%s:%s%s%s%s%s" % (filename,
                                        L[:pos],
                                        StartOfHit,
                                        pattern,
                                        EndOfHit,
                                        L[pos+len(pattern):])

if __name__ == "__main__":
        import sys,glob,getopt

        # Use getopt to parse the -p and -m options.
        # The -p option has an associated value. The -m option
        # does not.
        # (Options with associated values are passed into getopt with
        # a ":" after them.)
        # getopt returns a list with two items. The first is a tuple of
        # the options processed. The second is what is left of
        # the command-line parameters after any options have
        # been processed.
```

```
# Getopt will now search for m option as well.
# Note that it does not
# have a colon after it because it has no associated value.

(options,remainder) = getopt.getopt (sys.argv[1:],"p:m")
pattern = None
MarkHits = 0
for (option,value) in options:
      if option == '-p':
            pattern = value
      #*** Check to see if -m switch specified
      elif option == '-m':
            MarkHits = 1
      else:
            sys.stderr.write ("Unknown option '%s'" %
              option)
if pattern == None:
            sys.stderr.write (
                  "Usage: %s -p pattern" % sys.argv[0]
                  "[filename]...[filename]")
            sys.exit()
if len(remainder)==0:
      sys.stderr.write (
            "No filename specified. "
            "Defaulting to test.xml\n")
      XMLGrep ("test.xml",pattern,MarkHits)
else:
      for a in remainder:
            for g in glob.glob(a):
                  # Process each parameter in turn
                  XMLGrep (g,pattern,MarkHits)
```

Notice the change to the XMLGrep function declaration XMLGrep(filename,pattern,MarkHits=0). Python allows you to specify *default values* to be associated with parameters to a function. If the function is called without values for the defaulted parameters, the defaults specified in the function declaration are used instead.

For example, a call to XMLGrep of the form XMLGrep ("foo.xml","bar") is perfectly valid. Within that call, the MarkHits parameter will have a value of 0, the specified default.

Two sample invocations of the new `xgrep` are shown below. In the first invocation, hit marking is enabled by the -m switch. In the second example, it is disabled because a -m switch is not specified:

```
CD-ROM reference=7046.txt
C>python xgrep.py -m -p sean staff.xml

staff.xml:<email>[sean]@digitome.com</email>
staff.xml:<web>http://www.digitome.com/[sean].html</web>
C>python xgrep.py -p sean staff.xml

staff.xml:<email>sean@digitome.com</email>
staff.xml:<web>http://www.digitome.com/sean.html</web>
```

7.7 | Introducing Regular Expressions

The Python standard library provides a module known as `re` for regular expression processing. For full information on `re`, see the documentation at `Doc\lib\module-re.html`. Also, a "how to guide" to regular expressions can be found at `http://www.python.org/doc/howto/`.

The simplest way to use the `re` module is to use the `search` function. It takes two parameters—the pattern and the string to be searched. If the search succeeds, the function returns an object known as a *match object*. If it fails, it returns `None`. Every match object provides methods called `start()` and `end()` that can be used to retrieve the start and end offsets of the matching string, respectively.

```
CD-ROM reference=7047.txt
>>> import re
>>> # Search for the string "Wo" in the string "Hello World"
>>> mo = re.search ("Wo", "Hello World")
>>> print mo
<re.MatchObject instance at 7fedd0>
>>> print mo.start()
6
>>> print mo.end()
8
```

Here is an example of using a regular expression to search for a simple attribute assignment in an XML document. We have an XML file that contains lines of the form:

```
CD-ROM reference=7048.txt
<Person height="6" weight = "200">
```

We want to match the height attribute assignment with a regular expression.

```
CD-ROM reference=7049.txt
>>> x = '<Person height = "6" weight = "200">'
>>> mo = re.search ('height = "\d+"',x)
>>> mo.start()
8
>>> mo.end()
20
>>> print "Match string is '%s'" % x[mo.start():mo.end()]
Match string is 'height = "6"'
```

The "\d" string in regular expressions means "match any digit." The string "\d+" means "match one or more digits." So, the pattern will work for any number of digits, as shown below.

```
CD-ROM reference=7050.txt
>>> x = '<Person height = "180" weight = "200">'
>>> mo = re.search ('height = "\d+"',x)
>>> print "Match string is '%s'" % x[mo.start():mo.end()]
Match string is 'height = "180"'
```

The pattern above depends on the existence of a single space both before and after the equal sign to match the height attribute assignment. If these spaces are missing, a match will not occur. The following failed match demonstrates the problem.

```
CD-ROM reference=7051.txt
>>> x = '<Person height ="180" weight = "200">'
>>> mo = re.search ('height = "\d+"',x)
>>> print mo
None
```

A good way to fix the problem would be to allow for any amount of white space—including no white space at all—on either side of the equal sign. The "\s" string in regular expressions means "match a white space character." The pattern "\s*" means "match zero or more white space characters." Putting "\s*" on either side of the equal sign solves the white space problem.

```
CD-ROM reference=7052.txt
>>> x = '<Person height ="180" weight = "200">'
>>> mo = re.search ('height\s*=\s*"\d+"',x)
>>> print "Match string is '%s'" % x[mo.start():mo.end()]
Match string is 'height ="180"'
>>> x = '<Person height=        "180" weight = "200">'
>>> mo = re.search ('height\s*=\s*"\d+"',x)
>>> print "Match string is '%s'" % x[mo.start():mo.end()]
Match string is 'height=        "180"'
```

It is a common occurrence with regular expressions to want to isolate a part of a matching string. In the example above, it would be useful to be able to separate the height value (the number "180") from the rest of the attribute assignment "height = ". Python enables you to do this by *grouping* parts of regular expressions and then retrieving them as separate units. A group is created by surrounding part of a regular expression with parentheses. The first group is known as group 1, the second as group 2, and so on. After a match, groups can be retrieved by group number. In the example below, a group is created surrounding the digits that make up the number assigned to the height attribute.

```
CD-ROM reference=7053.txt
>>> x = '<Person height=        "180" weight = "200">'
>>> mo = re.search ('height\s*=\s*("\d+")',x)
>>> print mo.groups()[0]
'180'
```

The groups() method of a match object returns a list of the groups contained in a regular expression match. By indexing into this list using the group number, the program can retrieve the text of the group. There is also a `group()` method which, given a group number, returns the contents of that group.

```
CD-ROM reference=7054.txt
>>> x = '<Person height=        "180" weight = "200">'
>>> mo = re.search ('height\s*=\s*("\d+')',x)
>>> print mo.group(1)
'180'
```

With the aid of groups, we can get back values for both the `height` and `weight` attributes in a single search, as shown below.

```
CD-ROM reference=7055.txt
>>> x = '<Person height=        "180" weight = "200">'
>>> mo = re.search
('height\s*=\s*("\d+")\s*weight\s*=\s*("\d+")>',x)
>>> print mo.groups()
>>> ('180', '200')
>>> # This first group is the height group
>>> print mo.groups()[0]
'180'
>>> # Can also access it with the group number (1)
>>> print mo.group(1)
'180'
>>> # This second group is the weight group
>>> print mo.groups()[1]
'200'
>>> # Can also access it with the group number (2)
>>> print mo.group(2)
'200'
```

When there are multiple groups, it can be a pain to try and remember what number corresponds to what group. Python allows groups to be named; then, the contents of a group can be retrieved either by name or by number. To name a group, wrap its name in angle brackets and add the string `"?P"` to the start of the group, as illustrated below.

```
CD-ROM reference=7056.txt
>>> x = '<Person height=        "180" weight = "200">'
>>> mo = re.search
```

```
('height\s*=\s*"(?P<height>\d+)"\s*weight\s*=\s*"(?P<weight>\
  d+)">',x)
>>> #Can use symbolic name to access the height group
>>> mo.group('height')
'180'
>>> #Group number still works
>>> mo.group(1)
'180'
>>> #Can use symbolic name to access the weight group
>>> mo.group('weight')
'200'
>>> #Group number still works
>>> mo.group(2)
'200'
```

We just need to cover two more little pieces of regular expression syntax and we will have enough done to integrate regular expressions into xgrep and start playing with it as a standalone program.

The "." character means "match any character except a newline." It is particularly useful in regular expressions. For example, the following pattern matches the element type name of simple XML end-tags.

```
CD-ROM reference=7057.txt
>>> x = '<Greeting>Hello World</Greeting>'
>>> mo = re.search ('(</.+>)',x)
>>> print mo.group(1)
'</Greeting>'
```

There is a problem lurking in this pattern, however, which is illustrated by the following example.

```
CD-ROM reference=7058.txt
>>> x = "<Greeting>Hello
World</Greeting><Farewell>Goodbye</Farewell>"
>>> mo = re.search ('(</.+>)',x)
>>> mo.group(1)
'</Greeting><Farewell>Goodbye</Farewell>'
```

You may find this result suprising. I certainly did the first time I came across it. Notice that the matched string extends from the beginning of the Greeting end-tag to the end of the Farewell end-tag. The reason is easy to understand once you look at the regular expression from Python's point of view.

We have asked it to match one or more characters bounded on the left hand side by `</` and bounded on the right hand side by `>`. The key point to note is that the `.+` pattern will happily match any `>` characters it comes across. The regular expression matcher keeps chewing through characters until it hits the last available `>`, which then terminates the match.

The string `"</Greeting><Farewell>Goodbye</Farewell>"` is a match because

- The first two characters, `</`, match the first part of the regular expression `</`

- The string
  `"Greeting><Farewell>Goodbye</Farewell"`
  matches the `.+` part of the regular expression

- The last character `>` matches the `>` part of the regular expression

The situation is illustrated in figure 7–1.

The default behavior of `+` and `*` in regular expressions is to be *greedy*. That is, they match as much text as possible. There are times

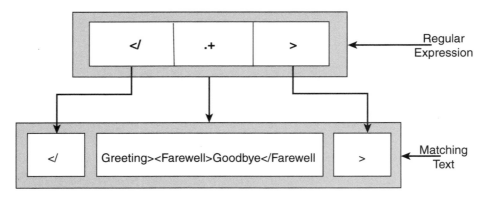

Figure 7–1   Greedy regular expression match.

when this is exactly what you want and there are times when it is not. You can switch between greedy and nongreedy mode by appending a ? to the + or * characters in the regular expression. Here is a nongreedy version of the end-tag matcher that fixes the problem.

```
CD-ROM reference=7059.txt
>>> x = "<Greeting>Hello World</Greeting><Farewell>
  Goodbye</Farewell>"
>>> mo = re.search ('(</.+?>)',x)
>>> mo.group(1)
'</Greeting>'
```

7.8 | Using Escape Sequences in Regular Expressions

The \ character is used in Python strings to indicate that the character or characters following the \ (backslash) are to be treated in a special way. Perhaps the most common example is the string "\n" which is interpreted to mean "ASCII linefeed" also known as "newline." There are many others including "\t" for tab and "\b" for backspace. For a full list, see section 2.4.1 of the Python Reference Manual.

Adding these special "escape codes" to regular expressions can be awkward because the \ character is also considered to be a special character by Python/Perl regular expressions. For example, consider the problem of matching the two character string "\n"—that is, a backslash character immediately followed by an "n" character.

```
CD-ROM reference=7060.txt
# Matching a "backslash N" string - incorrect first attempt
import re
BackslashN = re.compile ("\n")
```

The problem with this is that the "\n" string is considered special by Python's string parser. The above regular expression matches a newline character rather than the intended two-character string.

The solution is to escape the backslash from Python's string with *another* backslash character.

```
CD-ROM reference=7061.txt
# Matching a backslashN character - correct second attempt
import re
BackslashN = re.compile ("\\n")
```

For long regular expressions or regular expressions involving a lot of literal backslashes, this doubling up of backslash characters inhibits readability. To counteract this, Python provides a simple way to escape an entire string from backslash interpretation. Simply prefix the string with an r as shown here.

```
CD-ROM reference=7062.txt
# Matching a backslashN character
import re
BackslashN = re.compile (r"\n")
```

7.9 | Compiling Regular Expressions

So far, we have performed regular expression matches by passing the required pattern into the search function provided by the re module.

As you can imagine, regular expressions can get quite complex. The bigger the regular expression, the more work the search function has to do to figure out what it means. The re module allows you to compile a regular expression into a *regular expression object,* as shown below.

```
CD-ROM reference=7063.txt
import re

EndTag = re.compile ("</(.+?)>")

f = open ('staff.xml','r')
for l in f.readlines():
    mo = EndTag.search (l)
    if mo:
        print mo.group(1)
```

In the above example, the regular expression is parsed once during the call to `compile`. It is this compiled regular expression object that is then used to perform the searches.

This approach also leads to more readable code because each of the compiled regular expressions can be given a useful mnemonic name such as `EndTag` above.

7.10 | Adding Regular Expressions to xgrep

Finally(!) it is time to add regular expression support to `xgrep`. Here is the code for the `XMLGrep` function of `xgrep.py` modified to allow the use of regular expressions.

```
CD-ROM reference=7064.txt
import string,os
#import regular expressions module
import re

def XMLGrep(filename,pattern,MarkHits=0):
    # Create a regular expression object out of the
    # specified pattern
    Pat = re.compile (pattern)

    # MarkHits is an optional parameter; it defaults to 0
    # if not specified.
    if MarkHits == 0:
        # Do not mark hits, make hit delimiters blank
        # strings.
        StartOfHit = ""
        EndOfHit = ""
    else:
        # Mark hits, make hit delimiters matching square
        # brackets.
        StartOfHit = "["
        EndOfHit = "]"
    f = open (filename,'r')
    for L in f.readlines():
```

```
mo = Pat.search (l)
# Does the string l match the regular expression
# object Pat?
# If it does, a "match object" is returned.
# If not, search() returns None.
if mo is not None:
        # We got a match with the regular expression
        # Print out the match, using match delimiters
        # to show the "hit"
        print "%s:%s%s%s%s%s" % (filename,
                    L[1:mo.start()],
                    StartOfHit,
                    L[mo.start():mo.end()],
                    EndOfHit,
                    L[mo.end():])
```

7.11 | xgrep in Action

In this section, we illustrate xgrep in action and, on the way, learn some more useful regular expression syntax.

An xgrep invocation to find simple XML start- and end-tags is shown below.

```
CD-ROM reference=7065.txt
C>type test.xml

<Greeting>
Hello <b>World</b>
<Farewell>
Goodbye</Farewell></Greeting>
CD-ROM reference=7066.txt
C>python xgrep.py -p "<.+?>" test.xml

test.xml:<Greeting>
test.xml:<b>World</b>
test.xml:<Farewell>
test.xml:<Farewell></Greeting>
```

The pattern simply looks for a start-tag or an end-tag. If there is more than one match per line, no extra actions are taken. To see the exact reason for a match occurring, use the -m option.

```
CD-ROM reference=7067.txt
C>python xgrep.py -m -p "<.+?>" test.xml
test.xml:[<Greeting>]
test.xml:[<b>]World</b>
test.xml:[<Farewell>]
test.xml:[<Farewell>]</Greeting>
```

The ^ character in a pattern restricts the pattern to match only if it starts at the beginning of a line, as illustrated below.

```
CD-ROM reference=7068.txt
C>type test.xml

<Greeting>
Hello World<Farewell>
Goodbye</Farewell></Greeting>

C>python xgrep.py -m -p "^<.+?>" test.xml

test.xml:[<Greeting>]
```

Notice that only the Greeting start-tag, which starts at the beginning of a line, causes a match.

The $ character appearing at the end of a pattern restricts the pattern to match only if it ends at the end of a line. In the following example, a match only occurs on lines that end with a > character.

```
CD-ROM reference=7069.txt
C>type test.xml

<Greeting>Hello World<Farewell>
Goodbye
</Farewell>
</Greeting>

C>python xgrep.py -m -p ">$" test.xml

test.xml:<Greeting>Hello World<Farewell[>]
test.xml:</Farewell[>]
test.xml:</Greeting[>]
```

Square brackets can be used in patterns to create sets of characters. A match occurs only if the relevant part of the searched string contains one of the characters from the set. The example below uses a set to match any line that begins with an H or an I character.

```
CD-ROM reference=7070.txt
C>type test.xml

<Greeting>
Hello
Indigo
<Farewell>
Goodbye
</Farewell>
</Greeting>

C>python xgrep.py -m -p "^[HI]" test.xml

test.xml:[H]ello
test.xml:[I]ndigo
```

The "-" character can be used within a set to create a range of characters. This example matches any line that starts with a capital letter.

```
CD-ROM reference=7071.txt

C>python xgrep.py -m -p "^[A-Z]" test.xml

test.xml:[H]ello
test.xml:[I]ndigo
test.xml:[G]oodbye
```

A set normally means "cause a match if the string contains one of these." You can reverse the meaning of set to mean "cause a match if the string *does not* contain one of these" by starting it with a ^ character. This is known as set *negation*.

This example matches any line that does not start with a capital letter. It illustrates the two distinct uses of ^. The first ^ restricts matches to those that start at the beginning of a line. The second ^ negates the character class and means "match any character that is not in the range A to Z."

```
CD-ROM reference=7072.txt
C>type test.xml

<Greeting>
Hello
Indigo
<Farewell>
Goodbye
</Farewell>
</Greeting>

C>python xgrep.py -m -p "^[^A-Z]" test.xml

test.xml:[<]Greeting>
test.xml:[<]Farewell>
test.xml:[<]/Farewell>
test.xml:[<]/Greeting>
```

Here is an example that matches lines that do not end in a > character.

```
CD-ROM reference=7073.txt
C>python xgrep.py -m -p "[^>]$" test.xml

test.xml:Hell[o]
test.xml:Indig[o]
test.xml:Goodby[e]
```

This example matches start-tags by excluding tags that begin with /.

```
CD-ROM reference=7074.txt
C>python xgrep.py -m -p "<[^/].+?>" test.xml

test.xml:[<Greeting>]
test.xml:[<Farewell>]
```

The backslash character \ can be used to escape special characters in regular expressions. This example finds lines that contain the string Mr.. The "." after the string Mr literally means "." thanks to the backslash that precedes it.

```
CD-ROM reference=7075.txt
C>type test.xml

<name>
```

```
Mr. Sean Mc Grath
</name>
```

```
C>python xgrep.py -m -p "Mr\." test.xml
test.xml:[Mr.] Sean Mc Grath
```

In this example, any man whose first name starts with "S" and ends with "n" is matched.

```
CD-ROM reference=7076.txt
C>type test.xml
<names>
<name>
Mr. Sean Mc Grath
</name>
<name>
Mr. Stephen Murphy
</name>
<name>
Mr. Sandy Duffy
</name>
</names>
```

```
C>python xgrep.py -m -p "Mr\. S.*?n " test.xml
```

```
test.xml:[Mr. Sean ]Mc Grath
test.xml:[Mr. Stephen ]Murphy
```

7.12 | Parsing XML with Regular Expressions

The XML specification document contains a rigorous definition of the structure of an XML document in the form of a *grammar*. This grammar lends itself to implementation in terms of (admittedly) complex regular expressions.

The xmllib library, which is part of the standard Python distribution, makes extensive use of regular expressions. It is well worth having a look at xmllib to get an idea of how serious regular-expression programming is done.

One particularly important point that xmllib illustrates well is that legibility of complex regular expressions is greatly improved if they are built from small pieces.

The following two lines of code are lifted straight from xmllib. Note how the entityref regular expression depends on the -Name regular expression.

```
CD-ROM reference=7077.txt
-Name = '[a-zA-Z-:][-a-zA-Z0-9.-:]*'     # valid XML name
entityref = re.compile('&(?P<name>' + -Name + ')[^-a-zA-Z0-
   9.-:]')
```

7.13 | Cautionary Tales

The examples I have used in this chapter combined with the fragment from the xmllib standard library strongly hint that XML can be gainfully processed with Python's regular-expression support. This is indeed the case, but a number of caveats need to be borne in mind.

Some things you can incur in an XML document can cause simple regular expression-based programs to go astray. Some of the more common "gotchas" are:

- Comments
- CDATA sections
- General entity references
- Single-quoted attribute value literals
- Document-type declaration subsets

If you do not use these features of XML (and feel confident that the XML you will have to process will never contain any of them), feel free to skip this section.

7.13.1 *Comments*

An XML document can contain comments. A comment consists of text bounded by the string <!– at the start of the comment and –> at the end of the comment.

Anything within the comment is not considered to be part of the document and can be thrown away by XML parsers. Both xmlv and xmln throw comments away as shown below.

```
CD-ROM reference=7078.txt
C>type gotcha.xml

<?xml version="1.0"?>
<!–
This is not a <foo> start tag
–>
<foo>
</foo>
C>xmln gotcha.xml

(foo
-\n
)foo
```

The following xgrep command is intended to match lines containing a foo start-tag in the file gotcha.xml. The xgrep utility knows nothing about XML comments, and thus the string "<foo>" in the comment causes a false match. We get two matches where there should really only be one.

```
CD-ROM reference=7079.txt
C>python xgrep.py -p "<foo>" -m gotcha.xml

gotcha.xml:This is not a [<foo>] start tag
gotcha.xml:[<foo>]
```

7.13.2 *CDATA Sections*

CDATA sections are parts of an XML document that are shielded from the XML parser. As a result they can contain the special characters < and & without being incorrectly interpreted as special by the parser. A CDATA section starts with `<[CDATA[` and ends with `]]>`. The following file contains a CDATA section.

```
CD-ROM reference=7080.txt
C>type gotcha.xml

<?xml version="1.0"?>
<foo>
this is some data. The following bit does not contain
a start-tag <![CDATA[
<foo>
]]>
</foo>

<p>
Parsing this file with xmln illustrates how the text "<foo>"
within the CDATA section has been treated as literal text:
C>xmln gotcha.xml

(foo
-\n
-this is some data. The following bit does not contain
-\n
-a start-tag
-\n
-<foo>
-\n
-\n
)foo
```

The `xgrep` utility knows nothing about CDATA sections and so the `"<foo>"` string in the CDATA section causes a false positive match.

```
CD-ROM reference=7081.txt
C>python xgrep.py -p "<foo>" -m gotcha.xml

gotcha.xml:[<foo>]this is some data.
gotcha.xml:a start-tag <![CDATA[[<foo>]
```

7.13.3   *Entity References*

XML documents can be stored in multiple pieces, known as entities. During parsing, a parser can expand references to entities and pass the expanded document on to the application.

A nonvalidating parser may or may not expand entities. They are not required to do so by the XML specification. The expat parser, on which xmln is based, by default does not expand entity references. The rxp parser, on which xmlv is based, does (as indeed it must do because it is a validating XML parser).

The following DTD declares the element type foo. It also declares an entity named stuff. The entity declaration connects the entity stuff with the content of the file bar.xml.

```
CD-ROM reference=7082.txt
C>type foo.dtd

<!ELEMENT foo (#PCDATA|foo)*>
<!ENTITY stuff SYSTEM "bar.xml">
```

The file gotcha.xml below contains a document type declaration and a reference to the entity stuff.

```
CD-ROM reference=7083.txt
C>type gotcha.xml

<?xml version="1.0"?>
<!DOCTYPE foo SYSTEM "foo.dtd">
<foo>
Some of the content of this document is external
to this entity. &stuff;
<foo>
```

Finally, here is bar.xml.

```
CD-ROM reference=7084.txt
C>type bar.xml

Here is some more <foo>content</foo>.
```

When the file `gotcha.xml` is parsed by `xmlv`, the entity `stuff` is fetched and its contents are added to the document. This behavior is illustrated by the following invocation of `xmlv`.

```
CD-ROM reference=7085.txt
C>xmlv gotcha.xml

(foo
-\nSome of the content of this document is external\nto this
entity. Here is some more
(foo
-content
)foo
-.\n
)foo
```

The `xgrep` utility knows nothing about entity references. So, although there are two `foo` elements in the above document, `xgrep` sees only one of them.

```
CD-ROM reference=7086.txt
C>python xgrep.py -p "<foo>" -m gotcha.xml

gotcha.xml:[<foo>]
```

7.14 | Avoiding False Positive Matches

We have seen how Python's regular expressions can be gainfully applied to XML. We have also seen that there are some "gotchas" with this approach to bear in mind when processing arbitrary XML that may use features such as comments, CDATA sections, and entity references.

How can we deal with these gotchas? Well, the most obvious answer is to use a full-blown XML parser to process the XML document. If, for example, you processed PYX generated from `xmln` or `xmlv`, the XML parser will insulate you from any false hits such as those shown in the above sections.

This approach—using an XML parser to create "events" and then processing the events—is a popular and powerful technique. We use it to enhance xgrep in the next chapter. The middle ground between "blind" regular-expression matching and using a full-blown XML parser is known as "shallow parsing."

7.15 | Shallow Parsing XML with Python Regular Expressions

It is possible to write a single regular expression that will tokenize XML into markup and data components. Robert D. Cameron has developed such a regular expression and presented it in the Markup Languages journal.[3]

The article included a Perl 5 implementation that was used by David Niergarth (jdnier@execpc.com) to produce a Python implementation. A sample REX application is shown below. It works by importing the XML-SPE regular expression from the REX module. This expression is then used with the findall function provided by the re module. Given a string and a regular expression, this function returns a list of nonoverlapping matches found in the string.

```
CD-ROM reference=7087.txt
import re
from REX import XML-SPE
if __name__ == '__main__':
xml = (
'<?xml version="1.0"?><greeting>'
    'Hello <b x = "1">Wor<?foo bar?>ld</b></greeting>'
)
print re.findall (XML-SPE,xml)
```

The output is shown below.

---

[3]"REX: XML shallow parsing with regular expressions," Markup Languages: Theory & Practice 1.3 (1999).

```
CD-ROM reference=7088.txt
['<?xml version="1.0"?>',
 '<greeting>',
 'Hello ',
 '<b x = "1">',
 'Wor',
 '<?foo bar?>',
 'ld',
 '</b>',
 '</greeting>']
```

REX is a useful tool when full-blown XML parsing is unavailable. I find it particularly useful in situations where I need to process pseudo-XML documents, that is, documents that contain XML-style markup but are not well formed and thus cannot be parsed with utilities such as xmln. Here is the code for REX.py. You will also find it on the accompanying CD-ROM.

```
CD-ROM reference=7089.txt

"""REX/Python

Created by David Niergarth <jdnier@execpc.com>

Based on Robert D. Cameron's REX/Perl 1.0.

Original copyright notice follows:

REX/Perl 1.0

Robert D. Cameron "REX: XML Shallow Parsing with Regular
Expressions", Technical Report TR 1998-17, School of
Computing Science, Simon Fraser University, November, 1998.
Copyright (c) 1998, Robert D. Cameron.
The following code may be freely used and distributed
provided that this copyright and citation notice remains
intact and that modifications or additions are clearly
identified.

"""
import re
TextSE             = "[^<]+"
UntilHyphen        = "[^-]*-"
Until2Hyphens      = UntilHyphen + "(?:[^-]" + UntilHyphen +
```

```
                                     ")*-"
CommentCE          = Until2Hyphens + ">?"
UntilRSBs          = "[^\\]]*](?:[^\\]]+])*]+"
CDATA-CE           = UntilRSBs + "(?:[^\\]>)" + UntilRSBs +
                     ")*>"
S                  = "[ \\n\\t\\r]+"
NameStrt           = "[A-Za-z-:]|[^\\x00-\\x7F]"
NameChar           = "[A-Za-z0-9-:.-]|[^\\x00-\\x7F]"
Name               = "(?:" + NameStrt + ")(?:" + NameChar +
                     ")*"
QuoteSE            = "\"[^\"]*\"|'[^']*'"
DT-IdentSE         = (S + Name + "(?:" + S + "(?:" +
                           Name + "|" + QuoteSE + "))*")
MarkupDeclCE       = "(?:[^\\]\"'><]+|" + QuoteSE + ")*>"
S1                 = "[\\n\\r\\t ]"
UntilQMs           = "[^?]*\\?+"
PI-Tail            = ("\\?>|" + S1 + UntilQMs + "(?:[^>?]" +
                           UntilQMs + ")*>")
DT-ItemSE          = ("<(?:!(?:-" +
                           Until2Hyphens +
                           ">|[^-]" +
                           MarkupDeclCE +
                           ")|\\?" +
                           Name +
                           "(?:" +
                           PI-Tail +
                           "))|%" +
                           Name + ";|" +
                           + S)
DocTypeCE          = (DT-IdentSE + "(?:" + S +
                           ")?(?:\\[(?:" + DT-ItemSE +
                           ")*](?:" + S + ")?)?>?")
DeclCE             = ("-(?:" + CommentCE +
                           ")?|\\[CDATA\\[(?:" +
                           CDATA-CE +
                           ")?|DOCTYPE(?:" + DocTypeCE +
                           ")?"
PI-CE              = Name + "(?:" + PI-Tail + ")?"
EndTagCE           = Name + "(?:" + S + ")?>?"
AttValSE           = "\"[^<\"]*\"|'[^<']*'"
ElemTagCE          = (Name + "(?:" + S + Name + "(?:" +
                           S + ")?=(?:" + S +
                           ")?(?:" + AttValSE +
                           "))*(?:" + S + ")?/?>?")
MarkupSPE          = ("<(?:!(?:" + DeclCE + ")?|\\?(?:"
```

```
                                  + PI-CE + ")?|/(?:" +
                                  EndTagCE + ")?|(?:" +
                                  ElemTagCE + ")?)")
XML-SPE                = TextSE + "|" + MarkupSPE

if __name__ == '__main__':
        xml = (
        '<?xml version="1.0"?><greeting>'
        Hello <b x = "1">Wor<?foo bar?>ld</b></greeting>'
        }
        print re.findall (XML-SPE,xml)
```

7.16 | Current Implementation of xgrep

To wrap up this chapter, you may want to glance over the code for xgrep as it currently stands.

```
CD-ROM reference=7090.txt
C>type xgrep.py

import strangest
import re

def XMLGrep(filename,pattern,MarkHits=0):
        Pat = re.compile (pattern)

        if MarkHits == 0:
                # Do not mark hits, make hit delimiters blank
                # strings.
                StartOfHit = ""
                EndOfHit = ""
        else:
                # Mark hits, make hit delimiters matching square
                # brackets.
                StartOfHit = "["
                EndOfHit = "]"
        f = open (filename,"r")
        for L in f.readlines():
```

```
                L = L[:-1]
                mo = Pat.search (l)
                if mo is not None:
                        # Print out the match, using match delimiters
                        # to show the "hit."
                        print "%s:%s%s%s%s%s" % (filename,
                                L[0:mo.start()],
                                StartOfHit,
                                L[mo.start():mo.end()],
                                EndOfHit,
                                L[mo.end():])

if __name__ == "__main__":
    import sys,glob,getopt

    # -p pattern to search for
    # -m turn on hit highlighting
    (options,remainder) = getopt.getopt (sys.argv[1:],"p:m")
    pattern = None
    MarkHits = 0
    for (option,value) in options:
        if option == '-p':
                pattern = value
        elif option == '-m':
                MarkHits = 1
        else:
                sys.stderr.write ("Unknown option '%s'" %
                  option)
    if pattern == None:
                sys.stderr.write (
                "Usage: %s -p pattern [-m] " % sys.argv[0]
                "[filename]...[filename]")
                sys.exit()
    if len(remainder)==0:
        sys.stderr.write (
            "No filename specified. "
            "Defaulting to test.xml\n")
        XMLGrep ("test.xml",pattern,MarkHits)
    else:
        for a in remainder:
                for g in glob.glob(a):
                        # Process each parameter in turn
                        XMLGrep (g,pattern,MarkHits)
```

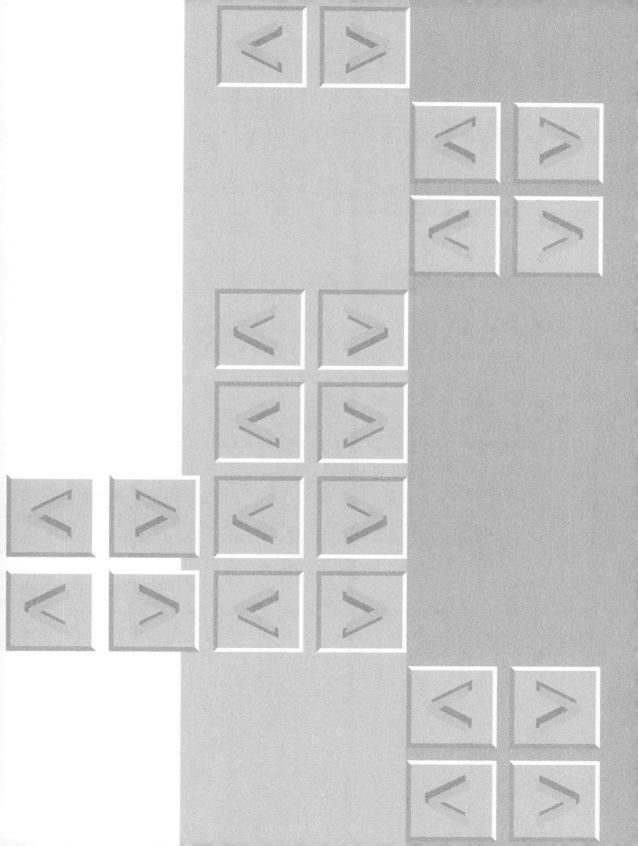

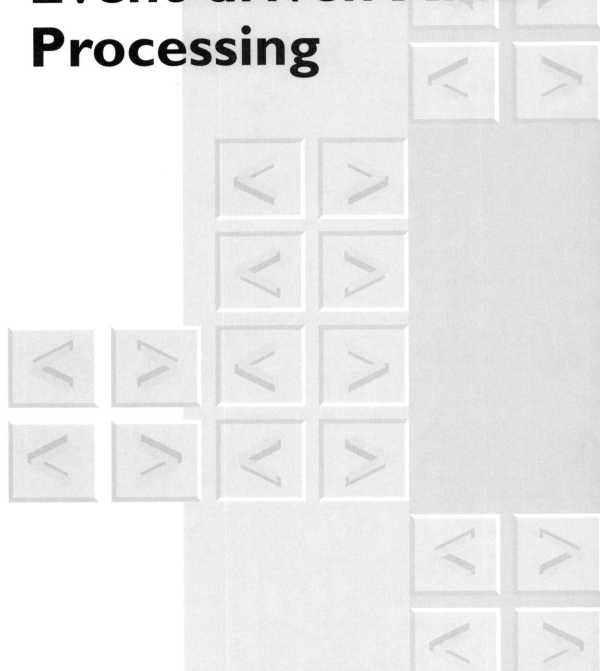

Event-driven XML Processing

I n chapter 7 we introduced regular expressions and built the
first phase of the xgrep utility. In this chapter, we extend
xgrep by making it XML-aware. That is, we give xgrep
the ability to work with the PYX notation generated from XML files
rather than process the plain text directly. This approach removes an
entire layer of problems that crop up when XML is processed directly.
Some of these problems were discussed at the end of the last chapter; we
recap the problem areas at the start of this chapter.

On the road to making xgrep XML-aware, we will take the opportunity to introduce some more Python facilities, such as bitwise
arithmetic operations and connecting to subprocesses via pipes. We
will also look at some more of the features of the getopt module for
command-line option processing.

8.1 | Making xgrep XML-Aware

The previous chapter showed that although using regular expressions to process XML directly is possible, it is not without its problems. Principal among the problems is that fully capturing the syntax of XML with regular expressions is unavoidably complex. I mentioned the fact that Python's standard library for simple XML processing—xmllib—uses regular expressions. By taking a look at xmllib, you can readily see how complex these regular expressions can get. For example, the following three regular expressions are lifted straight from xmllib.py. They illustrate what is involved in capturing the full syntactic structure of the XML declaration.

```
CD-ROM reference=8001.txt
_S = '[ \t\r\n]+'

_opS = '[ \t\r\n]*'

xmldecl = re.compile('<\?xml'+_S+
                'version'+_opS+'='+_opS+'(?P<ver-
                sion>'+_QStr+')'+
                '(?:'+_S+'encoding'+_opS+'='+_opS+
                  "(?P<encoding>'[A_Za_z][_A_Za_z0
                  _9._]*'|"
                '"[A_Za_z][_A_Za_z0_9._]*"))?'
                '(?:'+_S+'standalone'+_opS+'='+_opS+
                  '(?P<standalone>\'(?:yes|no)\'|"
                  (?:yes|no)"))?'+
                _opS+'\?>')
```

So far, xgrep has treated the files it is passed as plain text files. Even if the input to xgrep is XML, it does not take advantage of this fact. We have seen how various syntactic constructs that can occur in XML can lead to false hits. Removing the possibility of such false hits is very difficult with regular expressions alone.

Here is an example document that illustrates some false hits which, when we make xgrep XML-aware, will cease to be a problem. The following (admittedly pathological) XML document is to be searched for the word "greeting."

```
CD-ROM reference=8002.txt
<!— This is a document with a greeting root element —>
<!DOCTYPE greeting [
<!ELEMENT greeting (#PCDATA)>
<!ATTLIST greeting quality (WARM|COLD|HOSTILE) "WARM">
]>
<greeting>
A greeting from greeting-land.
<?greeting x=1?>
</greeting>
```

The following xgrep invocation illustrates the many false hits this XML document will generate.

```
CD-ROM reference=8003.txt
```

```
C>python xgrep.py -m -p greeting greeting.xml
```

```
greeting.xml:<!— This is a document with a [greeting] root
element —>
greeting.xml:<!DOCTYPE [greeting] [
greeting.xml:<!ELEMENT [greeting] (#PCDATA)>
greeting.xml:<!ATTLIST [greeting] quality (WARM|COLD|HOSTILE)
  "WARM">
greeting.xml:<[greeting]>
greeting.xml:A [greeting] from greeting-land.
greeting.xml:<?[greeting] x=1?>
greeting.xml:</[greeting]>
```

Of these eight hits, only one is actually character data. How can we remove the false hits? One look at the complexity of the full regular expression for the XML declaration shown at the start of this section should be enough to convince you that making xgrep XML-aware by rolling our own regular expressions is a lot of work!

A far more pragmatic approach would be to build xgrep on top of an existing parser implementation and process the post-XML parse output—PYX, for example. Routing XML files through xmln or xmlv gives us a mechanism for removing false hits because we can easily differentiate character data from markup in the PYX notation. We get a nice, clean stream of "events" corresponding to start-tags, end-tags, character data, and so on. No need for complex regular expressions.

8.2 | Invoking xmln from xgrep

Routing the XML file through `xmln` and picking up the output is made easy by Python's `popen` function, which can be found in the `os` module. You simply provide it with the command you want executed and it returns a file object. By reading from this file object, you read the output of the executed command.

```
CD-ROM reference=8004.txt
>>> import os
>>> f = os.popen ("xmln greeting.xml")
>>> f.readlines()
['(greeting\012', 'Aquality WARM\012', '-\\n\012',
'-A greeting from greeting-land.\012', '-\\n\012',
'?greeting x=1\012', '-\\n\012', ')greeting\012']
>>> f.close()
```

In the code above, the `popen` function creates a "pipe" connection to the output of the command `xmln greeting.xml`. The full output is read in one go by the `readlines()` method, which returns a list of lines. Finally, the file object is closed.

Note the occurrences of `\012`. This is Python's way of showing a linefeed character (character 10 in ASCII). Every line of data returned from `readlines` ends in one of these.

8.3 | Adding PYX Support for xgrep

We need to add a reasonable amount of new code to `xgrep` in this chapter. We will also take the opportunity of modularizing the code a little. We introduce a separate function, `XMLGrepEvents`, to handle the PYX event-based form of XML-aware processing. This reorganization will stand us in good stead when we add another form of XML-aware processing in the next chapter.

In the code below, a `-e` switch has been added to tell `xgrep` to function in "event mode." In this mode, `xgrep` treats files as XML files and processes the output of xmln rather than processing the text of the XML file directly.

The existing XMLGrep function has not been modified in any way and so is not reproduced here.

```
CD-ROM reference=8005.txt
import string,os
import re

def XMLGrepEvents (filename,pattern,MarkHits=0):
    """

    XML-aware version of XMLGrep. Uses xmln as an event source
    """
    Pattern = re.compile (pattern)

    if MarkHits == 0:
        # Do not mark hits, make the hit delimiters
        # blank strings.
        StartOfHit = ""
        EndOfHit = ""
    else:
        # Mark hits, make hit delimiters matching
        # square brackets.
        StartOfHit = "["
        EndOfHit = "]"

    # Open a pipe connection to the output of the
    # xmln invocation.
    f = os.popen ("xmln %s" % filename)

    for L in f.readlines ():
        L = L[:-1]
        # Character data events lines always
        # start with a "-".
        if L[0] == '-':
            mo = Pattern.search (l)
            if mo is not None:
                # Print out the match, using match
                # delimiters to show the "hit".
                print "%s:%s%s%s%s%s" % (filename,
                    # The slice starts at 1 to
                    # remove the "-"
                    L[1:mo.start()],
                    StartOfHit,
```

```
                                    L[mo.start():mo.end()],
                                    EndOfHit,
                                    L[mo.end():])
if __name__ == "__main__":
    import sys,glob,getopt

    MarkHits = 0
    UseEventStyle = 0

    # -e use event style
    # -p pattern to search for
    # -m turn on hit highlighting
    (options,remainder) = getopt getopt (sys.argv[1:],"p:me")
    pattern = None
    for (option,value) in options:
        if option == '-p':
            pattern = value
        elif option == '-m':
            MarkHits = 1
        elif option == '-e':
            UseEventStyle = 1
        else:
            sys.stderr.write ("Unknown option '%s'" %
                option)
    if pattern == None:
            sys.stderr.write (
                "Usage: %s  -p pattern [-e] [-m] " %
                    sys.argv[0]
                "[filename]...[filename]")
            sys.exit()
    if len(remainder)==0:
        sys.stderr.write (
            "No filename specified. "
            "Defaulting to test.xml\n")
        XMLGrep ("test.xml",pattern,MarkHits)
    else:
        for a in remainder:
            for g in glob.glob(a):
                # Process each file in turn using
                # either event style or plain text style.
                if UseEventStyle:
                    XMLGrepEvents
                        (g,pattern,MarkHits)
                else:
                    XMLGrep (g,pattern,MarkHits)
```

Here is an invocation of the new xgrep with the troublesome greeting.xml that caused the false hits earlier in this chapter. Note how all the false hits have disappeared.

```
CD-ROM reference=8006.txt
C>python xgrep.py -e -m -p greeting greeting.xml
greeting.xml:A [greeting] from greeting-land.
```

8.4 | Adding XML Search Features to xgrep

The current code is a good start on the road to an XML-aware grep, but there are a number of improvements we can make quite easily. Now seems as good a time as any to add them. We will allow xgrep to do the following.

■ Use a validating source of XML events (i.e., xmlv)

■ Match on attribute names

■ Match on attribute values

■ Match on processing instructions

■ Match on element type names

Adding these to the code is a lot easier than dreaming up a sensible way to specify them with single-letter command options! Thankfully, Python's getopt library supports the use of *multicharacter* command options that are preceded with two rather than one hyphen. Here are the new options we will add.

■ --V Turn on validation

■ --AN Match on attribute names

- ■ --AV Match on attribute values

- ■ --PI Match on processing instructions

- ■ --ETN Match on element type name

Here is the code. A lot has changed! We will discuss the changes once you have had a chance to look over the code.

```
CD-ROM reference=8007.txt
C>type xgrep.py

import string,os
import re

# Use "bits" to store boolean options.
MARK_HITS                       =    1
USE_EVENT_STYLE                 =    2
USE_TREE_STYLE                  =    4
VALIDATE                        =    8
MATCH_ATTRIBUTE_NAME            =   16
MATCH_ATTRIBUTE_VALUE           =   32
MATCH_PROCESSING_INSTRUCTION    =   64
MATCH_ELEMENT_TYPE_NAME         =  128
MATCH_CHARACTER_DATA            =  256


# PrintMatch subroutine called from many places in the code
# prints the match details.
def PrintMatch(filename,description,line,mo,StartOfHit,
  EndOfHit):
      print "%s%s:%s%s%s%s%s" % (filename,
              description,
              line[1:mo.start()],
              StartOfHit,
              line[mo.start():mo.end()],
              EndOfHit,
              line[mo.end():])
# XML-aware grepping using event source -- either xmln or xmlv
# depending on VALIDATE option.
def XMLGrepEvents (filename,pattern,options):
      Pattern = re.compile (pattern)

      if options & MARK_HITS:
          StartOfHit = "["
```

```
            EndOfHit = "]"
    else:
            StartOfHit = ""
            EndOfHit = ""

    if options & VALIDATE:
            f = os.popen ("xmlnv %s" % filename)
    else:
            f = os.popen ("xmln %s" % filename)

    for L in f.readlines():
            L = L[:-1]
            if L[0] == 'A':
                    # Attribute event
                    if options & MATCH_ATTRIBUTE_NAME:
                            name = string.split (L[1:])[0]
                            mo = Pattern.search (name)
                            if mo is not None:
                                    PrintMatch (filename,
                                                "(Attribute Name)",
                                                L[1:],
                                                mo,
                                                StartOfHit,
                                                EndOfHit)

                    if options & MATCH_ATTRIBUTE_VALUE:
                            value = string.join (
                                string.split (L[1:])[1]," ")
                            mo = Pattern.search (value)
                            if mo is not None:
                                    PrintMatch (filename,
                                                "(Attribute Value)",
                                                L[1:],
                                                mo,
                                                StartOfHit,
                                                EndOfHit)

            if L[0] == '?':
                    # Processing Instruction Event
                    if options &
                       MATCH_PROCESSING_INSTRUCTION:
                            mo = Pattern.search (L[1:])
                            if mo is not None:
                                    PrintMatch (filename,
                                                "(Processing
                                                  Instruction)",
```

```
                                        L[1:],
                                        mo,
                                        StartOfHit,
                                        EndOfHit)

        if L[0] == '(':
            # Start-tag event
            if options & MATCH_ELEMENT_TYPE_NAME:
                mo = Pattern.search (L[1:])
                if mo is not None:
                    PrintMatch (filename,
                                "(Element Type
                                  Name)",
                                L[1:],
                                mo,
                                StartOfHit,
                                EndOfHit)

        if L[0] == '-':
            # Character data event
            if options & MATCH_CHARACTER_DATA:
                mo = Pattern.search (L[1:])
                if mo is not None:
                    PrintMatch (filename,
                                "(Character Data)",
                                L[1:],
                                mo,
                                StartOfHit,
                                EndOfHit)
def XMLGrep(filename,pattern,options):
    Pat = re.compile (pattern)

    if options & MARK_HITS:
        StartOfHit = "["
        EndOfHit = "]"
    else:
        StartOfHit = ""
        EndOfHit = ""

    f = open (filename,"r")
    for L in f.readlines():
        L = L[:-1]
        mo = Pattern.search (l)
        if mo is not None:
            PrintMatch (filename,
```

```
                                    "",
                                    1,
                                    mo,
                                    StartOfHit,
                                    EndOfHit)
if __name__ == "__main__":
    import sys,glob,getopt
    pattern = None

    # The default option is to match on character data.
    OptionsBitmap = MATCH_CHARACTER_DATA

    (options,remainder) = getopt.getopt (
        sys.argv[1:],"p:mev",["AN","AV","PI","ETN"])
    for (option,value) in options:
        if option == '-p':
            pattern = value
        elif option == '-m':
            OptionsBitmap = OptionsBitmap | MARK_HITS
        elif option == '-e':
            OptionsBitmap = OptionsBitmap |
                USE_EVENT_STYLE
        elif option == '-v':
            OptionsBitmap = OptionsBitmap | VALIDATE
        elif option == '--AN':
            OptionsBitmap = OptionsBitmap |
                MATCH_ATTRIBUTE_NAME
            OptionsBitmap = OptionsBitmap &
                ~MATCH_CHARACTER_DATA
        elif option == '--AV':
            OptionsBitmap = OptionsBitmap |
                MATCH_ATTRIBUTE_VALUE
            OptionsBitmap = OptionsBitmap &
                ~MATCH_CHARACTER_DATA
        elif option == '--PI':
            OptionsBitmap = OptionsBitmap | \
                MATCH_PROCESSING_INSTRUCTIONS
            OptionsBitmap = OptionsBitmap &
                ~MATCH_CHARACTER_DATA
        elif option == '--ETN':
            OptionsBitmap = OptionsBitmap | \
                MATCH_ELEMENT_TYPE_NAME
            OptionsBitmap = OptionsBitmap &
                ~MATCH_CHARACTER_DATA
        else:
```

```
                    sys.stderr.write ("Unknown option '%s'" %
                        option)

    if pattern == None:
                    sys.stderr.write ("Usage: %s " % sys.argv[0])
                    sys.stderr.write (
                        "-p pattern [-e] [-m] [-v] "
                        "[--AV|--AN|--ETN|--PI][file]...
                            [file]")
                    sys.exit()

    if len(remainder)==0:
            sys.stderr.write (
                "No filename specified. Defaulting to
                    test.xml\n"
                )

            if OptionsBitmap | USE_EVENT_STYLE:
                    XMLGrepEvents ("test.xml",
                                    pattern,
                                    OptionsBitmap)
            else:
                    XMLGrep ("test.xml",
                            pattern,
                            OptionsBitMap)
    else:
            for a in remainder:
                    for g in glob.glob(a):
                            # Process each file in turn using
                            # either event style or plain text
                            # style.
                            if OptionsBitmap | USE_EVENT_STYLE:
                                    XMLGrepEvents (g,pattern,
                                        OptionsBitmap)
                            else:
                                    XMLGrep (g,pattern,OptionsBitMap)
```

As you can see, quite a bit has changed in the new xgrep code. In the sections below, we talk about the major changes, namely:

- Use of long option names in getopt

- Use of "bit twiddling" to handle the many options available

- The match printing function

8.5 | Using Long Option Names in getopt

Python's `getopt` library supports the use of multicharacter option names. On a command line, these are preceded by two hyphens. You tell `getopt` what multiline options to look for by passing in a third parameter to the `getopt` call. The third parameter is an array of strings as can be seen here:

```
CD-ROM reference=8008.txt
      (options,remainder) = getopt.getopt (
                   sys.argv[1:],"p:mev",["AN","AV","PI",
                   "ETN"])
```

This code instructs `getopt` to watch for `--AN`, `--AV`, `--PI` and `--ETN`. These can be freely mixed with the single-character options `-p`, `-m`, `-e` and `-v`.

8.6 | Using "Bit Twiddling" to Handle the Many Options Available

Perhaps the most striking change in the code is the handling of all the command-line options in the code. There are nine on/off options to `xgrep` at this point. We could have separate variables for each one, like this.

```
CD-ROM reference=8009.txt
MarkHits = 0
UseEventStyle = 0
UseTreeStyle = 0
Validate = 0
MatchAttributeName = 0
MatchAttributeValue = 0
MatchProcessingInstruction = 0
MatchElementTypeName = 0
MatchCharacterData = 0
```

We could then set these to 1 as required when processing the results from `getopt`. We could then pass them into `XMLGrepEvents`, where they would be needed to decide how to perform matches.

An alternative approach has been used that keeps all the boolean variables in one integer variable called `options`. The key thing to notice is that each bit of the integer represents a different on/off option. Figure 8–1 shows the options flag when the `MARK_HITS`, `USE_EVENT_STYLE`, and `MATCH_ELEMENT_TYPE_NAME` options have been enabled.

The numbers assigned to the options correspond to the number that will set the option to "on." For example, `MATCH_ATTRIBUTE_NAME` is the fifth bit (counting right to left), which is the binary number 10000, which is 16 decimal.

To turn on a particular option, Python's bitwise OR operator "|" is used. This example turns on `MATCH_ELEMENT_TYPE_NAME`.

```
CD-ROM reference=8010.txt
    options = options | MATCH_ELEMENT_TYPE_NAME
```

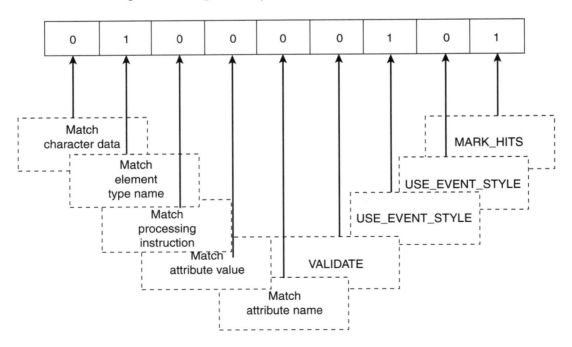

Figure 8–1   Storing multiple boolean variables in a single integer by using bits.

To turn a particular option off, Python's bitwise AND operator & is used in conjunction with the bitwise negation operator ~.

```
CD-ROM reference=8011.txt
    options = options & ~MATCH_ELEMENT_TYPE_NAME
```

8.7 | The Match Printing Function

With the addition of all the command-line options, there are now a total of six points in the code where a match needs to be printed out. Five of these occur in the XML-aware XMLGrepEvents and one occurs in the non-XML-aware XMLGrep function. Rather than duplicate the printing code six times, we introduced a subroutine. A side effect is having a single place to make code changes if we want to modify the way xgrep generates its output.

8.8 | Some Examples

The following example is an XML-aware grep for phrases beginning with "g" and ending in "t." The search is restricted to character data. Therefore, we do not get any false hits such as the <greeting> start-tag.

```
CD-ROM reference=8012.txt
C>python xgrep1.py -m -p g.*t -e  greeting.xml

greeting.xml(Character Data): [greeting from greet]ing-land.
```

The pattern here, g.*t is a Python regular expression. Notice how the output includes not only the filename, but also the type of XML event that caused the match—in this case, character data. Notice also how the resultant match has "skipped over" the "t" in the the first occurrence of "greeting" and extended as far as the second one. This is a consequence of the fact that Python pattern matching is, by default, *greedy* as discussed in chapter 7.

Here is the nongreedy version:

```
CD-ROM reference=8013.txt
C>python xgrep1.py -m -p g.*?t -e  greeting.xml

greeting.xml(Character Data): [greet]ing from greeting-land.
```

This time the * character in the regular expression is followed by a question mark ?. This has the effect of changing the match from greedy to nongreedy. That is, the first occurrence of a "t" after a "g" will cause a match.

The example below uses the same search pattern but this time searches element type names only.

```
CD-ROM reference=8014.txt
C>python xgrep1.py -m -p g.*?t __ETN greeting.xml

greeting.xml(Element Type Name):[greet]ing
```

As a final example, this invocation of xgrep matches any attribute called "number" that contains the number "10."

```
CD-ROM reference=8015.txt
C>type phones.xml
<phones>
<phone number = "096-36038"/>
This text with the number 10 in it will not confuse xgrep
<?neither will this number 10 ?>
<!- or indeed, this number 10 ->
<phone number = "01-6621056"/>
<phone number = "096-36039"/>
</phones>

C>python xgrep1.py -m -p .*10.* -AV foo.xml
foo.xml(Attribute Value):[number 01-6621056]
```

8.9 | Generalizing the Idea of Event-Based XML Processing

The event-based programming style has a long history in the field of structured document processing. Long before XML came into existence, it was a common approach to HTML processing. Python's HTML processing library, `htmllib`, takes an event-driven approach.

Long before HTML, the event-driven style was a common approach to SGML processing. In fact, a number of programming languages such as OmniMark and Balise have been created specifically to support the event-driven structured SGML-processing paradigm. General-purpose scripting languages such as Perl, Tcl, and indeed Python are also often used with SGML, typically using James Clark's `sgmls` and `nsgmls` parsers as event sources.[1]

In `xgrep`, events are retrieved from the event source through the use of the `readline()` method. The code follows the general pattern, sometimes known as the "read ahead/read replace" pattern, shown below.

```
CD-ROM reference=8016.txt

Parser = StartParser ("greeting.xml")
e = GetEvent(Parser)
while e:
        if e.Type == START_TAG:
                if e.ElementTypeName=="part":
                        #do this
                elif e.ElementTypeName=="chapter"
                        #do this
        elif e.Type == END_TAG:
                if e.ElementTypeName=="part":
                        #do this
```

---

[1]In my book *ParseMe.1st—SGML for Software Developers,* also in this series, you can read how Python, Perl, and C++ can be used to process SGML with a variety of approaches, including event processing.

```
        elif e.ElementTypeName=="chapter"
                #do this


            . . .
      elif ...:


    . . .
    e = GetEvent(Parser)
```

As the complexity of processing increases, this pattern leads to longer and longer nested conditionals in one large `while` loop. This code can get unwieldy.

One technique to deal with the problem is to *dispatch* events to special *handler functions,* like this.

```
CD-ROM reference=8017.txt
def HandleStartTag(e):
            if e.ElementTypeName=="part":
                #do this
            elif e.ElementTypeName=="chapter"
                #do this

def HandleEndTag(e):
            if e.ElementTypeName=="part":
                #do this
            elif e.ElementTypeName=="chapter"
                #do this

Parser = StartParser ("greeting.xml")
e = GetEvent(Parser)
while e:
      if e.Type == START_TAG:
            HandleStartTag(e)
      elif e.Type == END_TAG:
            HandleEndTag(e)


            . . . .
      elif ...:


    . . .
    e = GetEvent(Parser)
```

This approach can be taken a stage further by leaving it up to the parser to call the handler functions rather than dispatching them manually, as follows.

```
CD-ROM reference=8018.txt
def HandleStartTag(e):
            if e.ElementTypeName=="part":
                #do this
            elif e.ElementTypeName=="chapter"
                #do this

def HandleEndTag(e):
            if e.ElementTypeName=="part":
                #do this
            elif e.ElementTypeName=="chapter"
                #do this

Parser = StartParser ("greeting.xml")
# Register a handler for start-tags.
Parser.RegisterStartTagHandler(HandleStartTag)
# Register a handler for end-tags.
Parser.RegisterEndTagHandler(HandleEndTag)
Parser.Go()
```

This approach—registering handlers (also known as *callbacks*) and then yielding control to the parser—is highly reminiscent of the event-driven approach usually used with Graphical User Interface programming.

A good real-world example of this technique in action is James Clark's expat parser, which was specifically designed to fit this processing style. In fact, we may have already executed a program that uses this style in chapter 3. Remember the testpyexpat.py program used to test the XML package? The code is reproduced here. Even without further comment from me, you should be able to see the event-driven architecture it uses.

```
CD-ROM reference=8019.txt
#! /usr/bin/env python

# Import the pyexpat xml parsing module.
from xml.parsers import pyexpat

# Create a test XML file as a Python string.
TestFile = """<?xml version="1.0"?>
<Employee>
      <Name>
```

```
                <Given>Sean</Given>
                <Family>McGrath</Family>
        </Name>
        <Extension>
        1234
        </Extension>
</Employee>
"""

# Create a function to be called whenever an element starts.
def StartElementHandler(Element,Attributes):
        print "Element %s has started" % Element

# Create a function to be called whenever an element ends.
def EndElementHandler(Element):
        print "Element %s has ended"  % Element

# Create a parser object.
parser = pyexpat.ParserCreate()

# Tell the parser about the "handlers" for starting and
# ending elements.
parser.StartElementHandler = StartElementHandler
parser.EndElementHandler = EndElementHandler

# Parse the test file.
result = parser.Parse(TestFile,1)

# Check the result code. A 0 means something went wrong.
if result == 0:
        print 'Error', pyexpat.ErrorString(parser.ErrorCode)
        print 'Line', parser.ErrorLineNumber
        print 'Column', parser.ErrorColumnNumber
```

8.10 | A Standardized Event-Driven Processing Model

Although the philosophical approach used in event-driven XML processing is clear, it seems that no two developers can agree on a naming convention for how to implement it!

For every XML parser, there is yet another variation on the event-driven processing approach that uses slightly different ways of registering callback functions, slightly different ways of passing parameters to callbacks, slightly different ways of terminating processing, and so on.

Luckily, there is a standard way to do it in the XML world in the form of SAX—simple API for XML. We will take a good look at SAX in chapter 10.

8.11 | Advantages and Disadvantages of Event-Driven Processing

The event-based processing style is in many ways an improvement over the regular expression-based approach. Letting a full-fledged XML parser process the raw text ensures a much more rigorous adherence to the XML specification than we could hope to achieve "by hand." However, there are disadvantages as well as advantages.

8.11.1   *Limited Event Types*

The processing we can perform with an event-driven style is affected by the nature of the events the underlying parser makes available to us. The `xmln` and `xmlv` utilities, for example, do not report comments, CDATA sections, or element type declarations as events.

It could be argued that the output format of `xmln` and `xmlv` should be extended to include notification for these types of events. However, this is a slippery slope. It is tempting to think that with a few more event types, everything of interest in the source XML will be available. Before you know it, you will find events for external entity references, notation declarations, internal document type declaration subsets, content models, defaulted attribute values, line ends within start-tags, attribute value specification delimiters. . . . Need I go on?

The beauty of the event-driven approach is that is focuses on the principal event types used in the majority of XML-processing applications. It does not attempt to cover them all.

8.11.2   *Parsing Context*

XML is designed so that parsers—both validating and nonvalidating—do not need to "look ahead" very far in documents before recognizing events such as start-tags, character data, and so on. From an event-driven processing perspective, this means that event handling can happen simultaneously with parsing. The parser does not need to keep any large amount of XML in memory. Consequently, the event-driven style can be used to process very large documents without processing-power problems.

On the downside, one consequence of the event-driven approach is that processing tasks that involve looking ahead at events yet to take place are more difficult to code. For example, given the following XML file, how would you code an application that prints out all invoices that contain at least three items?

CD-ROM reference=8020.txt

```
<invoices>
    <invoice>
        <item name="shoes" cost="10.00"/>
        <item name="socks" cost="1.00"/>
    </invoice>
    <invoice>
        <item name="shoes" cost="10.00"/>
        <item name="socks" cost="1.00"/>
    </invoice>
    <invoice>
        <item name="shoes" cost="10.00"/>
        <item name="socks" cost="1.00"/>
        <item name="trousers" cost="100.00"/>
    </invoice>
    <invoice>
        <item name="shoes" cost="10.00"/>
    </invoice>
</invoices>
```

I will leave you to think about that. When we get on to the Pyxie library later in the book, we will create some solutions to this problem—some using an event-driven approach and some using a more powerful but more resource-hungry approach based on tree structures stored in memory.

8.12 | In Conclusion

We have seen how the event-driven approach cuts out a lot of potential trouble spots for processing XML by leaving the handling of XML syntax in the safe hands of an XML parser.

We now have a version of xgrep that doubles as a plain text grepping tool and an XML-aware grepping tool. It has its faults, but even as it stands, it is a useful utility.

In the next chapter, we will extend xgrep further, but for now, we close out this chapter with a couple of small changes to xgrep.

Before we finish this chapter, we will improve the PrintMatch function. Currently, it prints its output on standard output with the print statement. This is likely to be a less-than-perfect behavior when the module is imported into larger programs, especially for GUI applications where the concept of "standard output" may not even exist.

We will pave the way towards a GUI front end for xgrep by allowing it to take a parameter to specify where the output should go.

Finally, the function previously known as XMLGrep has been renamed to TextGrep to more readily differentiate it from its XML-aware cousin (who will be joined by another cousin in the next chapter).

Here is the complete code for xgrep with these changes incorporated. You might like to look over this code before proceeding to the next chapter.

```
CD-ROM reference=8021.txt
import string,os
import re

# Use "bits" to store boolean options.
```

```
MARK_HITS                    =    1
USE_EVENT_STYLE              =    2
USE_TREE_STYLE               =    4
VALIDATE                     =    8
MATCH_ATTRIBUTE_NAME         =   16
MATCH_ATTRIBUTE_VALUE        =   32
MATCH_PROCESSING_INSTRUCTION =   64
MATCH_ELEMENT_TYPE_NAME      =  128
MATCH_CHARACTER_DATA         =  256


# PrintMatch subroutine called from many places in the code
# prints the match details.
def PrintMatch(filename,description,line,mo,StartOfHit,
  EndOfHit,out):
      out.write ("%s%s:%s%s%s%s%s\n" % (filename,
                                        description,
                                        line[1:mo.start()],
                                        StartOfHit,
                                        line[mo.start():
                                          mo.end()],
                                        EndOfHit,
                                        line[mo.end():])
# XML-aware grepping using event source — either xmln or xmlv
# depending on VALIDATE option.
def XMLGrepEvents (filename,pattern,options,out=sys.stdout):
      print options
      Pat = re.compile (pattern)

      if options | MARK_HITS:
          StartOfHit = "["
          EndOfHit = "]"
      else:
          StartOfHit = ""
          EndOfHit = ""

      if options & VALIDATE:
          f = os.popen ("xmlnv %s" % filename)
      else:
          f = os.popen ("xmln %s" % filename)

      for L in f.readlines():
          L = L[:-1]
          if L[0] == 'A':
              # Attribute event
              if options & MATCH_ATTRIBUTE_NAME:
                  name = string.split (L[1:])[0]
```

```
        mo = Pat.search (name)
        if mo is not None:
                PrintMatch (filename,
                            "(Attribute Name)",
                            L[1:],
                            mo,
                            StartOfHit,
                            EndOfHit,
                            out)

    if options & MATCH_ATTRIBUTE_VALUE:
        value = string.join (
            string.split (L[1:])[1]," ")
        mo = Pat.search (value)
        if mo is not None:
                PrintMatch (filename,
                            "(Attribute Value)",
                            L[1:],
                            mo,
                            StartOfHit,
                            EndOfHit,
                            out)

if L[0] == '?':
    # Processing Instruction Event
    if options & MATCH_PROCESSING_INSTRUCTION:
        mo = Pat.search (L[1:])
        if mo is not None:
                PrintMatch (filename,
                            "(Processing
                              Instruction)",
                            L[1:],
                            mo,
                            StartOfHit,
                            EndOfHit,
                            out)

if L[0] == '(':
    # Start-tag event
    if options & MATCH_ELEMENT_TYPE_NAME:
        mo = Pat.search (L[1:])
        if mo is not None:
                PrintMatch (filename,
                            "(Element Type
                              Name)",
                            L[1:],
```

```python
                                                mo,
                                                StartOfHit,
                                                EndOfHit,
                                                out)

            if L[0] == '-':
                    # Character data event
                    if options & MATCH_CHARACTER_DATA:
                            mo = Pat.search (L[1:])
                            if mo is not None:
                                    PrintMatch (filename,
                                                "(Character Data)",
                                                L[1:],
                                                mo,
                                                StartOfHit,
                                                EndOfHit,
                                                out)
def TextGrep(filename,pattern,options,out=sys.stdout):
    """
    Straight text grepping algorithm
    """
    Pat = re.compile (pattern)

    # Set up hit markers.
    if options & MARK_HITS:
            StartOfHit = "["
            EndOfHit = "]"
    else:
            StartOfHit = ""
            EndOfHit = ""

    f = open (filename,"r")
    for L in f.readlines():
            # Strip off new line
            L = L[:-1]
            mo = Pat.search (l)
            if mo is not None:
                    # Found a match — print it. The second
                    # parameter is a blank string because
                    # this is only used to show context (e.g.,
                    # Element, Atttribute, Character Data)
                    # when performing XML-aware grepping.
                    PrintMatch (filename,
                                "",
                                l,
                                mo,
```

```
                              StartOfHit,
                              EndOfHit,
                              out)

if __name__ == "__main__":
    import sys,glob,getopt

    pattern = None

    # The default option is to match on character data.
    OptionsBitmap = MATCH_CHARACTER_DATA

    (options,remainder) = getopt.getopt (
            sys.argv[1:],
            "p:mev",
            ["AN","AV","PI","ETN"])

    for (option,value) in options:
        if option == '-p':
        pattern = value
        elif option == '-m':
                OptionsBitmap = OptionsBitmap | \
                                        MARK_HITS
        elif option == '-e':
                OptionsBitmap = OptionsBitmap | \
                                        USE_EVENT_STYLE
        elif option == '-v':
                OptionsBitmap = OptionsBitmap | \
                                        VALIDATE
        elif option == '--AN':
                OptionsBitmap = OptionsBitmap | \
                                        MATCH_ATTRIBUTE
                                        _NAME
                OptionsBitmap = OptionsBitmap & \
                                        ~MATCH_CHARACTER
                                        _DATA
        elif option == '--AV':
                OptionsBitmap = OptionsBitmap | \
                                        MATCH_ATTRIBUTE
                                        _VALUE
        OptionsBitmap = OptionsBitmap & \
                                        ~MATCH_CHARACTER
                                        _DATA
        elif option == '--PI':
                OptionsBitmap = OptionsBitmap | \
                                        MATCH_PROCESSING_
```

```
                                           INSTRUCTIONS
                OptionsBitmap = OptionsBitmap & \
                                    ~MATCH_CHARACTER
                                    _DATA
        elif option == '--ETN':
                OptionsBitmap = OptionsBitmap | \
                                    MATCH_ELEMENT_TYPE
                                    _NAME
                OptionsBitmap = OptionsBitmap & \
                                    ~MATCH_CHARACTER
                                    _DATA
        else:
                sys.stderr.write ("Unknown option '%s'" % 
                  option)

    if pattern == None:
                sys.stderr.write ("Usage: %s " % sys.argv[0])
                sys.stderr.write (
                    "-p pattern [-e] [-m] [-v] "
                    "[--AV|--AN|--ETN|--PI] [file]...
                       [file]")
                sys.exit ()

    if len(remainder)==0:
        # No filename specified — default to test.xml.
        if OptionsBitmap | USE_EVENT_STYLE:
            XMLGrepEvents (open(test.xml,"r"),
                                pattern,
                                OptionsBitmap)
        else:
            TextGrep (sys.stdin,
                            pattern,
                            OptionsBitMap)
    else:
        for a in remainder:
            for g in glob.glob(a):
                # Process each file in turn, using
                # either an XML-aware event style or
                # a straight text style.
                # Output is to standard output.
                if OptionsBitmap | USE_EVENT_STYLE:
                    XMLGrepEvents (g,pattern,
                        OptionsBitmap)
                else:
                    TextGrep (g,pattern,
                        OptionsBitMap)
```

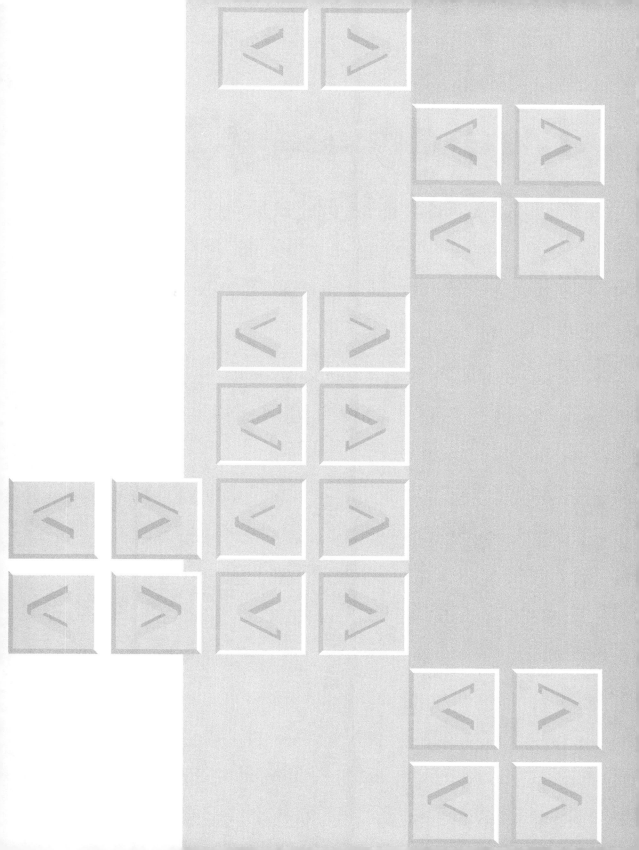

Tree-driven XML Processing

I n chapter 8, we made xgrep XML-aware by allowing it to feed off the PYX notation produced by xmln and xmlv.

In this chapter, we extend xgrep again by allowing it to answer queries like these.

- Find "Sean" anywhere within a name element.

- Print the text content of price elements.

- Count the number of invoice elements that have an overdue child element.

All the above queries share a common characteristic: They are most easily answered by modelling XML as a hierarchical structure. Answering queries like these with xgrep as it currently stands is not possible.

We can find "Sean" in data content easily, but we cannot *restrict* matches to "Sean" occurring somewhere within a name element.

What we need to answer these questions easily is a way of manipulating XML as a tree structure. Tree processing is at the heart of the

Pyxie library, and this chapter will serve as a warm-up for the development of the Pyxie in chapter 12. We will use the tree-processing functionality developed in this chapter in the file `pyxie.py`.

Consider the following XML file.

```
CD-ROM reference=9001.txt
<?xml version="1.0"?>
<bills>
<metadata>
Sean created this file.
</metadata>
<bills.services>
 <invoices>
  <invoice>
   <name>Sean Mc Grath</name>
   <description>Consultancy</description>
   <price><dollars>12</dollars><cents>50</cents></price>
   <overdue/>
  </invoice>
 <invoice>
  <name>Aine Mc Grath</name>
  <description>Consultancy</description>
  <price><dollars>32</dollars><cents>70</cents></price>
  <paid/>
 </invoice>
 </invoices>
</bills.services>
<bills.goods>
<invoices>
  <invoice>
   <name>Aoife Mc Grath</name>
   <description>Computers</description>
   <price><dollars>1250</dollars><cents>00</cents></price>
  </invoice>
 <invoice>
  <name>Niamh Mc Grath</name>
  <description>Paper</description>
  <price><dollars>56</dollars><cents>20</cents></price>
  <overdue/>
 </invoice>
</invoices>
</bills.goods>
</bills>
```

Thinking of this as a hierarchical structure, we can visualize this XML file, as shown in figure 9–1.

Let us think about the first of the queries we wish to find an answer to, namely, the occurrences of "Sean" within name elements.

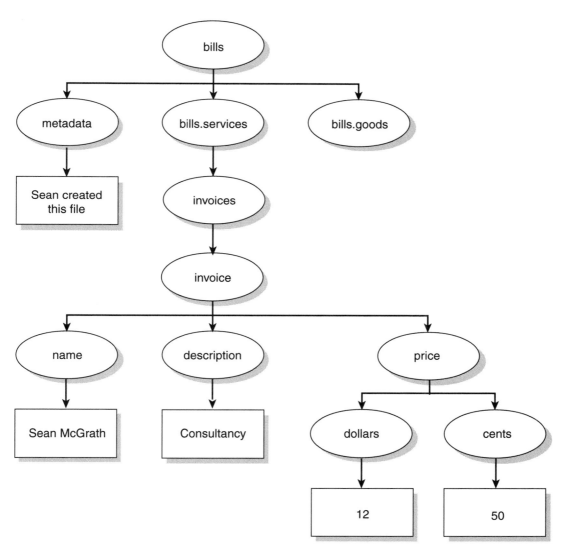

Figure 9–1   Visualizing an XML file as a hierarchical structure.

We need to create a Python data structure that allows us to navigate from node to node in this tree structure. Finding "Sean" within name elements is then reduced to the problem of finding "Sean" within text and then checking that somewhere in the ancestry of the matching node, we encounter a name element.

9.1 | Modelling a Node

In figure 9–1, element nodes are represented by ellipses, and data nodes are represented by rectangles. Although they are clearly different types of node, they share some common characteristics, namely, they can be linked top, bottom, left, and right to other nodes.

The fact that the two node types are different yet share some common characteristics points strongly to an implemention that involves a class hierarchy. The base of the hierarchy will be the xNode class, as shown below.

```
CD-ROM reference=9002.txt
class xNode:
      def __init__(self):
            self.Up = self.Down = self.Left = self.Right = None
```

Element nodes can be implemented as a subclass of xNode called xElement. Objects of type xElement will inherit the pointers to Up, Down, Left, and Right from the parent class, xNode. They will also have some storage for items particular to element nodes, namely, the element type name and any attributes.

```
CD-ROM reference=9003.txt
class xElement (xNode):
      def __init__(self,ElementTypeName):
            xNode.__init__(self)
            self.ElementTypeName = ElementTypeName
            self.AttributeValues = {}
```

Data nodes are also subclassed from xNode. The extra item we need here is storage for the actual text.

```
CD-ROM reference=9004.txt
class xData (xNode):
    def __init__(self,str):
        xNode.__init__(self)
        self.Data = str
```

So, we now have `xElement` nodes and `xData` nodes, and we have all the necessary "scaffolding" in place to allow us to join them into hierarchies. Collectively, a hierarchy of these nodes will form a tree structure. The structure is rooted at a single node known as the *root node*.

9.2 | Navigating a Tree

When doing tree navigation, it is useful to be able to keep track of a current position in a tree. A sensible place to put that functionality would be in a tree object—that is, implement the navigation functionality as methods of a tree class. We will create a class `xTree` to act as the top-level XML document object.

```
CD-ROM reference=9005.txt
class xTree:
def __init__(self):
self.RootNode = None
self.CurPos = None
```

In the constructor above, we have allocated storage for `RootNode`, which references the root node in the tree. We have also allocated storage for `CurPos`—the current position in the tree. When a tree is created, `CurPos` starts out being the same as `RootNode`, but it can be moved from node to node with the following methods.

```
CD-ROM reference=9006.txt
    def Down(self):
        """
        Move current position to the node below the
          current node.
        """
```

```
                    self.CurPos = self.CurPos.Down

        def Up(self):
            """
            Move current position to the node above the
            current node.
            """
            self.CurPos = self.CurPos.Up

        def Right(self):
            """
            Move current position to the node that is to
            the right of the current node.
            """
            self.CurPos = self.CurPos.Right

        def Left(self):
            """
            Move current position to the node that is to
            the left of the current node.
            """
            self.CurPos = self.CurPos.Left

        def Home(self):
            """
            Move the current positon back to the root element.
            """
            self.CurPos = self.RootNode
```

9.3 | Building xTree Structures

We can now navigate at will through an xTree structure, but how do we build the structure in the first place?

We could build up the structure "by hand" by using xTree, xData, and xElement objects.

```
CD-ROM reference=9007.txt
t = xTree()
t.RootNode = xElement("greeting")
t.CurPos = r.RootNode
t.Down()
t.CurPos.Bottom = xData("Hello World")
```

This program builds a tree that corresponds to the following XML document.

```
CD-ROM reference=9008.txt
<greeting>
Hello World
</greeting>
```

To better see the correspondence between the Python data structure and the XML file, let us add a couple of methods that will allow us to print XML from these structures easily.

You will remember from chapter 5 that Python allows you to take control over how an object is printed by overriding the special `__repr__` method.

The `__repr__` method for xData nodes is straightforward—it simply needs to return the string variable it uses to hold the data in the node.

```
CD-ROM reference=9009.txt
class xData(xNode):
    def __init__(self,str):
        xNode.__init__(self)
        self.Data = str

    def __repr__(self):
        return self.Data
```

For xElement nodes, the situation is a little trickier. We need to:

■ Create a string representation of the the start-tag

■ Allow all child nodes to create their own string representation

■ Create a string representation of the end-tag

Assume for the moment the existence of a utility function children that returns a list of child nodes of the current node. We can write the `__repr__` for an xElement node like this.

```
CD-ROM reference=9010.txt
# Create the start-tag.
```

```
res = '<%s>' % self.ElementTypeName
# Allow each of the children to recursively provide their own
# textual representation.
for c in Children(self):
    res = res + `c`
# Create the end-tag.
res = res + '</%s>' % self.ElementTypeName
```

We are nearly there. The last thing we need is the ability to print an xTree or, more powerfully, the part of an xTree rooted at the current position. Here is the code.

```
CD-ROM reference=9011.txt
class xTree:
    def __init__(self):
        self.RootNode = None
        self.CurPos = None

    def __repr__(self):
        return '<?xml version="1.0"?>\n' + `self.CurPos`
```

Note the back-ticks, which cause Python to ask the enclosed object to produce its textual representation. There is also a repr function that achieves the same thing, so we could have written the code like this:

```
CD-ROM reference=9012.txt
        return '<?xml version="1.0"?>\n' + repr(self.CurPos)
```

We can now create an XML file programmatically and then print it out as an XML file.

```
CD-ROM reference=9013.txt
t = xTree()
t.RootNode = xElement("greeting")
t.CurPos = t.RootNode
t.Down()
t.Down = xData("Hello World")
t.Home()
print `t`
```

The output of this program is shown below.

```
CD-ROM reference=9014.txt
```

```
<?xml version="1.0"?>
<greeting>Hello World</greeting>
```

To better show off how the algorithm recursively handles child nodes, we will create a more deeply nested structure to test the printing capability.

```
CD-ROM reference=9015.txt
C>type treebuild.py

from pyxie import *

t = xTree()
t.RootNode  = xElement("TABLE")
t.CurPos = t.RootNode
t.CurPos.Down = xElement("TR")
t.Down()
t.CurPos.Down = xElement("TD")
t.Down()
t.CurPos.Down = xElement("P")
t.Down()
t.CurPos.Down = xElement("STRONG")
t.Down()
t.CurPos.Down = xData("Hello World")
t.Home()
print `t`
```

The output of this program is shown below. The XML has been pretty-printed to show its hierarchical structure.

```
CD-ROM reference=9016.txt
C>python treebuild.py

<?xml version="1.0"?>
<TABLE>
 <TR>
   <TD>
     <P>
      <STRONG>
       Hello World
      </STRONG>
     </P>
   </TD>
  </TR>
</TABLE>
```

9.4 | Building an xTree By Using PYX

Building xTree objects programmatically is useful for testing but not much fun. What we need is an algorithm that will read PYX format and create an xTree from it. This algorithm works by keeping track of the current position in the tree as the tree is built from PYX events. A variable known as PasteDown keeps track of the direction in which new nodes should be appended to the tree, that is, beneath the current node (PasteDown == 1) or to the right of the current node (PasteDown == 0).

```
CD-ROM reference=9017.txt
def PYX2xTree(self,f):
    # Use a stream of PYX to create a tree structure.
    # Create a temporary root node.
    self.RootNode = xElement("TEMP")
    # Set the current position to the root node.
    self.CurPos = self.RootNode
    # Initial pasting direction for new nodes is downward.
    PasteDown = 1
    for L in f.readlines():
        # Chop off the new line
        L = L[:-1]

        if L[0] == '(':
            # A start-tag event
            # Grab the element type name.
            etn = L[1:]
            # Create an xElement node to hold the element.
            element = xElement(etn)
            if PasteDown:
                # Create necessary node
                # inter connections, given that the
                # new node will be beneath the
                # current node.
                self.CurPos.Down = element
                element.Up = self.CurPos
                self.CurPos = element
            else:
                # Create necessary node
                # inter connections, given that the
```

```
                            # new node will be to the right of the
                            # current node.
                            self.CurPos.Right = element
                            element.Left = self.CurPos
                            element.Up = self.CurPos.Up
                            self.CurPos = element
                            # Having pasted right, new paste
                            # direction
                            # will be downward.
                            PasteDown = 1

            elif L[0] == ')':
                    # End-tag event
                    if not PasteDown:
                            # If currently pasting right, move
                            # up one in the hierarchy.
                            self.CurPos = self.CurPos.Up
                    PasteDown = 0

            elif L[0] == '_':
                    # Character data
                    datum = xData(l[1:])
                    if PasteDown:
                            # Create necessary node
                            # inter connections, given that
                            # the new node will be beneath the
                            # current node.
                            self.CurPos.Down = datum
                            datum.Up = self.CurPos
                            self.CurPos = datum
                            PasteDown = 0
                    else:
                            # Create necessary node
                            # inter connections, given that
                            # the new node will be to the right
                            # the current node.
                            self.CurPos.Right = datum
                            datum.Left = self.CurPos
                            datum.Up = self.CurPos.Up
                            self.CurPos = datum

# Get rid of temporary root node.
temp = self.RootNode.Down
self.RootNode.Down = None
temp.Up = None
```

```
self.RootNode = temp
self.CurPos = self.RootNode
return self
```

9.5 | A Test Harness for Pyxie

Now that we can load XML that has been converted to PYX notation and re-create an XML document from the tree, we can add a simple test harness to the `pyxie.py` module. The code creates a tree from the XML document supplied as its first parameter. The tree is then "serialized" to XML as output.

```
CD-ROM reference=9018.txt
if __name__ == "__main__":
    import os,sys
    t = BuildTree (os.popen("xmln " + sys.argv[1]))
    print `t`
```

Here is an example of the test harness in action.

```
CD-ROM reference=9019.txt
C>type greeting.xml
<greeting>
Hello World.
</greeting>
```

```
C>python pyx.py greeting.xml
```

```
<?xml version="1.0"?>
<greeting>\nHello World.\n</greeting>
```

9.6 | Handling Line Ends

One small problem remains. Note the \n strings in the above output. These are literally the two characters "\" followed by "n" as the PYX format reports line ends in this escaped form. Before creating an xTree, we need to decode these into real line ends. The decode function below does the work.

```
CD-ROM reference=9020.txt
def Decode(s):
        return string.replace (s,"\\n","\n"))
```

We now need to call this function before creating any new xData nodes.

The PYX2String method:

```
CD-ROM reference=9021.txt
                    elif L[0] == '_':
                            datum = xData(l[1:])
```

```
CD-ROM reference=9022.txt
                    elif L[0] == '_':
                            datum = xData(Decode(l[1:]))
```

We now get correct line ends in the regenerated XML created by the test harness.

```
CD-ROM reference=9023.txt
C>python pyx.py greeting.xml

<?xml version="1.0"?>
<greeting>
Hello World.
</greeting>
```

9.7 | A Syntax for Tree Processing with xgrep

So far so good. We have the beginnings of a Python data structure for loading arbitrary XML files into fully navigable data structures. We can carry over all the existing xgrep syntax and add a collection of optional qualifiers. The presence of one of these qualifiers can be used to cause xgrep to work in tree mode.

- ■ **--parent** Match if parent element has the specified element type name

- ■ **--ancestor** Match if list of ancestors contains the specified element type name

- ■ **--child** Match if a child of the matching element has the specified element type name

- ■ **--descendant** Match if a descendant of the matching element has the specified element type name

- ■ **--sibling** Match if a sibling of the matching element has the specified element type name

With the above syntax changes, here is how we can express the three queries with which we began this chapter.

Find "Sean" Anwhere within a name *Element:*
```
CD-ROM reference=9024.txt
C>python xgrep.py -m -p sean --parent name bills.xml
```

Print the Text Content of price *Elements:*
```
CD-ROM reference=9025.txt
C>python xgrep.py -p.* --ancestor price bills.xml
```

Print an XML Document for Each invoice
Element That Has an overdue *Child Element:*
```
CD-ROM reference=9026.txt
C>python xgrep.py --ETN invoice --descendant overdue bills.xml
```

9.8 | Adding Support for Attributes

You may have noticed that we have an AttributeValues dictionary in the xElement class but the PYX2xTree methods currently do not process them. Let us rectify that. The first thing we need to do is change PYXTree to process the PYX notation for attributes.

```
CD-ROM reference=9027.txt
            elif L[0] == 'A':
                i = string.index (L," ")
                aName = L[1:i]
                aValue = L[i+1:]
                self.CurPos.AttributeValues[aName] =
                    aValue
```

The __repr__ method of xElement also needs to change in order to output (name,value) pairs for attributes when re-creating XML.

```
CD-ROM reference=9028.txt
    def __repr__(self):
        if len(self.AttributeValues) == 0:
            res = '<%s>' % self.ElementTypeName
        else:
            res = '<%s' % self.ElementTypeName
            for (aName,aValue) in self.Attribute
              Values.items():
                aValue = string.replace(aValue,'"','"')
                res = res + ' %s = "%s"' % (aName,
                    aValue)
            res = res + ">"
        for c in Children(self):
            res = res + `c`
        res = res + '</%s>' % self.ElementTypeName
        return res
```

9.9 | Some Utility Bits and Pieces

9.9.1 *Descendants*

In order to implement the --descendant command-line switch, we need to be able to find a list of all descendant nodes. This is a classic example of a recursive function that occurs very often in XML tree processing.

In the code below, notice that the auxillary method `Descendants1` does most of the real work. The `Descendants` function serves to initialize the result list, which is passed into `Descendants1` and then returned.

```
CD-ROM reference=9029.txt
class xTree:
    def Descendants1(self,res,n):
        """
        Add descendants of node "n" to the result list "res."
        This is an internal recursive method invoked from
        the Descendants method.
        """
        if n is None:
            return
        pos = n.Down
        if pos is None:
            return
        res.append (pos)
        self.Descendants1(res,pos)
        while pos.Right:
            res.append (pos)
            self.Descendants1(res,pos)
            pos = pos.Right

    def Descendants(self,n=None):
        """
        Create a list of the descendants of the current node
        or the specified node. Most of the work is done by
        the recursive Descendants1 method.
        """
        self.PushPos()
        if n==None:
            n = self.CurPos
        res = []
        self.Descendants1(res,n)
        self.PopPos()
        return res
```

9.9.2 The AtElement and AtData Functions

We need to know if the current position in the `xTree` is an element, that is, if it is an instance of the `xElement` class.

```
CD-ROM reference=9030.txt
    def AtElement(self):
        """
        Return true if current position is an Element.
        """
        return isinstance (self.CurPos,xElement)
```

We need to know if the current position in the xTree is a data node (an instance of the xData class).

```
CD-ROM reference=9031.txt
    def AtData(self):
        """
        Return true if current position is character data.
        """
        return isinstance (self.CurPos,xData)
```

9.9.3 *The Seek Method*

With functions such as Ancestors/Descendants, it is useful to be able to set the current position in a tree in order to use the convenience methods such as Up, Down, AtElement and AtData. We introduce a Seek method for this purpose.

```
CD-ROM reference=9032.txt
    def Seek (self,Node):
        """
        Set the current position to the specified node.
        """
        self.CurPos = Node
```

9.10 | Implementing XMLGrepTree

We now have all the bits and pieces we need to add a tree-driven XML processing mode to xGrep. The bulk of the code changes are in the new function XMLGrepTree.

```
CD-ROM reference=9033.txt
```

```
# XML-aware grepping using event source--either xmln or xmlv
# depending on VALIDATE option.

def XMLGrepTree (filename,pattern,options,out,context=""):
    if options & VALIDATE:
        # Use xmlv as a PYX event source.
        f = os.popen ("xmlv %s" % filename)
    else:
        # Use xmln as a PYX event source.
        f = os.popen ("xmln %s" % filename)

    # Create an empty tree.
    tree = xTree()
    tree.PYX2xTree(f)
    f.close()

    Pattern = re.compile (pattern)

    if options & MARK_HITS:
        StartOfHit = "["
        EndOfHit = "]"
    else:
        StartOfHit = ""
        EndOfHit = ""
    NodeList = pyx.Descendants(tree.Root())
    for Node in NodeList:
        tree.Seek(Node)
        if tree.AtData():
            if options & MATCH_CHARACTER_DATA:
                mo = Pattern.search (tree.GetData())
                if mo:
                    if CheckContext (options,
                        tree,context):
                        PrintMatch (
                            filename,
                            "{Character Data}",
                            tree.GetData(),
                            mo,
                            StartOfHit,
                            EndOfHit,
                            out)
        elif tree.AtElement():
            if options & MATCH_ATTRIBUTE_NAME:
                for (a,v) in Node.Attributes():
                    mo = Pattern.search (a)
```

```
                     if mo:
                          if CheckContext(options,
                              tree,context):
                              PrintMatch (
                                   filename,
                                   "{Attribute
                                     Name}",
                                   a,
                                   mo,
                                   StartOfHit,
                                   EndOfHit,
                                   out)
                 if options & MATCH_ATTRIBUTE_VALUE:
                     for (a,v) in Node.Attributes():
                          mo = Pattern.search (v)
                          if mo:
                              if CheckContext(options,
                                  tree,context):
                                  PrintMatch (
                                       filename,
                                       "{Attribute
                                         Value",
                                       v,
                                       mo,
                                       StartOfHit,
                                       EndOfHit,
                                       out)
```

Most of the work in handling the command-line options has been relegated to a `CheckContext` function.

CD-ROM reference=9034.txt
```
def CheckContext (options,tree,context):
    if options & PARENT_CONTEXT:
        node = tree.CurPos.Up
        if node and node.ElementTypeName==context:
            return 1
        return 0
    if options & ANCESTOR_CONTEXT:
        for Node in pyx.Ancestors(tree):
            if Node.ElementTypeName==context:
                return 1
        return 0
    if options & CHILD_CONTEXT:
```

```
        for Node in pyx.Children(tree):
            if Node.ElementTypeName==context:
                return 1
        return 0
    if options & DESCENDANT_CONTEXT:
        for Node in pyx.Descendants(tree):
            if Node.ElementTypeName==context:
                return 1
        return 0
    if options & SIBLING_CONTEXT:
        for Node in pyx.Siblings(tree):
            if pyx.IsxElement(Node):
                if Node.ElementTypeName==context:
                    return 1
        return 0
```

9.11 | A Standardized Tree-Driven XML Processing Model

Tree-based processing of XML (and indeed HTML) is such a useful thing that the W3C has put forward a standard API for it known as the DOM—Document Object Model. The DOM is the subject of chapter 11.

The DOM has the advantage that it is becoming familiar to more and more programmers. However, like any language-independent API, it is a compromise. PYX tree creation and navigation is very Python specific but is more natural to program in Python than the DOM. There is no reason why the DOM should not be supported as a layer on top of Pyxie, thus providing Python programmers with the option to work at the standardized API level or at the Python-specific level.

9.12 | Advantages and Disadvantages of Tree-Driven XML Processing

The main advantage of tree-driven XML processing is that being able to navigate the structure at will leads to code that is easier to understand

and maintain. The disadvantage is that building and manipulating trees as in-memory data structures is more resource intensive. The sheer size of an XML file might make it impossible to load it into your computer's memory. There are times when the simplicity of tree-based processing must be sacrificed to allow very large files to be processed.

However, it is not as cut and dried as all that. As we will see later on, Pyxie provides *sparse trees*, which is a pleasant compromise providing the simplicity of tree-based processing with the resource efficiency of event-based processing.

9.13 | Some Examples

At the beginning of this chapter, we saw three examples of searches that require hierarchical context. In the short sections below, solutions to these three queries are illustrated.

9.13.1 *Find "Sean" Anywhere Within a Name Element*

We use the following small `staff` file to illustrate this query.

```
CD-ROM reference=9035.txt
C>type staff.xml

<staff>
<department name="Technical">
<person>
<title>Technical Director</title>
<name>
<given>Sean</given>
<family>McGrath</family>
</name>
<email>Sean@digitome.com</email>
<web>http://www.digitome.com/Sean.html</web>
</person>
</department>
</staff>
```

We can use the xgrep -ancestor switch to restrict the match for "Sean" to be within name elements only:

CD-ROM reference=9036.txt

C>python xgrep.py -m -p Sean --ancestor name staff.xml

staff.xml{Character Data}:[Sean]

Compare this with the result if we omit the --ancestor switch.

CD-ROM reference=9037.txt

C>python xgrep.py -m -p Sean staff.xml

staff.xml:given>[Sean]</given>
staff.xml:email>[Sean]@digitome.com</email>
staff.xml:web>http://www.digitome.com/[Sean].html</web>

9.13.2   *Print the Text Content of Price Elements*

We use the following XML file to illustrate this query.

```
CD-ROM reference=9038.txt
<?xml version="1.0"?>
<bills>
<metadata>
Sean created this file.
</metadata>
<bills.services>
 <invoices>
  <invoice>
   <name>Sean McGrath</name>
   <description>Consultancy</description>
   <price><dollars>12</dollars><cents>50</cents></price>
   <overdue/>
  </invoice>
 <invoice>
  <name>Aine McGrath</name>
  <description>Consultancy</description>
  <price><dollars>32</dollars><cents>70</cents></price>
  <paid/>
 </invoice>
```

```
</invoices>
</bills.services>
<bills.goods>
<invoices>
  <invoice>
   <name>Aoife McGrath</name>
   <description>Computers</description>
   <price><dollars>1250</dollars><cents>00</cents></price>
  </invoice>
 <invoice>
  <name>Niamh McGrath</name>
  <description>Paper</description>
  <price><dollars>56</dollars><cents>20</cents></price>
  <overdue/>
 </invoice>
</invoices>
</bills.goods>
</bills>
```

We can restrict the match to character data within price elements by specifying a wildcard pattern and restricting the match to have a price ancestor element.

```
CD-ROM reference=9039.txt
C>python xgrep.py -m -p.* --ancestor price bills.xml

bills.xml{Character Data}:[12]
bills.xml{Character Data}:[50]
bills.xml{Character Data}:[32]
bills.xml{Character Data}:[70]
bills.xml{Character Data}:[1250]
bills.xml{Character Data}:[00]
bills.xml{Character Data}:[56]
bills.xml{Character Data}:[20]
```

9.13.3   *Count the Number of Invoice Elements that Have an Overdue Descendant Element*

We can restrict matches to invoice elements having an overdue element descendants with the --descendant option. We will use the same bills.xml file as in the last example.

```
CD-ROM reference=9040.txt
C>python xgrep.py -m -p invoice[^s] --ETN --descendant
  overdue bills.xml
bills.xml{Element Type Name:[invoice]
bills.xml{Element Type Name:[invoice]
```

Note the use of the [^s] in the regular expression. This inclusion avoids hits on the invoices element that would be generated if we left it out.

```
CD-ROM reference=9041.txt
C>python xgrep.py -m -p invoice --ETN --descendant overdue
  bills.xml

bills.xml{Element Type Name:[invoice]s
bills.xml{Element Type Name:[invoice]
bills.xml{Element Type Name:[invoice]s
bills.xml{Element Type Name:[invoice]
```

A more robust way to avoid the false hits would be to anchor the "invoice" pattern to the start and end of the string like this.

```
CD-ROM reference=9042.txt
C>python xgrep.py -m -p ^invoice$ --ETN --descendant overdue
  bills.xml

bills.xml{Element Type Name:[invoice]
bills.xml{Element Type Name:[invoice]
```

9.14 | Bringing It All Together

We end this chapter with a complete copy of the finished xgrep.

```
CD-ROM reference=9043.txt
import string,os,sys
import re
from pyxie import *

# Use "bits" to store boolean options
MARK_HITS                     = 1
USE_EVENT_STYLE               = 1 << 1
```

```
USE_TREE_STYLE                   = 1 << 2
VALIDATE                         = 1 << 3
MATCH_ATTRIBUTE_NAME             = 1 << 4
MATCH_ATTRIBUTE_VALUE            = 1 << 5
MATCH_PROCESSING_INSTRUCTION     = 1 << 6
MATCH_ELEMENT_TYPE_NAME          = 1 << 7
MATCH_CHARACTER_DATA             = 1 << 8
PARENT_CONTEXT                   = 1 << 9
ANCESTOR_CONTEXT                 = 1 << 10
CHILD_CONTEXT                    = 1 << 11
DESCENDANT_CONTEXT               = 1 << 12
SIBLING_CONTEXT                  = 1 << 13


# PrintMatch subroutine called from many places in the code
# prints the match details.
def PrintMatch(filename,description,line,mo,StartOfHit,
  EndOfHit,out):
      out.write ("%s%s:%s%s%s%s%s%s\n" % (filename,
                                description,
                                line[1:mo.start()],
                                StartOfHit,
                                line[mo.start():mo.end()],
                                EndOfHit,
                                line[mo.end():]))

def CheckContext (options,tree,context):
    if options & PARENT_CONTEXT:
        node = tree.GetUp()
        if node and node.ElementTypeName==context:
            return 1
        return 0
    if options & ANCESTOR_CONTEXT:
        for Node in tree.Ancestors():
            if Node.ElementTypeName==context:
                return 1
        return 0
    if options & CHILD_CONTEXT:
        for Node in tree.Children():
            if isinstance(Node,xElement) and\
Node.ElementTypeName==context:
                return 1
        return 0
    if options & DESCENDANT_CONTEXT:
        for Node in tree.Descendants():
            if isinstance(Node,xElement) and\
```

```
Node.ElementTypeName==context:
                    return 1
        return 0
    if options & SIBLING_CONTEXT:
        for Node in tree.Siblings():
            if isinstance(Node,xElement):
                if Node.ElementTypeName==context:
                    return 1
        return 0


# XML-aware grepping using event source --either xmln or xmlv
# depending on VALIDATE option.
def XMLGrepTree (filename,pattern,options,out,context=""):
    if options & VALIDATE:
        f = os.popen ("xmlnv %s" % filename)
    else:
        f = os.popen ("xmln %s" % filename)

    tree = PYX2xTree (f)
    f.close()

    Pattern = re.compile (pattern)

    if options & MARK_HITS:
        StartOfHit = "["
        EndOfHit = "]"
    else:
        StartOfHit = ""
        EndOfHit = ""

    NodeList = tree.Descendants()
    for Node in NodeList:
        tree.Seek(Node)
        if tree.AtData():
            if options & MATCH_CHARACTER_DATA:
                mo = Pattern.search (tree.Data)
                if mo:
                    if CheckContext (options,tree,
                        context):
                        PrintMatch (
                            filename,
                            "{Character Data}",
                            tree.Data,
                            mo,
```

```
                                    StartOfHit,
                                    EndOfHit,
                                    out)

elif tree.AtElement():
    if options & MATCH_ATTRIBUTE_NAME:
        for (a,v) in Node.Attributes():
            mo = Pattern.search (a)
            if mo:
                    if CheckContext(options,
                        tree,context):
                            PrintMatch (
                                    filename,
                                    "{Attribute
                                      Name}",
                                    a,
                                    mo,
                                    StartOfHit,
                                    EndOfHit,
                                    out)
    elif options & MATCH_ATTRIBUTE_VALUE:
        for (a,v) in Node.Attributes():
            mo = Pattern.search (v)
            if mo:
                    if CheckContext(options,
                        tree,context):
                            PrintMatch (
                                    filename,
                                    "{Attribute
                                      Value",
                                    v,
                                    mo,
                                    StartOfHit,
                                    EndOfHit,
                                    out)
    elif options & MATCH_ELEMENT_TYPE_NAME:
        mo = Pattern.search (tree.Element
            TypeName)
        if mo:
                if CheckContext(options,tree,
                    context):
                            PrintMatch (
                                    filename,
                                    "{Element
                                      Type Name",
```

```
                                          tree.Element
                                            TypeName,
                                          mo,
                                          StartOfHit,
                                          EndOfHit,
                                          out)


    def TextGrep(filename,pattern,options,out=sys.stdout):
        Pattern = re.compile (pattern)

        if options & MARK_HITS:
            StartOfHit = "["
            EndOfHit = "]"
        else:
            StartOfHit = ""
            EndOfHit = ""

        f = open (filename,"r")
        for L in f.readlines():
            L = L[:-1]
            mo = Pattern.search (L)
            if mo is not None:
                PrintMatch (
                    filename,
                    "",
                    L,
                    mo,
                    StartOfHit,
                    EndOfHit,
                    out)
if __name__ == "__main__":
        import sys,glob,getopt

        pattern = None
        context = ""

        # The default option is to match on character data
        OptionsBitmap = MATCH_CHARACTER_DATA

        (options,remainder) = getopt.getopt (
            sys.argv[1:],
            "p:mev",
            ["AN","AV","PI","ETN","parent=",
             "ancestor=","child=","descendant=",
```

```
        "sibling="])
for (option,value) in options:
    if option == '-p':
        pattern = value
    elif option == '-m':
        OptionsBitmap = OptionsBitmap | MARK_HITS
    elif option == '-e':
        OptionsBitmap = OptionsBitmap | USE_EVENT
            _STYLE
    elif option == '-v':
        OptionsBitmap = OptionsBitmap | VALIDATE
    elif option == '--AN':
        OptionsBitmap = OptionsBitmap | MATCH
            _ATTRIBUTE_NAME
        OptionsBitmap = OptionsBitmap & ~MATCH
            _CHARACTER_DATA
    elif option == '--AV':
        OptionsBitmap = OptionsBitmap | MATCH
            _ATTRIBUTE_VALUE
        OptionsBitmap = OptionsBitmap & ~MATCH
            _CHARACTER_DATA
    elif option == '--PI':
        OptionsBitmap = OptionsBitmap | \
            MATCH_PROCESSING_INSTRUCTIONS
        OptionsBitmap = OptionsBitmap & ~MATCH
            _CHARACTER_DATA
    elif option == '--ETN':
        OptionsBitmap = OptionsBitmap | MATCH
            _ELEMENT_TYPE_NAME
        OptionsBitmap = OptionsBitmap & ~MATCH
            _CHARACTER_DATA
    elif option == '--parent':
        OptionsBitmap = OptionsBitmap | PARENT
            _CONTEXT
        # Turn on tree mode.
        OptionsBitmap = OptionsBitmap | USE_TREE
            _STYLE
        context = value
    elif option == '--ancestor':
        OptionsBitmap = OptionsBitmap |
        ANCESTOR_CONTEXT
        # Turn on tree mode.
        OptionsBitmap = OptionsBitmap | USE_TREE
            _STYLE
        context = value
```

```
        elif option == '--child':
            OptionsBitmap = OptionsBitmap | CHILD
              _CONTEXT
            # Turn on tree mode.
            OptionsBitmap = OptionsBitmap | USE_TREE
              _STYLE
            context = value
        elif option == '--descendant':
            OptionsBitmap = OptionsBitmap | DESCENDANT
              _CONTEXT
            # Turn on tree mode.
            OptionsBitmap = OptionsBitmap | USE_TREE
              _STYLE
            context = value
        elif option == '--sibling':
            OptionsBitmap = OptionsBitmap | SIBLING
              _CONTEXT
            # Turn on tree mode.
            OptionsBitmap = OptionsBitmap | USE_TREE
              _STYLE
            context = value
        else:
            sys.stderr.write ("Unknown option '%s'" %
              option)

    if pattern == None:
            sys.stderr.write ("Usage: %s " % sys.argv[0])
            sys.stderr.write (
                "_p pattern [-e] [-m] [-v] "
                "[--AV|--AN|--ETN|--PI] "
                "[--parent|--ancestor|--child|"
                "--descendant|--sibling] [file]...
                  [file]")
            sys.exit()
    if len(remainder)==0:
        # No filename specified --default to test.xml
        if OptionsBitmap & USE_EVENT_STYLE:
            XMLGrepEvents (open("test.xml","r"),
                                 pattern,
                                 OptionsBitmap)
        elif OptionsBitmap & USE_TREE_STYLE:
            print "calling  xml grep tree"
            XMLGrepTree (open("test.xml","r"),
                                 pattern,
                                 OptionsBitmap,
```

```
                                sys.stdout,
                                context)
            else:
                    TextGrep (sys.stdin,pattern,OptionsBitMap)
    else:
            for a in remainder:
                    for g in glob.glob(a):
                            # Process each file in turn, using
                            # either event style or plain text
                              style.
                            # Output is to standard output.
                            if OptionsBitmap & USE_EVENT_STYLE:
                                    XMLGrepEvents (g,pattern,
                                        OptionsBitmap)
                            elif OptionsBitmap & USE_TREE_STYLE:
                                    XMLGrepTree (g,
                                                        pattern,
                                                        Options
                                                          Bitmap,
                                                        sys.stdout,
                                                        context)
                            else:
                                    TextGrep (g,
                                                        pattern,
                                                        OptionsBitmap,
                                                        sys.stdout)
```

Just Enough SAX

10

In this chapter, we examine one of the most widely implemented APIs used to process XML documents. SAX (Simple API for XML) is a simple, event-oriented API that supports the event-driven programming style discussed in chapter 8.

10.1 | History

The easiest route to an understanding of what SAX is and why it was created is via some background information about the very early days of XML and XML software development. The story begins with Peter Murray-Rust—pioneering XML software developer and creator of the xml-dev mailing list.[1]

---

[1]This mailing list has become something of an institution in the XML development world. To subscribe, send an e-mail to `majordomo@scml.org` with the message: subscribe xml-dev.

Peter was one of the first developers to create an XML-based application in the form of Jumbo—an XML browser based on the Java programming language. Jumbo began life as browser for XML documents conforming to the Chemical Markup Language DTD (CML). Since then, it has expanded in scope to become a general-purpose XML editing/viewing tool.

Originally, Peter developed his own XML parsing routines for Jumbo in the Java programming language. As development of XML progressed, powerful XML parsers began to appear, notably Ælfred by Dave Megginson, Lark by Tim Bray, and NXP by Norbert Mikula. Peter wanted to be able to configure Jumbo to use these different parsers. That is, he wanted to be able to swap XML parsers in and out of Jumbo without making code changes to Jumbo itself. The ability to swap XML parsers in an application is useful for a number of reasons:

- Parsers differ in their level of conformance to the XML specification.

- Parsers differ in the amount of memory they use.

- Parsers differ in the speed with which they parse XML.

- Nonvalidating parsers differ in their treatment of certain XML features such as external entities and defaulted attributes.

- Parsers differ in the quality of location information provided with error messages.

As things stood at the time, swapping parsers was not easy. It became evident to Peter Murray-Rust and others communicating on the xml-dev list that the emerging family of XML parsers had common core event-driven functionality for example, notifying applications when start-tags, end-tags, processing instructions, character data, and so on appear in the XML document.

However, each parser exposed this functionality *differently* in its API. Take the concept of notifying an application of the presence of character data as an example. One parser might provide a `charac-ters` method, another might use the name `chardata`. One might provide an array of characters with a length indicator, another might provide a string object, and so on.

Peter christened the phenomenon of multiple incompatible APIs to XML parsers "YAXPAPI" (Yet Another XML Parser API). Discussion on the xml-dev mailing list led to the idea of a standardized API that would allow XML application developers to swap XML parsers in and out of their applications without code changes at the application level.

The name SAX was adopted for the standardization effort.[2] Work on SAX started in December 1997, with David Megginson doing the lion's share of the work. David made regular postings to xml-dev on SAX design questions, often with his own view of the pros and cons of each choice. Enthusiastic discussion would follow each new set of questions or design choices. David would assimilate all the debate, make a decision, and move on to the next set of design decisions.

This process continued at breakneck speed for a month or so, and the first draft of SAX appeared during January of 1998. The API was developed in the Java programming language but care was taken not to introduce language dependencies into it. Where functionality was considered useful but specific to the Java programming language, it was separated out into a language-specific section to make it easier for developers to port SAX to other languages.

Five months of implementation experience and fine tuning followed, culminating in the birth of SAX 1.0 in May 1998. Jon Bosak of Sun Microsystems, one of XML's founding fathers and chairman of the W3C's XML Activity, kindly offered use of his `xml.org` domain name for the Java version of the SAX package for the Java platform; that domain now bears the name `org.xml.sax`.

---

[2]At one point, the acronym JAX—Java API for XML— was considered instead of SAX. I pointed out that this is somewhat rude in my country (slang for, um, restroom) and SAX was used instead.

The decision to avoid Java programming language dependencies in SAX soon bore fruit. Python was the first to emerge with a full-featured SAX implementation developed by Lars Marius Garshol. There is a C++ version, and a Perl implementation is ongoing. Other languages are expected to follow suit as SAX support in the XML industry grows.

Although SAX has proved very popular among the XML development community, it has no official standing within the W3C unlike, for example, the DOM API, which was developed by a W3C working group. (The DOM API is the subject of chapter 11.)

Although SAX is not *wired* to the Java programming language or to object-oriented languages, it is fair to say that SAX maps more easily to languages that support an object-oriented approach. An understanding of OO concepts is very useful in understanding SAX. In particular, an understanding of the Java platform concept of an interface is important.

10.2 | The Concept of an "Interface"

Chapter 5 briefly mentioned the Java platform concept of an *interface* in the context of Python's type system. If you are comfortable with the material in section 5.3 from that chapter, then the Java platform concept of an interface should readily make sense to you. If you are less than comfortable with that material, this coverage might solidify it for you.

Interfaces are closely related to the object-oriented programming concept of *inheritance*. Inheritance in turn is closely related to the way our minds organize concepts into hierarchies. These hierarchies form a powerful and natural way to model concepts in software. For example, my mental hierarchy for airplanes is shown in figure 10–1.

This might be a good hierarchy with which to model aircraft in software and it might not. It all depends on the application under development. Another perfectly good airplane hierarchy is shown in figure 10–2.

Clearly, there are many ways to build these hierarchies. A key skill in object-oriented design is picking the best hierarchy given the task at hand and potential future applications of the models under consideration. Continuing with the aeronautical theme, how would you or-

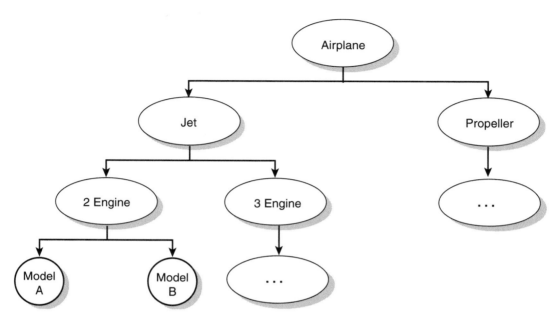

Figure 10–1 A hierarchy of airplane types.

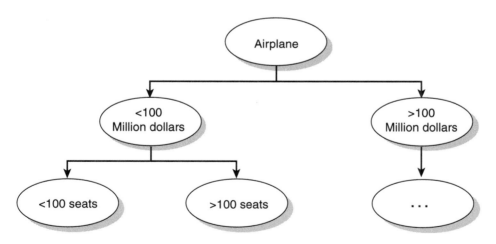

Figure 10–2 An alternative airplane type hierarchy.

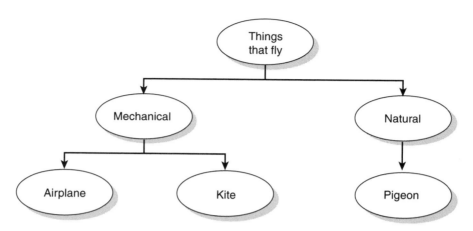

Figure 10–3 A hierarchy incorporating kites, pigeons, and airplanes.

ganize the concepts of airplane, kite, and pigeon into a hierarchy? One way to do it is shown in figure 10–3.

Now, airplanes and pigeons are very different things. There is a good chance that real-world software concerned with airplanes and pigeons would not use a hierarchy like that illustrated in figure 10–3. That said, airplanes and pigeons are clearly *related* by the fact that they both can fly.

As a software writer, you would expect to be able to ask software models of airplanes and pigeons to fly—even if they belong to completely different class hierarchies. This idea is illustrated in figure 10–4.

In figure 10–4, there are two classification hierarchies: Fixed Assets and Animals. Although airplanes and pigeons are in different hierarchies, we would like to be able to ask both of them to fly. In object-oriented design parlance, we would like to be able to send them both the *fly* message.

Relating this to XML processing, we might have classes in application areas as diverse as financial trading, hospital administration, and molecular biology, all requiring XML-processing capabilities. Each class is likely to be part of a natural hierarchy of classes to do with financial trading, hospital administration, etc.

One way to provide XML-processing capabilities would be to get each class to inherit from the XML-processing class in addition to its application area class. This technique is known as *multiple inheritance.*

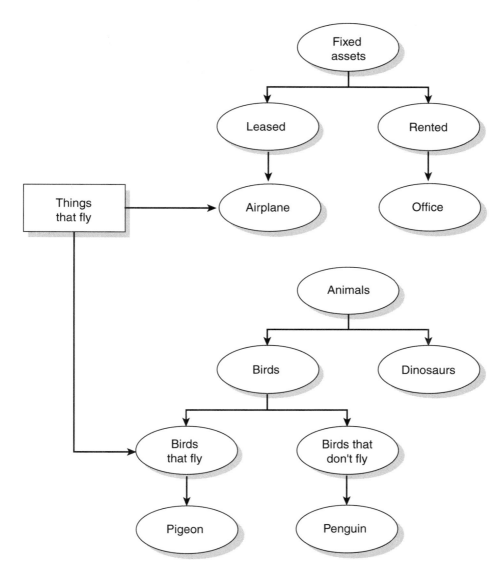

Figure 10–4   Combining hierarchies.

In the code fragment below, the class myFinancialTradingSystem is classified as both a FinancialTradingSystem and an XMLProcessor.

```
CD-ROM reference=10001.txt

class XMLProcessor:
    def StartElement(self,etn,attrs):
        pass

    def EndElement(self,etn,attrs):
        pass

    ...

class myFinancalTradingSystem (FinancialTradingSystem,
  XMLProcessor):
    def StartElement(self,etn,attrs):
        # Do something with an XML element and its
        # attributes

    def ShortSqueezeTheSilverMarket(self,Amount):
        # Perform a trade
```

Multiple inheritance is supported by a variety of object-oriented languages, including Python and C++. However, multiple inheritance can cause problems for language implementors and programmers alike. We will not go into the debate here. Suffice it to say that multiple inheritance is not universally acknowledged as a good idea.

The designers of the Java platform opted not to support multiple inheritance but to provide a facility to get the advantages of it without the perceived disadvantages. This is the Java concept of an *interface*.

Simply put, classes in the Java programming language are organized into single inheritance hierarchies. Any given class will have one and only one base class. However, any given class can support any number of interfaces. An interface specification is a collection of message names. Any class that provides implementations of the messages in the interface specification is said to *implement* the interface. By making the interface specification explicit in the language, Java compilers can check to make sure that classes that promise to implement interfaces do so properly.

Developers using SAX, for example, will state in their Java source code that the application implements one or more SAX interfaces.

The Java compiler can then check the source code to ensure that all the methods that need to be defined to implement the methods in the SAX interfaces have indeed been implemented.

Python does not currently provide any syntax for expressing interface specifications. As in Smalltalk before it, interfaces are more of a common convention than a language feature. It is up to the Python programmer to ensure that classes that should implement a particular interface actually do so.

10.3 | Overview of the SAX Specification

SAX consists of seven interfaces and three classes expressed in Java programming language syntax. The number of interfaces involved might sound somewhat daunting at first. In reality, only a subset of these are likely to be of interest to the majority of XML application developers because SAX caters to the needs of both XML parser developers and XML application writers.

The seven interfaces are:

- **DocumentHandler** Handling of start-tag, end-tags, character data, and so on.

- **AttributeList** Handling attributes

- **Parser** Parsing XML documents

- **ErrorHandler** Handling of parsing errors

- **DTDHandler** Handling of notation and entity declarations

- **EntityResolver** Handling of locating external entities

- **Locator** Supplying of location information from the parser to the application

The three classes are:

- **HandlerBase** A class that implements default document handling interfaces

- **InputSource** A class that provides all the information needed about an XML entity

- **SAXException** SAX exception handling

We will concentrate on one class and three interfaces:

- HandlerBase class

- DocumentHandler interface

- AttributeList interface

- ErrorHandler interface

10.4 | The HandlerBase Class

Four of the seven SAX interfaces are concerned with document handling:

- DocumentHandler

- ErrorHandler

- DTDHandler

- EntityResolver

We will take a close look at the first two of these later on. Together, these four interfaces comprise 14 different methods for handling aspects of document processing. The HandlerBase class implements

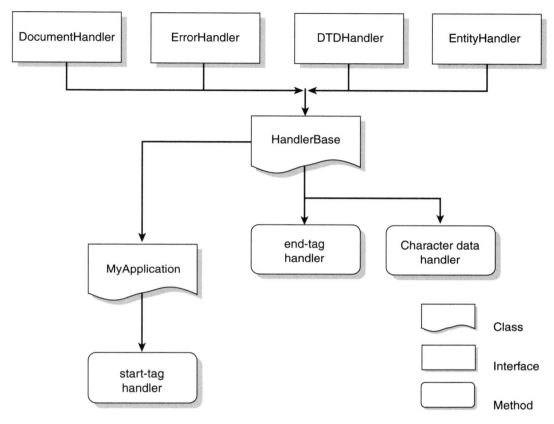

Figure 10–5 Implementing an interface.

default methods for all four interfaces. That is, all 14 methods required by the interfaces are defined, but they do not do anything.

Why is this useful? It is useful because it makes writing SAX applications very easy—simply make your class inherit from `Handler-Base` and you have implemented all four interfaces. You can simply override the methods that you actually need rather than provide stub implementions of those you do not need.

This concept is illustrated in figure 10–5.

The `HandlerBase` class lives in the file `saxlib.py`. It looks like this.

```
CD-ROM reference=10002.txt
class HandlerBase(EntityResolver,
                        DTDHandler,
                        DocumentHandler,
                        ErrorHandler):

    def __init__(self):
        pass
```

The handlers for the methods that make up each of the four interfaces are found in their respective classes. The `HandlerBase` class inherits the implementation of these methods through Python's inheritance mechanism.

Here is a fragment of the `DocumentHandler` class that shows some of the stub method implementations.

```
CD-ROM reference=10003.txt
class DocumentHandler:
    def startElement(self, name, atts):
        "Handle an event for the beginning of an element."
        pass

    def characters(self, ch, start, length):
        "Handle a character data event."
        pass

        ...
```

For example, imagine an application that is interested in nothing except start-tags. All that is necessary is a class derived from `HandlerBase` that implements the `startElement` method.

```
CD-ROM reference=10004.txt
from xml.sax import saxexts, saxlib, saxutils

class myHandler (saxlib.HandlerBase):
    def startElement (self, ElementTypeName, Attributes):
        print "Start-tag for ", ElementTypeName
```

10.5 | The DocumentHandler Interface

DocumentHandler is the main interface in SAX from a SAX application development perspective. It establishes handlers for start-tags, end-tags, processing instructions, character data, and so on. There are eight methods in the interface. The full stub interface looks like this.

```
CD-ROM reference=10005.txt

class DocumentHandler:
    def characters(self, ch, start, length):
        "Handle a character data event."
        pass

    def endDocument(self):
        "Handle an event for the end of a document."
        pass

    def endElement(self, name):
        "Handle an event for the end of an element."
        pass

    def ignorableWhitespace(self, ch, start, length):
        "Handle an event for ignorable whitespace in element
           content."
        pass

    def processingInstruction(self, target, data):
        "Handle a processing instruction event."
        pass

    def setDocumentLocator(self, locator):
        "Receive an object for locating the origin of SAX
           document events."
        pass

    def startDocument(self):
        "Handle an event for the beginning of a document."
        pass

    def startElement(self, name, atts):
```

```
    "Handle an event for the beginning of an element."
    pass
```

We take a closer look at each method and provide a code example of each one in the sections below.

10.5.1   *The startDocument Method*

This method is called at the very start of a document parse. SAX guarantees that this method is called before any other methods in the interface with the exception of `setDocumentLocator`. This makes it very useful for housing initialization code such as opening files, allocating data structures, and so on.

```
CD-ROM reference=10006.txt
from xml.sax import saxlib

class MySAXApplication (saxlib.HandlerBase):
    def startDocument(self):
        print "Start of Document"
```

10.5.2   *The endDocument Method*

This method is called at the very end of a document parse. It is a handy place to put cleanup code such as closing files, deleting data structures, and so on.

```
CD-ROM reference=10007.txt
from xml.sax import saxlib

class MySAXApplication (saxlib.HandlerBase):
    def endDocument(self):
        print "End of Document"
```

10.5.3   *The startElement Method*

This method is called when a start-tag and associated attributes are recognized in the XML document. The `Attributes` parameter implements another SAX interface called `AttributeList`, which is discussed later.

Note that the `AttributeList` object is *transient*. It is only valid for the life of the call to `startElement`. To keep a permanent copy of an attribute list, you must make a copy of it during this method.

```
CD-ROM reference=10008.txt
from xml.sax import saxlib

class MySAXApplication (saxlib.HandlerBase):
    def startElement(self,ElementTypeName, Attributes):
        LocalAttributes = []
        print "Start of Element", ElementTypeName
        for i in range (0,Attributes.getLength()):
            # Copy out attribute name and value into
            # local list.
            LocalAttributes.append (
                Attributes.getName(i),
                Attributes.getValue(i))
```

10.5.4   *The endElement Method*

This method is called whenever an end-tag is recognized in the XML document.

```
CD-ROM reference=10009.txt
from xml.sax import saxlib

class MySAXApplication (saxlib.HandlerBase):
    def endElement(self,ElementTypeName):
        print "End of Element ", ElementTypeName
```

Note that empty elements also trigger `endElement` events. For empty elements, the `endElement` event happens directly after the `startElement` event.

10.5.5   *The characters Method*

This method is called when character data is recognized in the XML document. The method takes three parameters: the first is a string, the second is an offset into the string at which the new chunk of character data starts, and the third parameter gives the length of the chunk.

```
CD-ROM reference=10010.txt
from xml.sax import saxlib

class MySAXApplication (saxlib.HandlerBase):
    def characters(self,chars,startOffset,Length):
        print "Character data", chars[startOffset:
            startOffset+Length]
```

An important aspect of XML parsers in general is that you cannot predict how much data will arrive in each call to the character handler. An XML parser is free to hand back chunks of character data in whatever sizes it likes. For example, consider this XML document:

```
CD-ROM reference=10011.txt
<test>
Hello World
</test>
```

A SAX application will receive one call to `startElement`, one call to `endElement`, but one or more calls to the `characters` method.

A second important point is that if the parser is nonvalidating, all character data—including white space—is routed through this method. If the parser is a validating XML parser, some white space (known in XML as ignorable white space) will be routed to the `ignorableWhitespace` method) discussed below.

10.5.6 *The ignorableWhitespace Method*

This method is called when ignorable white space is recognized in an XML document. Validating XML parsers are required to differentiate between normal and ignorable white space. In theory, nonvalidating parsers can do this if they have parsed and understood the element content models, but they are not required to differentiate by the XML 1.0 recommendation.

```
CD-ROM reference=10012.txt
from xml.sax import saxlib

class MySAXApplication(saxlib.HandlerBase)
    def ignorableWhitespace(self,chars,startOffset,Length):
        print "Ignorable White Space",
        print chars[startOffset:startOffset:Length]
```

10.5.7 *The processingInstruction Method*

This method is called when a processing instruction is recognized in the XML document.

```
CD-ROM reference=10013.txt
from xml.sax import saxlib

class MySAXApplication(saxlib.HandlerBase):
    def processingInstruction(self,target,data):
        print "Processing Instruction Target",target
        print align print "Processing Instruction Data",data
```

10.5.8 *The setDocumentLocator Method*

The SAX specification strongly urges, but does not require, implementors to provide a means of tracking locations in XML documents via the Locator interface. The setDocumentLocator method will be called by the parser with a Locator object that can be used to find out about where the XML parser is in the source XML document.

The parser calls this method once at the very start of the parsing process—that is, before the startDocument event. In the example below, a SAX application prints out the line number for each start-tag event.

```
CD-ROM reference=10014.txt
from xml.sax import saxlib

class MySAXApplication (saxlib.HandlerBase):
    def setDocumentLocator (self,L):
        self.MyLocatorObject = L
```

```
def startElement (self,ElementTypeName,Attributes):
    print "start-tag for ", ElementTypeName, "on line"
    print self.MyLocatorObject.getLineNumber()
```

The intent of the `Locator` interface is to provide the application with the location of the first piece of data after the data that caused the event. For example, in the document below, the line number associated with the `test` start-tag event is 4.

```
CD-ROM reference=10015.txt
<test
x = "1"
y = "2"
>Hello World
</test>
```

10.6 | The AttributeList Interface

As we have seen, the `startElement` handler in the `DocumentHandler` interface receives attributes in an object that implements the `AttributeList` interface.

The Python implementation of the `AttributeList` interface is in the file `saxlib.py` and looks like this.

```
CD-ROM reference=10016.txt
class AttributeList:
    def getLength(self):
        "Return the number of attributes in list."
        pass

    def getName(self, i):
        "Return the name of an attribute in the list."
        pass

    def getType(self, i):
        """Return the type of an attribute in the list.
        (Parameter can be either integer index or attribute
        name.)"""
        pass

    def getValue(self, i):
```

```
"""Return the value of an attribute in the list.
(Parameter can be either integer index or attribute
name.)"""
pass
```

We take a closer look at each method and provide a code example of each one in the sections below.

10.6.1   *The getLength Method*

This method retrieves the number of attributes associated with a start-tag.

```
CD-ROM reference=10017.txt
from xml.sax import saxlib

class MySAXApplication (saxlib.HandlerBase):
    def startElement (self,ElementTypeName,a):
        print "Start-tag for element ", ElementTypeName
        print "Total Attributes = ", a.getLength()
```

10.6.2   *The getName Method*

This method retrieves the name of an attribute associated with an element start-tag. It takes an integer parameter and returns the i'th parameter in the AttributeList structure. This method is primarily used in iterations in conjunction with the getLength method. In the example below, the startElement handler prints the names of the attributes associated with the start-tag.

```
CD-ROM reference=10018.txt
from xml.sax import saxlib
class MySAXApplication (saxlib.HandlerBase):

    def startElement (self,ElementTypeName, a):
        print "Start-tag for element ", ElementTypeName
        i = 0
        while i < a.getLength():
            print "Attribute Name ",a.getName(i)
            i = i + 1
```

Since attribute ordering is never significant in XML, you cannot know in what order the attributes will appear. That is, just because the attributes appear in a particular order in the source document does not mean they will appear in that order in the `AttributeList` structure.

10.6.3   *The getValue Method*

This method retrieves the value associated with an attribute. The method comes in two flavors. It can be called with an integer parameter to return the value of the i'th attribute in the `AttributeList`. Alternatively, it can be called with a string parameter. The value of the attribute with the name matching the string parameter is returned.

In this example, the integer parameter version of `getValue` is used with the `getLength` method.

```
CD-ROM reference=10019.txt
from xml.sax import saxlib

class MySAXApplication (saxlib.HandlerBase):

    def startElement (self,ElementTypeName,a):
        print "Start-tag for element ",ElementTypeName
        AttributeCount = a.getLength()
        i = 0
        while i < a.getLength():
            print "Attribute value ",a.getValue(i)
```

In the example below, the attribute name `quantity` is passed into `getValue` to retrieve the value of the attribute named `quantity`.

```
CD-ROM reference=10020.txt
from xml.sax import saxlib

class MySAXApplication (saxlib.HandlerBase):

    def startElement (self,ElementTypeName,a):
        print "Start-tag for element ",ElementTypeName
        Quantity = a.getValue("quantity")
```

10.6.4   *The getType Method*

This method retrieves the type associated with an attribute. Like getValue, the method comes in two flavors. It can be called with an integer parameter to return the type of the i'th attribute in the AttributeList. Alternatively, it can be called with a string parameter to return the type of the attribute with the matching name.

In this example, the integer parameter version of getType is used with the getLength method to print the types of all the attributes.

```
CD-ROM reference=10021.txt
from xml.sax import saxlib

class MySAXApplication (saxlib.HandlerBase):

    def startElement (self, ElementTypeName, a):
        print "Start-tag for element ",ElementTypeName
        AttributeCount = a.getLength()
        i = 0
        while i < a.getLength():
            print "Attribute type ",a.getType(i)
            i = i + 1
```

The attribute type is returned as a string. It can have the following values:

- CDATA

- ENTITY

- ENTITIES

- NOTATION

- ID

- IDREF

- IDREFS

- NMTOKEN

- NMTOKENS

Nonvalidating parsers are not required to process attribute declarations. As a result, they can return CDATA for all of the attribute types listed above.

10.7 | The ErrorHandler Interface

The ErrorHandler interface gives SAX application developers control over what happens when parsing errors are encountered. The XML 1.0 recommendation differentiates between two types of errors:

- **error**—This is a violation of the rules of the XML 1.0 specification. Conforming software is allowed to both detect and attempt to recover from this type of error, but it must report the error to the application. For example, it is an error for an element to have two attributes of type ID.

- **fatal error**—This is an error that conforming software must detect and report to the application. After a fatal error, a parser is allowed to continue processing in order to detect more errors, but it must not continue to parse the XML. In SAX terms, this means it must cease calling handlers in the DocumentHandler interface.

The ErrorHandler interface supports these two types of XML errors, using methods called, naturally enough, error and fatalError. The interface also supports a third type of error known as *warning*. This is intended for conditions that are neither errors nor fatal errors as defined in XML 1.0. For example, if a parser encounters multiple attribute declarations for the same element type, it may issue a warning. This is not an error condition and processing must continue unaffected.

The ErrorHandler interface class in saxlib.py looks like this.

```
CD-ROM reference=10022.txt
class ErrorHandler:
```

```
    def error(self, exception):
        "Handle a recoverable error."
        pass

    def fatalError(self, exception):
        "Handle a non-recoverable error."
        pass

    def warning(self, exception):
        "Handle a warning."
        pass
```

By default, SAX parsers ignore all errors except for fatal errors, for which they throw exceptions. To get the parser to stop throwing exceptions and call the warning/fatal/error methods of the `ErrorHandler` interface, the SAX application calls the `setErrorHandler` method of the `Parser` object, as shown below.

```
CD-ROM reference=10023.txt
from xml.sax import saxlib

class MySAXHandler (saxlib.HandlerBase):

    def error (self,ErrorInfo):
        print "Error %d %d" % (
            ErrorInfo.getLineNumber(),
            ErrorInfo.getColumnNumber()
            }

    def warning (self,ErrorInfo)
        print "Warning %d %d" % (
            ErrorInfo.getLineNumber(),
            ErrorInfo.getColumnNumber())

    def fatalError (self,ErrorInfo)
        print "Fatal Error %d %d" % (
            ErrorInfo.getLineNumber(),
            ErrorInfo.getColumnNumber())
        sys.exit()
# Main line
# Create a new XML parser object.
Parser = XMLParser()

# Create an instance of the MySAXHandler class.
```

```
Handler = MySAXHandler()

# Tell the parser object where the DocumentHandler is.
Parser.setDocumentHandler (Handler)

# Tell the parser object where the errorHandler is.
Parser.setErrorHandler (Handler)

// Parse a document.
Parser.parse("greeting.xml")
```

10.8 | A SAX Inspection Application

In this section, we develop a useful application that converts a sequence of SAX events into an XML document. This application is a useful debugging tool because it allows you to see at a glance the precise sequence of events generated by any SAX-compliant parser.

Given an XML document like this

```
CD-ROM reference=10024.txt
<Greeting x = "y">Hello World</Greeting>
```

the application generates this:

```
CD-ROM reference=10025.txt
<?xml version="1.0"?>
<!DOCTYPE SAXShow SYSTEM "SAXShow.dtd">
<SAXShow>
<Document>
<Element name="Greeting">
<Attribute name = "x" type = "CDATA" value="y"/>
<chars>Hello World</chars>
</Element>
</Document>
</SAXShow>
```

We will start with the DTD for the event sequence.

```
CD-ROM reference=10026.txt
<!ELEMENT SAXShow (DocumentLocator?,Document)>
```

```
<!ELEMENT Document (PI*,(Element|WS|PI|chars)*)>
<!ELEMENT Element (Attribute*,(Element|WS|PI|chars)*)>
<!ATTLIST Element name CDATA #REQUIRED>
<!ELEMENT Attribute EMPTY>
<!ATTLIST Attribute
              name  CDATA #REQUIRED
              type  CDATA #REQUIRED
              value CDATA #REQUIRED>
<!ELEMENT PI EMPTY>
<!ATTLIST PI
              target CDATA #REQUIRED
              data CDATA #REQUIRED>
<!ELEMENT DocumentLocator EMPTY>
<!ELEMENT WS (#PCDATA)>
<!ELEMENT chars (#PCDATA)>
```

Note how DTD syntax crisply captures quite a lot of information about the time ordering of SAX-generated events. Here is the code for `saxshow.py`.

```
CD-ROM reference=10027.txt
C>type saxshow.py
"""
A utility to create an XML document describing the order in
which SAX events have been called in processing an XML docu-
ment
"""
from xml.sax import saxlib,saxexts

class myHandler (saxlib.HandlerBase):
    """
    SAX document handler to create an XML document conforming
    to the saxshow DTD
    """
    def characters(self, ch, start, length):
        "Character data handler"
        print "<chars>%s</chars>" % ch[start:start+length]

    def endDocument(self):
        "End of document handler"
        print "</Document>"

    def endElement(self, name):
        "End of element handler"
```

```
                print "</Element>"

        def ignorableWhitespace(self, ch, start, length):
                "Ignorable white space (validating XML parsers only)"
                print '<WS>%s</WS>"  % ch[start:start+length]

        def processingInstruction(self, target, data):
                "Processing instruction handler"
                print '<PI target="%s" data="%s"/>' % (target,data)

        def setDocumentLocator(self, locator):
                "Parser has provided a document locator object"
                print '<SetDocumentLocator/>'

        def startDocument(self):
                "Start of document handler"
                print '<Document>'

        def startElement(self, name, atts):
                "Start of element handler"
                print '<Element name="%s">' % name
                for i in range (0,atts.getLength()):
                        print '<Attribute name = "%s"' %
                          atts.getName(i)
                                'type = "%s"' % atts.getType(i)
                                'value="%s"/>' % atts.getValue(i)
def SAXShow(fo):
        # Given an XML file object (fo), parse the XML, generating
        # an output XML document conforming to the saxshow DTD.
        # Create a document event handler.
        h = myHandler()
        # Create a SAX parser.
        parser = saxexts.make_parser()
        # Tell the parser about the document handler.
        parser.setDocumentHandler(h)
        # Print header of output document.
        print '<?xml version="1.0"?>'
        print '<!DOCTYPE SAXShow SYSTEM "SAXShow.dtd">'
        # Root element is SAXShow.
        print '<SAXShow>'
        parser.parseFile (fo)
        print '</SAXShow>'

if __name__ == "__main__":
        import sys
        SAXShow (open(sys.argv[1],"r"))
```

The following simple XML file illustrates the SAXShow application
in action.

```
CD-ROM reference=10028.txt
<names>
<name x = "y">
Mr. Sean Mc Grath
</name>
<name>
Mr. Stephen Murphy
</name>
<name>
Mr. Sandy Duffy
</name>
</names>


CD-ROM reference=10029.txt
C>python SAXShow.py test.xml
<?xml version="1.0"?>
<!DOCTYPE SAXShow SYSTEM "SAXShow.dtd">
<SAXShow>
<Document>
<Element name="names">
<chars>
</chars>
<Element name="name">
<Attribute name = "x" type = "CDATA" value="y"/>
<chars>
</chars>
<chars>Mr. Sean Mc Grath</chars>
<chars>
</chars>
</Element>
<chars>
</chars>
<Element name="name">
<chars>
</chars>
<chars>Mr. Stephen Murphy</chars>
<chars>
</chars>
</Element>
<chars>
</chars>
```

```
<Element name="name">
<chars>
</chars>
<chars>Mr. Sandy Duffy</chars>
<chars>
</chars>
</Element>
<chars>
</chars>
</Element>
</Document>
</SAXShow>
```

We can validate this XML document and generate PYX at the same time by piping the output through xmlv.

```
CD-ROM reference=10030.txt

C>python saxshow.py test.xml | xmlv
(SAXShow
-\n
(Document
-\n
(Element
Aname
-\n
...
```

We can validate the generated XML document without generating any PYX by redirecting standard output to the null device.

```
CD-ROM reference=10031.txt
```
Windows   C>**python saxshow.py test.xml | xmlv >nul**

No output appears on standard output, indicating that the generated XML document passed a validating XML parse. ■

```
CD-ROM reference=10032.txt
```
Linux $**python saxshow.py test.xml | xmlv /dev/null**

No output appears on standard output, indicating that the generated XML document passed a validating XML parse. ■

We can get a graphical view of the SAX event sequence order by simply displaying the resultant document in the C3 viewer.

```
CD-ROM reference=10033.txt
C>python saxshow.py test.xml > res.xml
C>python c3.py res.xml
```

A screenshot of res.xml in the C3 viewer is shown in figure 10–6. Note how making the output an XML file has led to some nice functionality for manipulating these files "for free." We can validate their structure with xmlv, we can view them in c3, we can use the XML-aware searching facilities of xgrep to locate particular SAX event sequences, and so on.

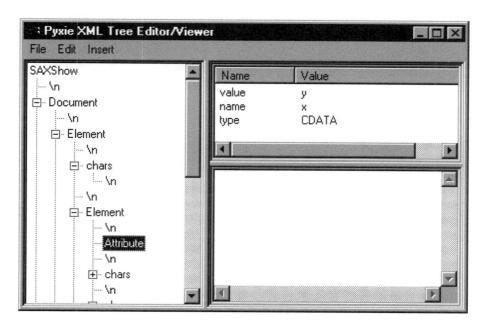

Figure 10–6   A SAXShow document viewed with the C3 XML viewer.

10.9 | SAX as a Source of PYX

We now have covered all the material on SAX required to build a SAX application that generates PYX. This facility will be part of the Pyxie library later on, but a standalone version of the routine is shown here to illustrate a SAX application.

```
CD-ROM reference=10034.txt
#! /usr/bin/env python

"""
Utility to create PYX notation from the default SAX-compliant
parser

Sean Mc Grath
XML Processing with Python
"""

# Import the SAX modules.
from xml.sax import saxexts, saxlib, saxutils
import string

def Encode (s):
    """
    Convert line ends to the two character sequence
    '\' followed by 'n'.
    """
    return  string.replace (s,"\n","\\n")

class myHandler (saxlib.DocumentHandler):
    def startElement(self,Element,Attributes):
        print "(%s" % Element
        # PYX attributes must be in alphabetical order
        # by attribute name.
        # Assemble a list of (name,value) pairs and
        # sort them.
        ListOfAttributes = []
        for i in range (0,Attributes.getLength()):
            ListOfAttributes.append
                ((Attributes.getName(i),
```

```
Encode(Attributes.getValue(i))))
            ListOFAttributes.sort()
            for (a,v) in ListOfAttributes:
                print "A%s %s" % (a,v)

        def characters(self,data,offset,length):
            print "-%s" % Encode(data[offset:offset+length])

        def processingInstruction (target, data):
            print "?target data"

        def endElement(self,Element):
            print ")%s"  % Element

        def error (self,exception):
            print "Parsing problem",exception
            sys.exit()

        def fatalErrror(self,exception):
            self.error(exception)

        def warning(Self,exception):
            self.error(exception)

def SAX2PYX(fo):
    # Create a SAX Document Handler.
    h = myHandler()
    # Create a SAX Parser.
    parser = saxexts.make_parser()
    # Tell the Parser where the document handler is.
    parser.setDocumentHandler(h)
    # Tell the Parser where the error handler is.
    parser.setErrorHandler(h)
    # Parse the file.
    parser.parseFile (fo)

if __name__ == "__main__":
    import sys
    SAX2PYX(open(sys.argv[1]))
```

We illustrate SAX2PYX in action with this XML document.

```
CD-ROM reference=10035.txt
C>type test.xml
```

```
<names>
<name x = "y">
Mr. Sean Mc Grath
</name>
<name>
Mr. Stephen Murphy
</name>
<name>
Mr. Sandy Duffy
</name>
</names>
```

C>**python sax2pyx.py test.xml**

```
(names
-\n
(name
Ax y
-\n
-Mr. Sean Mc Grath
-\n
)name
-\n
(name
-\n
-Mr. Stephen Murphy
-\n
)name
-\n
(name
-\n
-Mr. Sandy Duffy
-\n
)name
-\n
)names
```

10.10 | Switching SAX Parsers

As mentioned at the start of this chapter, one of the big advantages of basing an XML application on SAX is that you can switch from XML parser to XML parser without making code changes.

In the demonstration programs of this chapter, you have seen numerous calls to the `make_parser` function provided in the `saxexts` (SAX extensions) module.

```
CD-ROM reference=10036.txt
parser = saxexts.make_parser()
```

When invoked with no parameters, `make_parser` will return the first SAX-compliant parser it finds installed. You can specify a parser to use by giving its name as a parameter to the `make_parser` call. In the example below, James Clark's `expat` parser is selected.

```
CD-ROM reference=10037.txt
    parser = saxexts.make_parser("xml.sax.drivers.drv_pyexpat")
```

To see a full list of the SAX drivers installed on your system, look in the `xml/sax/drivers` subdirectory. This subdirectory also gives you the correct names to use when requesting specific parsers with the `make_parser()` function. Table 10.1 provides a partial list.

Table 10.1   Drivers for SAX-Compliant Parsers

Driver	*Description*
`drv_htmllib.py`	The HTML parsing library from the Python distribution.
`drv_pyexpat.py`	James Clark's `expat` non-validating XML parser. A good parser to use when parsing speed is of the essence.
`drv_sgmllib.py`	The SGML parsing library from the Python distribution. This parser is written in Python. It is a non-validating SGML parser. It makes no attempt to infer the presence of any tagging.
`drv_sgmlop.py`	The optimized SGML parsing library from the Python distribution by Fredrick Lundh. Use this as a plug-in replacement if you have previously used `drv_sgmllib` for a big speed increase.

(continued)

Table 10.1   Drivers for SAX-Compliant Parsers (continued)

Driver	Description
drv_xmldc.py	An XML scanner by Dan Connolly.
drv_xmllib.py	The XML parser from the Python distribution by Sjoerd Mullender. This is a non-validating XML parser written in Python.
drv_xmlproc.py	The non-validating version of xmlproc by Lars Marius Garshol. This is written in Python.
drv_xmlproc_val.py	The validating version of xmlproc by Lars Marius Garshol. This is the only validing XML parser in the Python XML package.
drv_xmltoolkit.py	The XML parser by David Scheres.

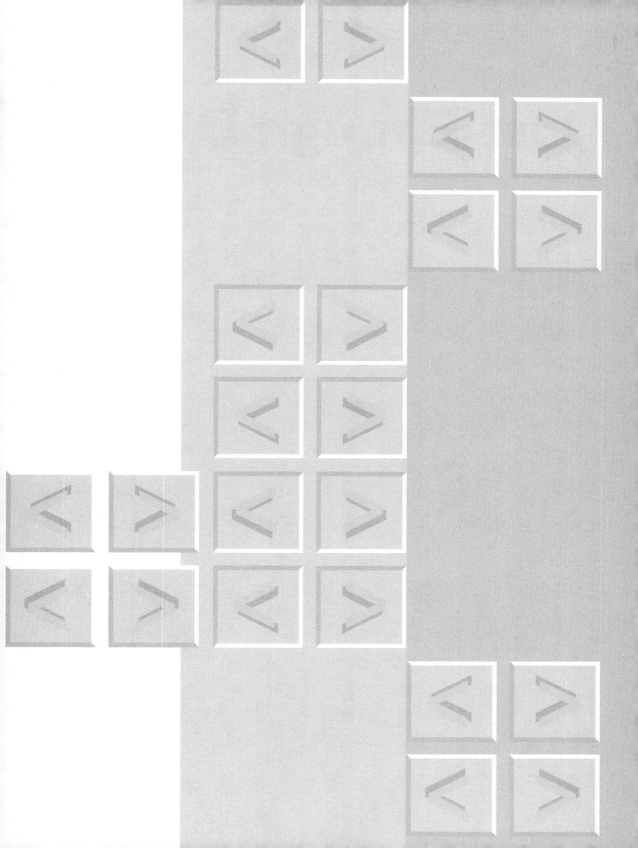

Just Enough DOM

T he DOM (Document Object Model) is a W3C initiative to standardize an API to both HTML and XML documents in a language-independent way. The DOM has its origins in Web browsers. A little history of Web browser evolution is useful in understanding what the DOM is and why it has been created.

11.1 History

The earliest web browsers simply *displayed* HTML. That is, there was nothing a programmer could do to change the way a document looked once it had been loaded into the browser. There was no programmatic access to the HTML document structure.

Later browsers provided access to the HTML structure. Most notably, the JavaScript scripting language and the Java programming language provided an API that a programmer could use to navigate an HTML document within the browser.

With the version 4 browsers, programmers could not only access but also *modify* the HTML displayed by the browser. Unfortunately, this powerful feature, known as *dynamic HTML*, was implemented with very different APIs in the Netscape and Microsoft browsers. This created a real headache for programmers wanting to make their HTML pages browser independent. The dynamic HTML issue made a standardized API to HTML from within the browser very desirable indeed.

While all this was happening, XML was appearing on the horizon. From a programming perspective, there is much in common between the API a programmer would use for HTML and the API a programmer would use for XML.

This commonality is not suprising given that HTML and XML are both SGML-based notations for the creation of hierarchical data structures. Figure 11–1 illustrates an HTML file viewed as a hierarchical structure. Figure 11–2 illustrates an XML file viewed as a hierarchical structure.

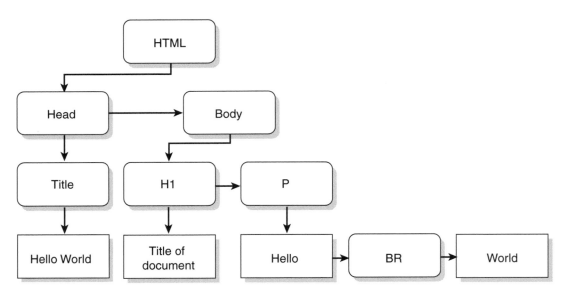

Figure 11–1   HTML viewed as a tree structure.

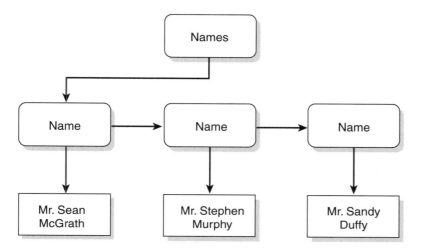

Figure 11–2   XML viewed as a tree structure.

Enter the DOM. The DOM harmonizes HTML and XML at the API level by providing core functionality that is applicable to both HTML and XML. This is known as the "DOM Level 1."[1]

The DOM is expressed in terms of language-independent *interfaces*. The word "interface" in DOM is analagous to the use of the word in SAX. That is, the DOM specifies functionality in terms of named collections of methods. Any class that implements the required interfaces can be a compliant DOM implementation.

A compliant DOM implementation must support DOM Level 1. In addition it may support either or both of the layers above the core which are known as "extended XML" and "HTML." This layering of the DOM API is shown in figure 11–3.

The DOM is programming language independent. The idea is that once programmers become familiar with the DOM API, they will be

---

[1]The reason for the "Level 1" qualification is that the DOM is under active development and DOM Level 2 is under development. Level 2 will build on level 1 and will provide new features, such as access to DTDs and control of the rendering process and event handling.

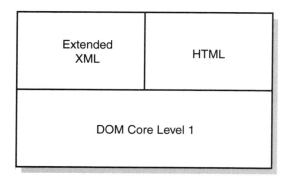

Figure 11–3   HTML and extended XML support built on top of core DOM level 1.

able to work with DOM implementations in a variety of languages and environments without a steep learning curve.

The DOM is a read/write API. As well as traversing the structure forward, backward, up, and down at will, you can create new structures, delete existing ones, and so on.

The DOM specification is written in OMG IDL—Object Management Group's Interface Definition Language. This language-independent syntax for expressing APIs is part of the CORBA specification.

Language bindings are provided for the Java programming language and ECMAScript (an industry-standard scripting language based on Sun's JavaScript and Microsoft's JScript).

11.2 | DOM Support in Python

Python has two DOM implementations. The first is commonly referred to as pyDOM. The second is known as 4DOM. pyDOM originated with Stéfane Fermigier and has been extensively worked on by Andrew Kuchling. 4DOM is the work of Fourthought Inc. (`http://www.fourthought.com`). One major difference between the two is that 4DOM is CORBA based and so can do distributed DOM processing.

The `pyDOM` package is part of the core Python XML library. The `4DOM` library is available at `http://www.fourthought.com`.

11.3 | The DOM Architecture

11.3.1 *The Concept of a Node*

The most fundamental concept in DOM is that of a *node*. A document is a collection of `Node` objects joined into a hierarchical structure. Each node has a `nodeType` variable that specifies what type of node it is. There are 12 node types in DOM level 1. More will be added in the future as more DOM levels are added. We concentrate on the four most important ones:

- **Document** An XML document has exactly one `Document` node. This is the container node for all other nodes. The first child of the `Document` node is the root element node of the XML or HTML document.

- **Element** Each element in an XML document has its own `Element` node. Attributes associated with an element are accessed via this node. Each attribute is represented by an **Attr** node.

- **Attr** Each attribute is stored in an `Attr` node.

- **Text** Character data chunks are stored in `Text` nodes.

As well as a `nodeType` variable, all nodes have `nodeName` and `nodeValue` variables. The meaning of these depends on the type of the node. In an `Element` node, for example, the `nodeName` variable contains the element type name and the `nodeValue` variable is set to `None`. In `Text` nodes, the `nodeName` variable is always set to `#text`, and the `nodeValue` variable is the data content of the node.

11.3.2 *The Concept of a Node List*

The second most fundamental concept in DOM is the concept of a *node list*. NodeLists are returned by many functions specified by the DOM and are indispensable for performing tree navigation and tree processing, as we will see.

11.3.3 *Linkages Between Nodes*

A collection of Nodes is structured into a hierarchy by the establishment of linkages between them. The DOM expresses the connections between nodes in terms of parent/child relationships. See figure 11–4.

As you can see in figure 11–4, all node objects have the following interconnection points:

■ **parentNode** All nodes with the exception of the Document node have a parentNode variable that points to

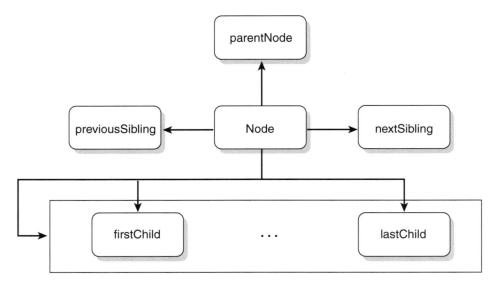

Figure 11–4 Linkages between DOM nodes.

the parent node. The `parentNode` variable for the single `Document` node is `None`.

- **firstChild** The first child of a node. If the node has no children, `firstChild` is `None`.

- **lastChild** The last child of this node. If the node has no children, `lastChild` is `None`.

- **previousSibling** If there is a preceding node with the same `parentNode`, then `previousSibling` points to it. If there is no such node, then `previousSibling` is `None`.

- **nextSibling** Analogous to `previousSibling` above.

- **childNodes** A list of the children of the node. If there are no children, `childNodes` is an empty `NodeList`.

11.4 | Accessing an XML File with pyDOM

The DOM specification purposely says nothing about the creation of the hierarchical data it provides access to. When the source is XML, one good way to load the DOM is through SAX events. In the program below, a SAX parser creates a DOM tree which then re-creates the XML document as output.

```
CD-ROM reference=11001.txt
C>type dom1.py

"""
Create a DOM tree structure from an XML file,
using a SAX parser.
"""
# Import the core DOM module.
from xml.dom import core

# Import the SAX DOM builder.
```

```
from xml.dom.sax_builder import SaxBuilder

# Import the SAX modules.
from xml.sax import saxexts,saxlib

import sys

# Create a SAX parser.
p = saxexts.make_parser()

# Create a SAX document handler which will build the DOM
# tree.
dh = SaxBuilder()

# Tell the parser about the document handler.
p.setDocumentHandler(dh)

# Parse the document.
p.parse(sys.argv[1])

p.close()

# The DOM object is available as the "document" instance
# variable.
doc = dh.document

print "Document element information",doc
print "Root element information",doc.firstChild

# Print the DOM object as XML.
print doc.toxml()


CD-ROM reference=11002.txt
C>type test.xml

<names>
<name x = "y">
Mr. Sean Mc Grath
</name>
<name>
Mr. Stephen Murphy
</name>
<name>
Mr. Sandy Duffy
</name>
```

```
</names>

c>python dom1.py test.xml

Root element information <DOM Document; root=<Element
'names'> >
<?xml version="1.0"?>
<names>
<name x='y'>
Mr. Sean Mc Grath
</name>
<name>
Mr. Stephen Murphy
</name>
<name>
Mr. Sandy Duffy
</name>
</names>
```

11.5 | Navigating a DOM Tree

In this example, which uses the same test.xml input file as the previous example, we print the data content of an XML document by traversing the tree, isolating the text nodes, and printing their contents.

```
CD-ROM reference=11003.txt
C>type dom2.py

"""
Print text by navigating DOM nodes.
"""
# Import the core DOM module.
from xml.dom import core

# Import the DOM SAX builder.
from xml.dom.sax_builder import SaxBuilder

# Import the SAX modules.
from xml.sax import saxexts,saxlib

import sys
```

```
def PrintText(nodelist):
    # Print the data content of a node list.
    for n in nodelist:
        if n.nodeType == core.TEXT_NODE:
            # For text nodes, data content is available as
            # the nodeValue instance variable.
            print n.nodeValue,
        elif n.nodeType == core.ELEMENT_NODE:
            # For element nodes, call PrintText,
            # recursively passing it the list
            # of children of the current node.
            PrintText(n.childNodes)


# Create a SAX parser
p = saxexts.make_parser()

# Create a SAX document handler which will build the DOM
  tree.
dh = SaxBuilder()

# Tell the parser about the document handler.
p.setDocumentHandler(dh)

# Parse the document.
p.parse(sys.argv[1])

doc = dh.document

PrintText (doc.documentElement.childNodes)
C>python dom2.py test.xml

Mr. Sean Mc Grath
Mr. Stephen Murphy

Mr. Sandy Duffy
```

11.6 | Walking a DOM Tree

The pyDOM package provides a number of utilities for processing DOM trees over and above what the DOM spec specifies. One of the most useful is the `Walker` class, which simplifies the process of walking an entire tree structure in top-down, left-to-right order.

In the example below, a class derived from `Walker` generates a subset of PYX from a DOM tree.

```
CD-ROM reference=11004.txt
"""
Walk a DOM Tree, generating PYX.
"""
# Import core DOM.
from xml.dom import core

# Import DOM walker utility class.
from xml.dom.walker import Walker

# Import DOM SAX builder.
from xml.dom.sax_builder import SaxBuilder

import string,sys
# Import SAX.
from xml.sax import saxexts,saxlib

def Encode(s):
    """
    Function to escape newlines for PYX notation
    """
    s = string.replace (s,"\n","\\n")
    return s

class myWalker (Walker):
    def startElement(self,n):
        print "(%s" % n.nodeName

    def endElement(self,n):
        print ")%s" % n.nodeName

    def doText(self, n):
        print "-%s" % Encode(n.nodeValue)
# Make a SAX parser.
p = saxexts.make_parser()
# Make a SAX builder (a SAX document handler).
dh = SaxBuilder()
# Tell the parser about the document handler.
p.setDocumentHandler(dh)
```

```
# Parse the document.
p.parse(sys.argv[1])
p.close()

doc = dh.document

myWalker().walk (doc.documentElement)
CD-ROM reference=11005.txt
C>python dom3.py test.xml

(names
-\n
(name
-\nMr. Sean Mc Grath\n
)name
-\n
(name
-\nMr. Stephen Murphy\n
)name
-\n
(name
-\nMr. Sandy Duffy\n
)name
-\n
)names
```

11.7 | Accessing Attributes

Attributes in the DOM are accessed from an element node by means of the `attributes` variable. Attributes are stored in a structure known as a `NamedNodeMap`. A `NamedNodeMap` is like a `NodeList` except that nodes in a `NamedNodeMap` can be retrieved, based on the value of their `nodeName` attribute.

In the following example, a DOM tree is traversed, and attribute names and values printed out by traversal of a `NamedNodeMap`.

```
CD-ROM reference=11006.txt
C>type dom4.py

"""
Printing attributes from a DOM tree
```

```
"""

from xml.dom import core
from xml.dom.walker import Walker
from xml.dom.sax_builder import SaxBuilder
import string,sys
from xml.sax import saxexts,saxlib

p = saxexts.make_parser()
dh = SaxBuilder()
p.setDocumentHandler(dh)
p.parse(sys.argv[1])
p.close()

doc = dh.document

def PrintAttributes(node):
    if node.nodeType == core.ELEMENT_NODE:
        attrs = node.attributes
        for i in range (0,attrs.get_length()):
            attr = attrs.item(i)
            print "Attribute name:",attr.name,
            print "Attribute value:",attr.value
        childNodes = node.childNodes
        for cnode in childNodes:
            PrintAttributes(cnode)

for n in doc.documentElement.childNodes:
    PrintAttributes(n)
```

CD-ROM reference=11007.txt
C>**type test1.xml**

```
<names>
<name x = "y">
Mr. Sean Mc Grath
</name>
<name a = "b" c = "d">
Mr. Stephen Murphy
</name>
<name e = "f">
Mr. Sandy Duffy
</name>
</names>
```

C>**python dom4.py test1.xml**

```
Attribute name: x Attribute value: y
Attribute name: c Attribute value: d
Attribute name: a Attribute value: b
Attribute name: e Attribute value: f
```

11.8 | Manipulating Trees

The DOM is a read/write API. In addition to reading the values in the document tree's nodes, it provides methods to rearrange and delete nodes. Consider the following XML document, which contains price information for some commodity.

```
CD-ROM reference=11008.txt
<?xml version="1.0"?>
<prices>
<price>12</price><price>10</price>
<price>54</price><price>9</price>
</prices>
```

The program below uses the DOM to reorder the price elements in ascending numerical order. It takes advantage of the fact that Python's built-in sort method for list objects allows a custom sort function to be used.

```
CD-ROM reference=11009.txt
"""
Example of rearranging a DOM tree
Sorts prices into descending order
"""
# Import core DOM.
from xml.dom import core
# Import the DOM SAX builder.
from xml.dom.sax_builder import SaxBuilder

import StringIO,string
# Import SAX.
from xml.sax import saxexts,saxlib

def ComparePrices(a,b):
    """
    Function to compare two branches of a DOM tree.
```

```
        The value of a branch is the character data
        in its first child.
        Function returns 0,-1 or 1 depending on an integer
        comparison of the values.
        """
        aprice = string.atoi(a.firstChild.nodeValue)
        bprice = string.atoi(b.firstChild.nodeValue)
        if aprice < bprice:
            return -1
        if aprice > bprice:
            return 1
        return 0

# Make a SAX Parser.
p = saxexts.make_parser()

# Make a DOM SAX builder (a document handler).
dh = SaxBuilder()

# Tell the parser about the document handler.
p.setDocumentHandler(dh)

# Parse a file created on-the-fly from
# this internal string.
p.parseFile(StringIO.StringIO (
        '<?xml version="1.0"?>'
        '<prices>'
        '<price>12</price><price>10</price>'
        '<price>54</price><price>9</price>'
        '</prices>'))
p.close()

# Retrieve the DOM object.
doc = dh.document

# Initialize list of nodes.
prices = []

while len (doc.documentElement.childNodes):
        # Iterate the list of child nodes,
        # cutting out each branch and appending
        # it to the prices list.
        prices.append(
            doc.documentElement.removeChild (
                doc.documentElement.firstChild)
            )
```

```
# Sort the list of DOM branches, using the
# custom sorting algorithm.
prices.sort (ComparePrices)

# Put them into reverse order.
prices.reverse()

# Reinsert the branches in the new numeric order.
for p in prices:
        doc.documentElement.appendChild(p)

# Output the sorted XML file.
print doc.toxml()
```

The output of the program, pretty-printed for legibility, is shown below.

```
CD-ROM reference=11010.txt
C>python dom5.py
<?xml version="1.0"?>
<prices>
  <price>54</price>
  <price>12</price>
  <price>10</price>
  <price>9</price>
</prices>
```

11.9 | Accessing an HTML File with pyDOM

In this program, an HTML file is loaded and re-created as an XML file. The principal difference between loading HTML and loading XML into the DOM is that an HTML-specific building module called HtmlBuilder is used.

```
CD-ROM reference=11011.txt
"""
Accessing an HTML document with DOM
"""
```

```
from xml.dom import core
from xml.dom.html_builder import HtmlBuilder
import StringIO,string

h = HtmlBuilder()
h.feed (
        '<html>'
        '<head>'
        '<title>'
        'Hello World'
        '</title>'
        '</head>'
        '<body>'
        '<h1>Title of document</h1>'
        '<p>Hello<br> World'
        '</html>')

doc = h.document

print doc.toxml()
CD-ROM reference=11012.txt
<HTML>
<HEAD>
<TITLE>Hello World</TITLE>
</HEAD>
<BODY>
<H1>Title of document</H1>
Hello</BR />World</P>
</BODY>
</HTML>
```

The output above is both HTML and XML. Figure 11–5 shows the output displayed in Internet Explorer 5.

As you will appreciate, having XML-compliant HTML makes a lot of engineering sense. You can use all your XML tools and techniques to process HTML. Figure 11–6 shows the output HTML/XML file displayed in the C3 XML viewer.

XML-compliant HTML is the subject of a W3C recommendation. See http://www.w3c.org for details.

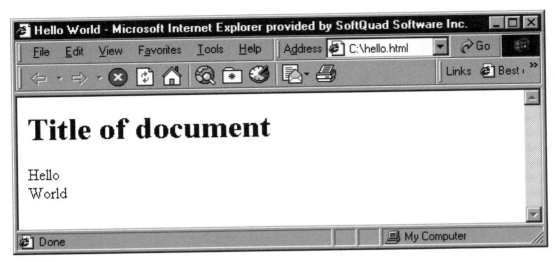

Figure 11–5   XML-compatible HTML viewed in Internet Explorer 5.

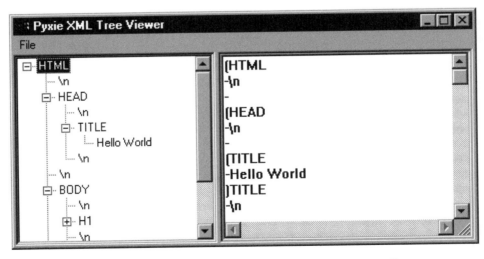

Figure 11–6   XML-compliant HTML displayed in the C3 XML viewer.

11.10 | Printing the Text of an HTML Document

The core level-1 DOM API is equally applicable to both HTML and XML documents. As a consequence, programs that rely simply on nodes and node navigation will be very similar in structure.

The following program prints the text content of an HTML document. The DOM building part is HTML specific, but the core tree traversal algorithm would work for XML files as well.

```
CD-ROM reference=11013.txt
C>type dom7.py

"""
Print text of a HTML document by navigating DOM nodes.
"""

#Import core DOM module.
from xml.dom import core

#Import DOM HTML Builder.
from xml.dom.html_builder import HtmlBuilder

import string

def PrintText(node):
    """
    Function to print the character data of
    a DOM branch.
    """
    if node.nodeType == core.TEXT_NODE:
        print node.nodeValue,
    elif node.nodeType == core.ELEMENT_NODE:
        ChildNodes = node.childNodes
        for cnode in ChildNodes:
            PrintText(cnode)

# Create a DOM HTML builder.
h = HtmlBuilder()

# Feed the builder some HTML.
```

```
h.feed (
      '<html>'
      '<head>'
      '<title>'
      'Hello World'
      '</title>'
      '</head>'
      '<body>'
      '<h1>Title of document</h1>'
      '<p>Hello<br> World'
      '</html>')
# Retrieve the DOM object.
doc = h.document

# Print out the character data.
PrintText (doc.documentElement)

CD-ROM reference=11014.txt
C>python dom7.py

Hello World Title of document Hello  World
```

11.11 | Changing Data Content in a DOM Tree

We have already seen how the DOM allows a tree structure to be rearranged. The content of text nodes can also be changed. In the program below, any telephone number matching the pattern "096 [number]" is changed to "+353 96 [number]". This task is made easy by the regular-expression-based substitution capabilities provided by Python's `re` module. The `sub` method replaces any regular expression matches with the specified string. The string can contain references to groups in the regular expression. The string `"\1"` refers to the first group, `"\2"` refers to the second group and so on. In the example below, the pattern `"096 (\d+)"` is used to locate telephone numbers that match the required pattern. Note the group surrounding the digits that follow `096`. This group can be referred to in the substitution string as `\1`, as shown below.

```
CD-ROM reference=11015.txt
"""
Change telephone numbers via regular expression substitution.
"""
from xml.dom import core
from xml.dom.walker import Walker
from xml.dom.sax_builder import SaxBuilder
from xml.sax import saxexts,saxlib

import StringIO

# Import regular expressions.
import re

TelephoneNumber = re.compile (r"096 (\d+)")

class myWalker (Walker):
    """
    A DOM walker to perform a regular expression:
    substitution
    """
    def doText(self, n):
    # Is this text node within a phone element?
  if n.parentNode.get_tagName()=="phone":
        d = n.nodeValue
        # Perform regular expression substitution
        # Note use of "\1" to refer to first group
        # in the regular expression.
        d = TelephoneNumber.sub (r"+353 96 \1",d)
        n.nodeValue = d
p = saxexts.make_parser()
dh = SaxBuilder()
p.setDocumentHandler(dh)
p.parseFile(StringIO.StringIO (
    '<?xml version="1.0"?>'
    '<offices>'
    '<office><name>Building 445</name><phone>096 36038
      </phone></office>'
    '<office><name>Building 42</name><phone>096 36039
      </phone></office>'
    '</offices>'))
p.close()

doc = dh.document

myWalker().walk (doc.documentElement)
```

```
print doc.toxml()
```

C>**python dom8.py**

```
<?xml version="1.0"?>
<offices>
 <office>
  <name>Building 445</name>
  <phone>+353 96 36038</phone>
 </office>
 <office>
  <name>Building 42</name>
  <phone>+353 96 36039</phone>
 </office>
</offices>
```

11.12 | Creating a Tree Programmatically

The Python DOM implementation provides a very useful class known as `Builder`. This class, an implementation of SAX `DocumentHandler`, uses SAX events to build a DOM tree structure. With `Builder`, it is straightforward to build an XML or HTML tree structure from scratch. As new nodes are added to the tree structure, `Builder` automatically keeps track of the current position, leading to easy-to-understand tree building code.

```
CD-ROM reference=11016.txt
```
C>**type dom9.py**

```
"""
Build an XML tree programmatically by using the DOM Builder
class.
"""

from xml.dom.builder import Builder

b = Builder()
b.startElement("names")
b.startElement("name",{"x":"y"})
```

```
b.text ("Mr. Sean Mc Grath")
b.endElement("name")
b.startElement("name")
b.text ("Mr. Stephen Murphy")
b.endElement("name")
b.startElement("name")
b.text ("Mr. Sandy Duffy")
b.endElement("name")
b.endElement("names")

print b.document.toxml()
```

The output below has been reformatted for legibility.

```
CD-ROM reference=11017.txt
C>python dom9.py

<?xml version="1.0"?>
<names>
 <name x='y'>Mr. Sean Mc Grath</name>
 <name>Mr. Stephen Murphy</name>
 <name>Mr. Sandy Duffy</name>
</names>
```

11.13 | Converting HTML to PYX by Using DOM

The HTML builder for Python's DOM implementation does a lot of work to infer the locations of missing tags. We can take advantage of this work to have a tool for parsing HTML into PYX format.

```
CD-ROM reference=11018.txt
C>type html2pyx.py

"""
Convert HTML to PYX via the DOM
"""

from xml.dom import core
from xml.dom.html_builder import HtmlBuilder
import string
```

```
def Encode (s):
    # Encode newlines for PYX output.
    return string.replace (s,"\n","\\n")

def OutputPYX(node):
    if node.nodeType == core.TEXT_NODE:
        print "-%s" % Encode(node.nodeValue)
    elif node.nodeType == core.ELEMENT_NODE:
        print "(%s" % node.nodeName
        children = node.childNodes
        for cnode in children:
            # Recurse for each child node.
            OutputPYX(cnode)
        print ")%s" % node.nodeName


def HTML2PYX(fileobj):
    # Create an HTML DOM Builder.
    h = HtmlBuilder()
    # Feed it the file object containing HTML.
    h.feed (fileobj.read())
    # Retrieve the DOM object.
    doc = h.document
    # Output PYX for the root element start-tag.
    print "(%s" % doc.documentElement.nodeName
    # Output PYX for all children (recursive).
    for node in doc.documentElement.childNodes:
        OutputPYX(node)
    # Output PYX for the root element end-tag.
    print ")%s" % doc.documentElement.nodeName


if __name__ == "__main__":
    import sys
    HTML2PYX(open(sys.argv[1],"r"))
```

An example of html2pyx in action is shown below. Note how the DOM HTML builder has automatically inferred the missing end-tags for the P and HTML elements.

```
CD-ROM reference=11019.txt
C>type hello.html

<html>
```

```
<head>
<title>Hello
</head>
<body>
<p>
Hello World
```

C>**python html2pyx test.html**

```
(HTML
-\n
(HEAD
-\n
(TITLE
-Hello\n
)TITLE
)HEAD
-\n
(BODY
-\n
(P
-\nHello World\n
)P
)BODY
)HTML
```

11.14 | Using PYX as a DOM Data Source

Here is a utility that allows PYX notation to act as a data source for DOM.

```
CD-ROM reference=11020.txt
"""
DOM builder from PYX notation source
"""

from string import *
from StringIO import StringIO
from xml.dom.builder import Builder
class pyxBuilder(Builder):
```

```
    def __init__(self):
        Builder.__init__(self)

    def decode(self,s):
        # Convert PYX escaped newlines to real newlines.
        return join (split (s,r"\n"),"\n")

    def feed(self, data):
        self.feedpyx(StringIO(data))

    def feedpyx(self, pyxStream):
        pyx = pyxStream.readline()
        while pyx != "":
            if pyx[0] == "(":
                elementname = pyx[1:-1]
                pyx = pyxStream.readline()
                dict={}
                while pyx[0] == "A":
                    [name,value] = split(pyx[1:-1],
                        " ", 1)
                    dict[name] = self.decode(value)
                    pyx = pyxStream.readline()
                self.startElement(elementname,dict)
                continue
            elif pyx[0] == ")":
                self.endElement(pyx[1:-1])
            elif pyx[0] == "?":
                [target, data] = split(pyx, " ", 1)
                self.processingInstruction(
                    target,
                    self.decode(data))
            else:
                assert pyx[0] == "-"
                self.text(self.decode(pyx[1:-1]))
            pyx = pyxStream.readline()
if __name__ == "__main__":
    import os,sys
    b = pyxBuilder()
    b.feedpyx(os.popen("xmln "+sys.argv[1]))
    print b.document.toxml()
```

```
C>python pyx_builder.py test.xml
<?xml version="1.0"?>
<names>
<name x='y'>
Mr. Sean Mc Grath
```

```
</name>
<name>
Mr. Stephen Murphy
</name>
<name>
Mr. Sandy Duffy
</name>
</names>
```

In this chapter, we have seen how Python's DOM implementation can be used to both navigate and rearrange XML and HTML documents. We have also seen how the DOM can be used to generate PYX and also how the DOM can use PYX as a source of hierarchical data.

It is now time to turn our attention to a purely Python-based XML processing library—Pyxie.

Pyxie: An Open Source XML-Processing Library for Python

12

I n this chapter, we develop the core Pyxie library, which will be used extensively in the examples that make up the rest of the book. This chapter is long and detailed and contains a lot of source code. You may want to go through the contents quickly in a first pass and then return for a detailed reading of particular sections as the need arises.

By the time you read this, the Pyxie library may well have grown beyond what is presented here! Please visit `http://www.pyxie.org` for the latest information.

Note that you are hereby cordially invited to improve/fix and contribute code to the Pyxie Open Source project. Get involved!

12.1 | What Is Pyxie?

Pyxie is an Open Source software development initiative, launched with this book. The goals of the Pyxie project are twofold:

- To build a powerful suite of XML processing tools in Python

- To evangalize Python in the XML development community at large

12.2 | Design Goals

Let us start by laying out some design goals:

- Pyxie shall provide a natural API to the Python developer.

- Pyxie shall support language-independent XML-processing APIs such as SAX and DOM as API layers on top of the core Pyxie API.

- Pyxie shall support both event-driven and tree-driven XML-processing paradigms.

- The extreme simplicity of the PYX notation shall not be compromised without good cause.

Let us look briefly at each of these design goals.

12.2.1 *Pyxie Shall Provide a Natural API to the Python Developer*

Pyxie programs should be both concise and easy to understand. This is best achieved by making use of Python facilities that support this goal. Facilities such as the flexible `for` loop, the ability to intercept access to an object's instance variables, the ability to get an arbitrary object to produce a textual description of itself, and so on.

As a consequence of this design decision, Pyxie is not easily portable to other languages. Making it portable to other languages would have made it less concise, less easy to understand, and a whole lot less fun:-) The Python world already has support for two language-independent XML-processing APIs in the form of SAX and DOM. (See next design goal.)

12.2.2 *Pyxie Shall Support Language-Independent XML-Processing APIs as Compatibility Layers on Top of the Core Pyxie API*

As a consequence of being language independent, APIs such as SAX and DOM tend to be lowest common denominator APIs. That is, they make minimal use of language-specific features to maximize portability to other languages. Although I do not use SAX and DOM APIs in my work, I can see the advantage of using them in certain circumstances.

I would like to see Pyxie support both SAX and DOM as layers *above* the Pyxie layer. The advantage of this approach is that a developer using Pyxie would have the option of using a language-independent API but would not be forced to do so.

12.2.3 *The Extreme Simplicity of the PYX Notation Shall Not Be Compromised Without Good Cause*

As you will have noticed, PYX is a very, very simple notation. It concentrates on providing the developer with information about the *logical* rather than the *physical* structure of an XML document. It does not concern itself with XML features such as external entities, notations, marked sections, and so on. The PYX notation could, in theory, be extended to support these constructs. However, extending the syntax of PYX is a slippery slope! Catering to markup information needs of all possible applications is tantamount to inventing a syntax that allows a byte-for-byte reconstitution of the original XML document.

If this is truly what your application needs, then you may be better off processing the source document lexically rather than relying on the tokenized output of an XML parser. A second alternative is to use an abstract formalism, known as *groves,* for the content of XML/SGML documents.[1]

It is important to note that the concept of PYX has not dropped out of thin air with the Pyxie project! There is an important historical precedent in the SGML world. The SGML standard[2] divides applications into two types: Structure-controlled and Markup-sensitive applications. Structure-controlled applications are only concerned with the logical structure of a document in terms of elements, attributes, data content, and so on. In the SGML standard, the set of information such applications are permitted to work with is defined as the Element Structure Information Set, commonly known as ESIS.

James Clark, at `http://www.jclark.com`, the author of the `expat` XML parser, is also the author of numerous excellent SGML-related tools. In particular, he wrote the `sgmls` and `nsgmls` SGML parsing applications that produce ESIS-compatible output. The PYX notation is modelled on James Clark's ESIS notation.[3]

12.3 | PYX Notation Processing

The most straightfoward (and least powerful) way of using the Pyxie library is to process the PYX notation directly. We have already seen numerous examples of the two command-line utilities, `xmln` and `xmlv`, that generate PYX output. We have seen how they can be used from within Python programs by use of the `popen` function. The

---

[1]For more information about groves and the grove paradigm, see a paper by Paul Prescod "Addressing the Enterprise: Why the Web needs Groves" `http://www` `.prescod.net/groves/shorttut/`

[2]ISO 8879:1986. For more information about SGML, see my book *ParseMe .1st–SGML, for Software Developers,* also in this series.

[3]You can find a comprehensive description of ESIS in my book *ParseMe.1st— SGML for Software Developers,* also in this series.

program below outputs the start-tags occurring in an XML document by processing the PYX-generated by xmln.

```
CD-ROM reference=12001.txt
C>type hello.xml

<?xml version="1.0"?>
<greeting>
Hello <b>World</b>
</greeting>

C>type p1.py

"""
Print start-tags from an XML document by processing PYX-
generated from xmln.
"""

import os,sys

pyx = os.popen ("xmln " + sys.argv[1])
for L in pyx.readlines():
        if L[0] == "(":
                print L[1:-1]

C>python p1.py hello.xml

greeting
b
```

The SAX support in the Python XML package can also be used as a source of PYX. This approach avoids "shelling out" to an external application such as xmln. Pyxie provides a function, SAX2PYX, that uses the default SAX parser to generate PYX. The following program produces the same output as the last program.

```
CD-ROM reference=12002.txt
C>type p2.py

"""
Print start-tags from an XML document by processing PYX-generated
from the default SAX-compliant parser.
"""
```

```
import sys
from pyxie import *
pyx = SAX2PYX(sys.argv[1])
for L in pyx.readlines():
        if L[0] == "(":
                print L[1:-1]
C>python p2.py hello.xml
greeting
b
```

It is often useful to be able to create PYX from ordinary Python strings containing well-formed XML. Pyxie provides a function, String2PYX, that does this.

```
CD-ROM reference=12003.txt
C>type p3.py

"""
Print start-tags from an XML document by processing PYX-generated
from a Python string containing XML.

"""

from pyxie import *

# Create a string containing XML.
hello = """
<?xml version="1.0"?>
<greeting>
Hello <b>World</b>
</greeting>
"""

pyx = String2PYX(hello)
for L in pyx.readlines():
        if L[0] == "(":
                print L[1:-1]

C>python p3.py hello.xml

greeting
b
```

The `String2PYX` function is used a lot in Pyxie programs and needs to be as fast as possible. Internally, the function uses the fastest XML parser supported by Python—the `pyExpat` module. Pyxie provides a function, `PyExpat2PYX`, that uses `PyExpat` to generate PYX. The program below illustrates how it is used.

```
CD-ROM reference=12004.txt
C>type p4.py

"""
Print start-tags from an XML document by processing PYX-generated
from PyExpat.
"""

import sys
from pyxie import *
pyx = PYExpat2PYX(open(sys.argv[1],"r"))
for L in pyx.readlines():
        if L[0] == "(":
                print L[1:_1]

C>python p4.py hello.xml

greeting
b
```

Pyxie also provides a function `File2PYX` that converts any XML file to PYX. Internally, this function also uses the `PyExpat` module.

In chapter 4, an `awk` "one liner" was used to produce PYX output indented to show the structure of the XML document. Here is a Python program that does the same thing.

```
CD-ROM reference=12005.txt
C>type p5.py

"""
Print PYX notation indented to show the structure of the
XML file.

"""
```

```
import sys
from pyxie import *

pyx = PYExpat2PYX(open(sys.argv[1],"r"))
Indent = 0
for L in pyx.readlines():
    if L[0] == "(":
        print "%s%s" % (Indent*" ",L[:-1])
        Indent = Indent + 1
    elif L[0] == ")":
        Indent = Indent - 1
        print "%s%s" % (Indent*" ",L[:-1])
    else:
        print "%s%s" % (Indent*" ",L[:-1])
```

C>python p5.py hello.xml

```
(greeting
 -\n
 -Hello
 (b
  -World
 )b
 -\n
)greeting
```

12.4 | Event-driven Processing

In chapter 10, we saw how the popular event-driven XML processing style can be used in Python with the Python implementation of the SAX API. Pyxie also provides event-driven XML-processing capabilities. Perhaps the biggest difference is that with Pyxie, event handlers can be named after the element types that they process. This is best illustrated by example. The following program has code to handle start-tags for greeting elements and end-tags for b elements. It also has a handler for data content that prints out the first four characters of the data.

```
CD-ROM reference=12006.txt
```
C>type p6.py

```
"""

Event-driven XML processing with Pyxie

"""

from pyxie import *

# Create a class derived from xDispatch.

class myHandler(xDispatch):
        #Handler for greeting start-tag
        def start_greeting(self,etn,attrs):
              print "Start-tag for 'greeting' element"

        #Handler for b end-tag
        def end_b (self,etn):
              print "End-tag for 'b' element"

        #Handler for character data
        def characters(self,data):
              print "character data: %s..." % data[:4]

import sys

# Create a myHandler object.
m = myHandler()

# Call its event handlers, using PYX generated from command-
# line argument.
m.Dispatch(File2PYX(sys.argv[1]))
```

C>python p6.py hello.xml

```
Start-tag for 'greeting' element
character data: \n...
character data: Hell...
character data: Worl...
End-tag for 'b' element
character data: \n...
```

Note how the handler methods are named after the elements they process. Handlers for start-tags have the start_ prefix. Handlers for end-tags have the end_ prefix. Pyxie event-driven programs are derived from the xDispatch base class. This class provides a

Dispatch method that looks after detecting and calling the handlers as required.

When processing XML using xDispatch derived classes, you can define default handlers for start- and end-tags. These will be called for any start- or end-tags that do not have their own dedicated handlers. In the program below, the default handlers are called for the b start-tag and the greeting end-tag.

```
CD-ROM reference=12007.txt

C>type p7.py

"""
Event-driven XML processing with Pyxie with
default event handlers
"""

from pyxie import *

# Create a class derived from xDispatch.

class myHandler(xDispatch):
    #Handler for greeting start-tag
    def start_greeting(self,etn,attrs):
        print "Start-tag for 'greeting' element"

    #Handler for b end-tag
    def end_b (self,etn):
        print "End-tag for 'b' element"

    #Handler for character data
    def characters(self,data):
        print "character data: %s..." % data[:4]

    #Default handler for end-tags
    def default_end(self,etn):
        print "Default end-tag handler called for '%s'" % etn

    #Default handler for start_tags
    def default_start(self,etn,attrs):
        print "Default start-tag handler called for '%s'" % etn
```

```
import sys
m = myHandler()
m.Dispatch(File2PYX(sys.argv[1]))
```

C>**python p7.py hello.xml**

```
python p7.py hello.xml
Start tag for 'greeting' element
character data: \n...
character data: Hell...
Default start-tag handler called for 'b'
character data: Worl...
End tag for 'b' element
character data: \n...
Default end-tag handler called for 'greeting'
```

Handlers for start-tags have access by means of a Python dictionary to any attributes present on the start-tag. The following program prints attributes for all elements except `table` elements.

```
CD-ROM reference=12008.txt
```

C>**type p8.py**

```
"""
Event-driven XML processing with Pyxie.
Attribute processing

XML Processing with Python
Sean Mc Grath

"""

from pyxie import *

# Create a class derived from xDispatch.

class myHandler(xDispatch):
    #Handler for table start-tag
    def start_table(self,etn,attrs):
        # Do not print out attributes for tables.
        pass

    #Default handler for start-tags
```

```
        def default_start(self,etn,attrs):
            for (n,v) in attrs.items():
                print "Attribute name:'%s' value:'%s'" % (n,v)
import sys
m = myHandler()
m.Dispatch(File2PYX(sys.argv[1]))
```

We will use the following XML file to illustrate this program. Note that the `border` attribute on the table element does not appear in the output when the program is executed.

```
CD-ROM reference=12009.txt
C>type tables.xml

<?xml version="1.0"?>
<foo>
hello world
<table border="1">
<tr><td>a</td><td>b></td></tr>
</table>
<B x = "42">
sdfsfd
</B>
<table>
<tr><td width="10">A</td><td>B></td></tr>
<tr><td>A1</td><td>B1</td></tr>
</table>
</foo>


C>python p8.py tables.xml

Attribute name:'x' value:'42'
Attribute name:'width' value:'10'
```

12.5 | Tree-driven Processing

In chapter 11, we saw how the W3C's Document Object Model (DOM) can be used with Python. Like the DOM, Pyxie provides a tree-oriented API to XML processing. In Pyxie, an `xTree` object provides tree-oriented access to the structure and content of an XML document. Once loaded into an xTree, an XML document can be navigated in any direction, its contents can be cut and pasted, and new structures can be added to the tree as required. Also, xTree objects can be used to re-create XML syntax by simply printing them.

In the following program, an xTree object is created from the hello.xml sample file of this chapter.

```
CD-ROM reference=12010.txt
"""
Simple tree-driven XML processing with Pyxie

"""

from pyxie import *

import sys
t = File2xTree (sys.argv[1])
print `t`
```

C>**python p9.py hello.xml**

```
<?xml version="1.0"?>
<greeting>
Hello <b>World</b>
</greeting>
```

Every node in an xTree object can be visited with a simple Python for loop. In this example, the data content of the hello.xml file is converted to upper case.

```
CD-ROM reference=12011.txt
```
C>**type p10.py**

```
"""
Converting data content to upper case, using
xTree

XML Processing with Python
Sean Mc Grath

"""

from pyxie import *
```

```
import sys
t = File2xTree (sys.argv[1])
for node in t:
      if isinstance(node,xData):
            node.Data = string.upper(node.Data)
print `t`
```

C>**python p10.py**

```
<?xml version="1.0"?>
<greeting>
HELLO <b>WORLD</b>
</greeting>
```

An xTree is made up of an interlinked collection of xElement and xData objects. The above program works by visiting each node in the xTree. It then checks to see if the current node is an xData node. If it is, its data content (available in the Data instance variable) is retrieved and converted to upper case.

In the program below, a for loop is again used to visit every node in the tree. This time, b elements are renamed to bold elements.

```
CD-ROM reference=12012.txt
```
C>**type p11.py**

```
"""
Converting b elements to bold elements using
xTree
"""

from pyxie import *

import sys
t = File2xTree (sys.argv[1])
for node in t:
      if isinstance(node,xElement):
            if node.ElementTypeName == "b":
                  node.ElementTypeName = "BOLD"
print `t`
```

C>**python p11.py**

```
<?xml version="1.0"?>
```

```
<greeting>
Hello <BOLD>World</BOLD>
</greeting>
```

Element nodes have an associated Python dictionary called `At-tributeValues`. This dictionary can be used to add or remove attributes. In the program below, all elements are given an `etn` attribute set to their element type name in upper case.

```
CD-ROM reference=12013.txt
C>type p12.py

"""
Add an etn attribute to all elements set
to their element type name in upper case,
using xTree.

"""

from pyxie import *
import sys
t = File2xTree (sys.argv[1])
for node in t:
      if isinstance(node,xElement):
            node.AttributeValues["etn"] =
string.upper(node.ElementTypeName)
print `t`
```

```
C>python p12.py

<?xml version="1.0"?>
<greeting etn = "GREETING">
Hello <b etn = "B">World</b>
</greeting>
```

12.6 | Tree Navigation

Pyxie maintains an *active node* for every `xTree` object. A variety of methods act on the tree, taking into account the currently active node. The most fundamental are the navigation primitives known as `Up`, `Down`, `Left`, and `Right`.

When an xTree is created, the active node is set to the root node. In the following program, the active position is moved downward twice, and the element type name of the new node is printed.

```
CD-ROM reference=12014.txt
"""
Print the element type name of the first,
Second-generation descendant of the root node.


"""

from pyxie import *

import sys
t = File2xTree (sys.argv[1])
t.Down()
t.Down()
print t.ElementTypeName

C>type hello.xml

<?xml version="1.0"?>
<greeting><hello><foo/></hello></greeting>
C>python p13.py hello.xml

foo
```

This XML document has purposely been created without any line ends. Essentially all line ends are significant in an XML document, and they can cause the creation of data nodes that just contain line ends. The easiest way to see this is to use the C3 document viewer. The line ends present in the following XML file are shown in figure 12–1.

```
CD-ROM reference=12015.txt
C>type hello.xml
<?xml version="1.0"?>
<greeting>
<hello>
<foo/>
</hello>
</greeting>
```

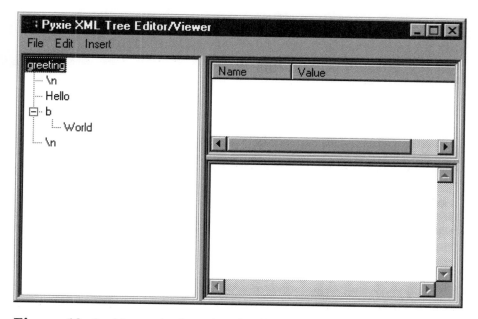

Figure 12–1 Line ends viewed in the C3 viewer.

Pyxie provides a function, `NormalizeWhiteSpaceSMG()`, that normalizes white space in the following way.

- A line end occurring immediately after a start-tag is removed.

- A line end occurring immediately before an end-tag is removed.

- No line end processing is performed for elements that have an `xml:space` attribute set to "preserve."

There are many, many ways to normalize white space, hence the "SMG" standing for "Sean McGrath" at the end of the function name. I am not suggesting that this is the only way to normalize white space! In the program below, the `NormalizeWhiteSpaceSMG` function is called after the `xTree` is created. As a result of the normalization, the b element is down 1, right 1, instead of down 2 from the root node.

```
CD-ROM reference=12016.txt
"""
Print the element type name of the first sibling
of the first child of the root node.
Normalize white space first.

"""

from pyxie import *

import sys
t = File2xTree (sys.argv[1])
NormalizeWhiteSpaceSMG(t)
t.Down()
t.Right()
print t.ElementTypeName
```

C>python p14.py hello.xml

b

12.7 | Tree Cut-and-Paste

Pyxies provides a `Cut` method that allows you to cut a piece out of a tree—the cutting is itself an `xTree` object. The `PasteDown` and `PasteRight` methods can be used to insert a tree into another tree. The `PasteDown` method positions the inserted tree, as the first child of the active node. The `PasteRight` method positions the inserted tree to the right of the active node.

In the following example, the b element is moved to the left of "Hello" with cut and paste operations.

```
CD-ROM reference=12017.txt
```
C>type p15.py

```
"""
Move b element to the left of "Hello" using
cut and paste operations.
"""
```

```
from pyxie import *

import sys
t = File2xTree (sys.argv[1])
NormalizeWhiteSpaceSMG(t)
t.Down()
t.Right()
t1 = t.Cut()
t.Home()
t.PasteDown(t1)
print `t`
```

```
C>python p15.py hello.xml
<?xml version="1.0"?>
<greeting><b>World</b>Hello </greeting>
```

12.8 | Node Lists

Pyxie provides a collection of functions for the creation and processing of lists of nodes. The Descendants method creates a Python list of all the nodes beneath the active position in an xTree. The following program creates a list of descendants of the root node and uses it to print the data content of an XML document backwards.

```
CD-ROM reference=12018.txt
C>type p16.py

" " "
Print the data content of an XML
document backwards.
" " "

from pyxie import *

import sys
t = File2xTree (sys.argv[1])
L = t.Descendants()
L.reverse()
for node in L:
        if isinstance(node,xData):
                strlist = list(node.Data)
                strlist.reverse()
```

```
                  print string.join(strlist,"")
```

C>python p16.py hello.xml

```
dlroW
 olleH
```

C>type AbleWasIEreISawElba.xml
```
<palindrome>
able was I ere I saw elba
</palindrome>
```

C>python p16.py ableWasIEreISawElba.xml

```
able was I ere I saw elba
```

The `Ancestors` method provides a list of ancestors of the current node. The following program uses the `Ancestors` method to print *fully qualified element names*. A fully qualified element name is one that contains the names of all the ancestors of the node, typically separated by ".".

```
CD-ROM reference=12019.txt
```
C>type tables.xml
```
<foo>
hello world
<table border="1">
<tr><td>a</td><td>b</td></tr>
</table>
<B x = "42">
sdfsfd
</B>
<table>
<tr><td width="10">A</td><td>B</td></tr>
<tr><td>A1</td><td>B1</td></tr>
</table>
</foo>
```

C>type p17.py

```
"""
Print fully qualified element names.

"""
```

```
from pyxie import *
import sys
t = File2xTree (sys.argv[1])
for node in t.Descendants():
        t.Seek(node)
        if t.AtElement():
                anc = t.Ancestors()
                fq = t.ElementTypeName
                for a in anc:
                        fq = a.ElementTypeName + "." + fq
                print fq
```

```
C>python p17.py tables.xml
```

```
foo.table
foo.table.tr
foo.table.tr.td
foo.table.tr.td
foo.B
foo.table
foo.table.tr
foo.table.tr.td
foo.table.tr.td
foo.table.tr
foo.table.tr.td
foo.table.tr.td
```

It is often the case that the only nodes of interest during an iteration of an xTree are xElement nodes. The Elements function acts as a filter—you provide it with a node list and it filters out the nonelement nodes. The following program also prints fully qualified element names.

```
CD-ROM reference=12020.txt
C>type p18.py
" " "
Print fully qualified element names
" " "

from pyxie import *

import sys
t = File2xTree (sys.argv[1])
for node in Elements(t.Descendants()):
```

```
    # iterate element nodes only
    t.Seek(node)
    anc = t.Ancestors()
    fq = t.ElementTypeName
    for a in anc:
        fq = a.ElementTypeName + "." + fq
    print fq

C>python p18.py tables.xml
foo.table
foo.table.tr
foo.table.tr.td
foo.table.tr.td
foo.B
foo.table
foo.table.tr
foo.table.tr.td
foo.table.tr.td
foo.table.tr
foo.table.tr.td
foo.table.tr.td
```

The Elements function has an optional second parameter specifying the element type names of interest. In the example below, fully qualified element names of tr and B elements only are printed.

```
CD-ROM reference=12021.txt
C>type p19.py
"""
Print fully qualified element names for a B element
Only.
"""

from pyxie import *

import sys
t = File2xTree (sys.argv[1])
for node in Elements(t.Descendants(),["tr","B"]):
    # iterate tr and B element nodes only
    t.Seek(node)
    anc = t.Ancestors()
    fq = t.ElementTypeName
    for a in anc:
        fq = a.ElementTypeName + "." + fq
    print fq
```

In a fashion analogous to the `Elements` function, the `DataNodes` function filters a nodelist to contain just `xData` nodes. The following program prints the data content of an XML document by traversing a list of its `xData` nodes.

```
CD-ROM reference=12022.txt
C>type p20.py

"""
Print data content of an XML file.

"""
from pyxie import *
import sys

t = File2xTree (sys.argv[1])
for node in DataNodes(t.Descendants()):
        t.Seek(node)
        data = string.strip(t.Data)
        if data:
                print data

C>python p20.py tables.xml

hello world
a
sdfsfd
A
A1
```

12.9 | Tree Walking

Walking a tree in Pyxie is analogous to walking a tree by using the event-driven style, with the exception that you have full access to the XML document structure. In this program, a function `Handler` is called twice for every node in the XML tree: once when the node is encountered "on the way down" in a depth-first, left-to-right tree walk, and again when the node is encountered "on the way up."

```
CD-ROM reference=12023.txt
C>type p21.py

"""
Print XML summary, using event-driven tree walk.

"""

from pyxie import *

def Handler(tree,StartOrEnd):
    if tree.AtElement():
        if StartOrEnd==1:
            print "Start Element:",tree.ElementTypeName
        else:
            print "End Element:",tree.ElementTypeName
    else:
        if StartOrEnd:
            print "data:%s..." % tree.Data[:4]


import sys
t = File2xTree (sys.argv[1])
NormalizeWhiteSpaceSMG(t)
t.Walk(Handler)

C>python p21.py
Start Element: greeting
data:Hell...
Start Element: b
data:Worl...
End Element: b
End Element: greeting
...
```

Pyxie also provides a `Dispatch` method on `xTree` objects that can be used to perform event-driven processing. The following program performs the same function as the last one but uses the `xTree` dispatch mechanism.

```
CD-ROM reference=12024.txt
"""
Print XML summary, using tree event dispatch.

"""

from pyxie import *

class Handler:
    def __init__(self,tree):
        self.tree = tree
        self.tree.Dispatch(self)

    def default_handler(self,StartOrEnd):
        if StartOrEnd:
            print "Start Element:", self.tree
                .ElementTypeName
        else:
            print "End Element:", self.tree
                .ElementTypeName

    def characters(self,StartOrEnd):
        if StartOrEnd:
            print "data:%s..." % self.tree.Data[:4]


import sys
t = File2xTree ("tables.xml")
NormalizeWhiteSpaceSMG(t)
Handler(t)
```

C>**python p22.py**

```
Start Element: greeting
data:Hell...
Start Element: b
data:Worl...
End Element: b
End Element: greeting
...
```

12.10 | Hybrid Event- or Tree-driven Processing

Tree-driven Pyxie programming is generally more pleasant than event-driven programming because you have full access to the XML document structure. There is a price to pay for this full access, however. Xtree-based processing is significantly more resource hungry than is xDispatch-based processing.

That said, it is often the case that the need for full tree access to an XML document is only necessary for fragments of the document. Perhaps the classic example of this is table structures such as HTML tables and CALS tables. It is very often painful to have to process these in an event-oriented fashion.

Pyxie provides a hybrid event- or tree-driven processing facility that allows you to start processing event-by-event and switch to tree-based processing as required. In the following program, the XML document is processed in a resource-efficient, event-oriented fashion except for table elements, which are processed in a tree-oriented fashion.

```
CD-ROM reference=12025.txt
C>type p23.py

"""
Hybrid Tree processing/Event Processing
Process table elements as trees.
Process rest of document as events.
XML Processing with Python
Sean Mc Grath
"""
from pyxie import *

class myHandler (xDispatch):
    def __init__(self):
        xDispatch.__init__(self)
        self.TableList = []

    def start_table(self,etn,attrs):
        print "Building tree from table element"
```

```
            # Push the table start-tag data back to be
            # redispatched
            self.PushElement(etn,attrs)
            # Append table to list of table mini-trees.
            self.TableList.append (PYX2Tree(self))

    def default_start(self,etn,attrs):
        print "start",etn

    def default_end(self,etn):
        print "end",etn

import sys
m = myHandler()
m.Dispatch(File2PYX(sys.argv[1]))
# TableList instance variable now contains a list
# of table elements -- each in its own tree structure.
for t in m.TableList:
    print "Table:"
    print `t`
```

```
C>type tables.xml
<foo>
hello world
<table border="1">
<tr><td>a</td><td>b></td></tr>
</table>
<B x = "42">
sdfsfd
</B>
<table>
<tr><td width="10">A</td><td>B></td></tr>
<tr><td>A1</td><td>B1</td></tr>
</table>
</foo>
```

```
C>python p20.py tables.xml

start foo
Building tree from table element
start B
end B
Building tree from table element
end foo
Table:
<?xml version="1.0"?>
```

```
<table border = "1"><tr><td>a</td><td>b></td></tr>
</table>
Table:
<?xml version="1.0"?>
<table><tr><td width = "10">A</td><td>B></td></tr>
<tr><td>A1</td><td>B1</td></tr>
</table>
```

12.11 | The Invoice Printing Problem Solved Three Ways

In section 8.11.2, the pros and cons of event-driven XML processing were discussed. The section posed the question, How would you write a program to print invoices from the following document that has at least three item elements?

```
CD-ROM reference=12026.txt
<invoices>
     <invoice>
          <item name="shoes" cost="10.00"/>
          <item name="socks" cost="1.00"/>
     </invoice>
     <invoice>
          <item name="shoes" cost="10.00"/>
          <item name="socks" cost="1.00"/>
     </invoice>
     <invoice>
          <item name="shoes" cost="10.00"/>
          <item name="socks" cost="1.00"/>
          <item name="trousers" cost="100.00"/>
     </invoice>
     <invoice>
          <item name="shoes" cost="10.00"/>
     </invoice>
</invoices>
```

The Pyxie program below solves this problem with three different algorithmic approaches:

- Event-driven processing style

- Tree-driven processing style

- Sparse tree-driven processing style

```
CD-ROM reference=12027.txt
C>type invoices.py

Data = """<invoices>
    <invoice>
        <item name="shoes" cost="10.00"/>
        <item name="socks" cost="1.00"/>
    </invoice>
    <invoice>
        <item name="shoes" cost="10.00"/>
        <item name="socks" cost="1.00"/>
    </invoice>
    <invoice>
        <item name="shoes" cost="10.00"/>
        <item name="socks" cost="1.00"/>
        <item name="trousers" cost="100.00"/>
    </invoice>
    <invoice>
        <item name="shoes" cost="10.00"/>
    </invoice>
</invoices>"""

from pyxie import *

def EventStyle():
    # Solve the invoice reporting problem by
    # using an event-driven Pyxie programming
    # style.
    #
    # Create a sub-class of xDispatch with
    # handlers for <item>, <invoice>, and </invoice>.
    #
    # 1. When an invoice element starts, reset
    # stored list of items.
    # 2. When an item starts, add to a list
    # of items.
    # 3. When an invoice ends, see if 3 or
    # more items have been accumulated.
    class MyHandler (xDispatch):
```

```
        def __init__(self,fo):
            xDispatch.__init__(self,fo)
            self.Items = []

        def start_item (self,etn,attrs):
            self.Items.append (attrs["name"],attrs
               ["cost"])

        def start_invoice (self,etn,attrs):
            self.Items = []

        def end_invoice (self,etn):
            if len(self.Items)>=3:
                print "<invoice>"
                for item in self.Items:
                    print "\t<item name=%s cost=
                    %s/>" %
                        (item[0],item[1])
                print "</invoice>"

    # Create an instance of the MyHandler class and
    # feed it PYX generated by parsing the Data
    # string.
    h = MyHandler(String2PYX(Data))
    # Start event dispatching.
    h.Dispatch()

def TreeStyle():
    # Solve the invoice reporting problem by
    # using a tree-driven Pyxie programming
    # style.
    #
    # 1. Create a tree.
    # 2. Walk the tree looking for invoice nodes.
    # 3. For each invoice node, get list of child
    #    elements.
    # 4. If there are 3 or more children, print
    #    the invoice.
    t = String2xTree(Data)
    for n in t:
        if t.AtElement("invoice"):
            items = Elements(t.Descendants())
            if len(items) >= 3:
                print `t`

def SparseTreeStyle():
```

```
# Solve the invoice reporting problem by
# using a sparse tree-driven Pyxie programming
# style.
#
# Create a subclass of xDispatch with
# a handler for <invoice>.
#
# 1. When an invoice element starts, build
#    a tree from that invoice.
# 2. For each invoice tree, get list of child
#    elements.
# 3. If there are 3 or more children, print
#    the invoice.

class MyHandler (xDispatch):
    def __init__(self,fo):
        xDispatch.__init__(self,fo)

    def start_invoice (self,etn,attrs):
        self.PushElement(etn,attrs)
        t = PYX2xTree(self)
        items = Elements(t.Descendants())
        if len(items) >= 3:
            print `t`


h = MyHandler(String2PYX(Data))
h.Dispatch()

if __name__ == "__main__":
    # Print all invoices having 3 or more items.
    # Three algorithms:
    # 1. Event Driven
    #    Fastest but most complex coding style
    # 2. Tree Driven
    #    Simple coding style but resource intensive
    # 3. Sparse Tree
    #    Reasonably simple coding style combined with
    #    memory efficiency
    EventStyle()
    TreeStyle()
    SparseTreeStyle()
```

12.12 | The Complete Source Code for the Pyxie Library

```
CD-ROM reference=12028.txt
#! /usr/bin/env python
"""
Pyxie
Core XML processing library
Version 0.5

XML Processing with Python
Sean Mc Grath

Introduction
_____
```

The Pyxie library provides facilities for processing XML. The library uses a simple notation to capture the information generated by XML parsers known as PYX.

PYX is a line-oriented notation in which the first character serves
to specify what type of parsing event the line represents:

First Character	Parsing Event
(	Start-tag
A	Attribute
)	End-tag
_	Data
?	Processing Instruction

Line ends and tabs occurring in data or attribute lines are escaped to "\" followed by "n" and "\" followed by "t", respectively.

Any process that generates information in PYX can be used as a data source for this library -- relational databases, HTML parsers, SGML parsers, XML parsers, latex parsers... whatever.

Facilities provided include:

    Tree-driven XML Processing (see xTree and related classes)
    Event-driven XML Processing (see the xDispatch class)
    Event-driven XML Processing with full Tree access
    (see the Dispatch method of xTree)
    Sparse Trees -- (see demo in test harness)
    A SAX-to-PYX driver to generate PYX from any SAX parser
    An SGML-like white space normalization function
    A Pyxie Exception class
    PYX encoder and decoder functions for handling escaped
    line ends/tabs

Tree-driven XML Processing

The xTree class provides:
    Navigational methods for moving current position around
    a tree structure
    Cut-and-Paste facilities
    Serialization to XML via repr
    Node list assembly methods such as Ancestors,
        Descendants, etc.
    Tree walking with callbacks to methods named after
        element type names
    A "Pythonic" tree-walking facility using a simple Python
        for loop
    An event dispatch facility (Dispatch) which can call
        handler methods in arbitrary Python classes

Event-driven XML Processing

The xDispatch class provides:
    Ancestor information available in a simple list struc-
    ture. Callbacks to methods named after element type
    names e.g., start_foo, end_foo. Default method handlers
    default_start and default_end. Callback for data con-
    tent (the characters method). Supports sparse tree
    building by allowing dispatched events to be pushed
    back onto the PYX stream (see demo in test harness)

The xDispatchMultiplexor class provides the ability to have
multiple event-driven "clients" processing a PYX event stream
in parallel.

See also the Pyxie project home page at http://www.pyxie.org.
There is a Pyxie mailing list. For more information, send e-mail
with just the word 'help' as subject or body to:

```
        pyxie_request@starship.python.net

"""
__version__ = "1.0"

import string

# Import c implementation of StringIO if available
try:
      import cStringIO
      StringIO = cStringIO
except ImportError:
      import StringIO


from exceptions import Exception

# An exception base class for Pyxie
# _____
class PyxieException (Exception):
      def __init__(self,s=""):
            self.problem = s
      def __str__(self):
            return self.problem


# An abstract base class for Pyxie nodes
# _____
class xNode:
      """
      xNode: All nodes in a Pyxie tree are derived from the
      xNode abstract base class.
      All nodes can be connected to other nodes, up, down,
      left and right.
      """
      def __init__(self):
            self.Up = self.Down = self.Left = self.Right = None



# A node representation of an XML element
# _____
class xElement (xNode):
      """
      xElement: A node representation of an XML element
      consisting of elment type name and attribute
      information
      """
```

```python
    def __init__(self,ElementTypeName):
        xNode.__init__(self)
        # An xElement must have an Element type name
        # (tag name).
        self.ElementTypeName = ElementTypeName
        # An xElement can have any number of attributes.
        # storage is of the form key/value in a Dictionary.
        self.AttributeValues = {}

    def __str__(self):
        """
        Return a meaningful representation of an xElement.
        """
        return ("xElement: "
                "Element Type Name='%s'. Attributes='%s'" % (
                    self.ElementTypeName,
                    `self.AttributeValues.items()`))
    def __repr__(self):
        """
        Return an XML serialization of an xElement.
        """
        if self.ElementTypeName == "?pi":
            # Processing instructions are stored
            # internally as a pseudo_element.
            res = "<?%s %s?>" % (
                    self.AttributeValues["target"],
                    self.AttributeValues["data"])
            return res
        if len(self.AttributeValues) == 0:
            # No attributes, so make ">" character
            # flush with element type name.
            res = '<%s>' % self.ElementTypeName
        else:
            # Emit start of start-tag
            res = '<%s' % self.ElementTypeName
            for (aName,aValue) in self.Attribute
              Values.items():
                    # Emit attribute name/value pairs.
                    # Double quotes always used, with
                    # internal double
                    # quotes escaped.
                    aValue = string.replace(aValue,'"',
                      "&quot;")
                    res = res + ' %s = "%s"' % (aName,aValue)
            # tack on the ">" to terminate the start-tag.
```

```
                    res = res + ">"
            # Need to process all children before emitting
            # end-tag.
            # This is a recursive process.
            # First, establish a list of all children.
            children = []
            pos = self.Down
            if pos:
                    children.append(pos)
                    while pos.Right:
                            pos = pos.Right
                            children.append(pos)

            # Iterate the list of children, invoking the
            #   __repr__ method on each one.
            for c in children:
                    res = res + `c`
            res = res + '</%s>' % self.ElementTypeName
            return res

# A node representation of XML character data
# _____
class xData (xNode):
    """

    xData: a node representation of XML data content
    """

    def __init__(self,str):
            xNode.__init__(self)
            self.Data = str

    def __str__(self):
            """

            Return a meaningful string representation of an
              xData object.
            Returns the first 10 characters.
            """

            return "xData (%s...)" % self.Data[:10]

    def __repr__(self):
            """

            Return the XML representation of an xData node.
            The XML representation of an xData node is simply the
            data content of the node.
            """

            return self.Data
        def __setslice__(self,i,j,s):
```

```
        """
        Convenience slicing method to allow assignment to
        a slice of the data content of an xData node
        """
        l = list(self.Data)
        l[i:j] = list(s)
        self.Data = string.join(l,"")

# xTree: A representation of an XML tree structure
# _____
class xTree:
    """
    xTree : a Python representation on an XML document
    as a hierarchical data structure made up of
    interconnected nodes
    """
    def __init__(self,rootnode=None):
        """
        Construct an xTree. A root node (xElement) can be
        provided if desired. (This is especially useful
        when doing sparse tree building.)
        """
        if rootnode:
            assert isinstance(rootnode,xNode)
            self.RootNode = rootnode
        else:
            self.RootNode = None
        self.CurPos = self.RootNode
        # Position stack supporting the PushPos
        # and PopPos functionality
        self.__PushStack = []

    def __getitem__(self,n):
        """
        Allow a tree to be iterated using Python's for loop
        """
        if n == 0:
            # Start of iteration, return root node.
            self.CurPos = self.RootNode
            return self.CurPos
        # We have been around the for loop at least
        # once, so return the "next" node. This is
        # the next node in a downward direction
        # or the next node in an easterly direction.
        if self.CurPos.Down:
            self.CurPos = self.CurPos.Down
```

```
                    return self.CurPos
            elif self.CurPos.Right:
                self.CurPos = self.CurPos.Right
                return self.CurPos
            else:
                while self.CurPos.Up and (not self.CurPos
                  .Right):
                    # Backtrack.
                    self.CurPos = self.CurPos.Up
                if self.CurPos.Right:
                    self.CurPos = self.CurPos.Right
                    return self.CurPos
                else:
                    # returning an IndexError terminates
                      the for loop.
                    raise IndexError("No more nodes in
                      xTree")

    def __getattr__(self,n):
        """
        Allow attributes of the current xElement or xData
        node to be accessed as attributes of the xTree
        object. Particularly useful for ElementTypeName
        and Data attributes. i.e., Instead of saying:
          "tree.CurPos.Data," can simply say "tree.Data".
        Instead of saying:
          "tree.CurPos.ElementTypeName", can simply say
          "tree.ElementTypeName".
        """
        if hasattr(self.CurPos,n):
            return getattr(self.CurPos,n)
        else:
            raise PyxieException (
            "No attribute '%s' on xTree or current
              xNode" % n)

    def __del__(self):
        """
        When an xTree is garbage collected, we need
        to break the circular
        references joining the xNode objects together.
        """
        self.ZapTree()

    def ZapTree(self):
        """
```

```
        Delete an xTree object completely by deleting the
        xNode objects attached to it. The xNodes are
        joined in a circular fashion and so the links
        need to be broken to allow Python's reference
        counting garbage collector to process them.
        """
        L = []
        # Create a list of all descendants of the root node
        self.Descendants1(L,self.RootNode)
        for n in L:
                # Iterate the list, breaking all links
                n.Up = n.Down = n.Left = n.Right = None

    def PushPos(self):
        """
        Push the current position onto a position stack
        for later retrieval via the PopPos method.
        """
        self.__PushStack.append(self.CurPos)

    def PopPos(self):
        """
        Pop a position from the position stack and make it
        the current position.
        """
        self.CurPos = self.__PushStack[-1]
        del self.__PushStack[-1]

    def AtElement(self,etn=None):
        """
        Predicate method. Is current position an Element?
        The optional argument allows the method to check
        for a particular element type name.
        """
        if not isinstance (self.CurPos,xElement):
            return 0
        if etn==None:
                return 1
        else:
            if self.ElementTypeName==etn:
                return 1
        return 0

    def AtData(self):
        """
        Predicate method. Is current position data?
```

```
        """
        return isinstance (self.CurPos,xData)

    def Home (self):
        """
        Set current position to root node.
        """
        self.CurPos = self.RootNode
        return self

    def Seek (self,Node):
        """
        Set current position to the specified node.
        """
        self.CurPos = Node

    def Down(self):
        """
        Set current position to first child of current node.
        """
        self.CurPos = self.CurPos.Down

    def HasDown(self):
        """
        Return true if current position has a child.
        """
        if self.CurPos.Down:
            return 1
        return 0

    def Up(self):
        """
        Set current position to parent of current node.
        """
        self.CurPos = self.CurPos.Up

    def GetUp(self):
        """
        Return parent of current node.
        """
        return self.CurPos.Up

    def HasUp(self):
        """
        Return true if current position has a parent.
        """
```

```
        if self.CurPos.Up:
            return 1
        return 0

def Right(self):
        """
        Set current position to first sibling of current node.
        """
        self.CurPos = self.CurPos.Right

def HasRight(self):
        """
        Return true if current position has a right sibling.
        """
        if self.CurPos.Right:
            return 1
        return 0

def Left(self):
        """
        Set current position to previous sibling of
          current node.
        """
        self.CurPos = self.CurPos.Left

def HasLeft(self):
        """
        Return true if current position has left sibling.
        """
        if self.CurPos.Left:
            return 1
        return 0

def Walk(self,func):
        """
        Walk the descendants of the current position, call-
        ing the specified function twice for each node:
        once "on the way down" and once "on the way up."
        """
        func(self,1)
        self.PushPos()
        for c in self.Children():
            self.Seek(c)
            # Recurse.
            self.Walk(func)
        self.PopPos()
```

```
            func(self,0)

    def WalkData(self,func):
        """
        Walk the data descendants of the current posi-
        tion, calling the specified function twice for
        each data node: once "on the way down" and once
        "on the way up."
        """
        if self.AtData():
            func(self,1)
        for c in self.Children():
            self.Seek(c)
            self.WalkData(func)
        if self.AtData():
            func(self,0)

    def WalkElements(self,func):
        """
        Walk the element descendants of the current posi-
        tion, calling the specified function twice for
        each element node: once "on the way down" and
        once "on the way up."
        """
        if self.AtElement():
            func(self,1)
        for c in self.Children():
            self.Seek(c)
            self.WalkElements(func)
        if self.AtElement():
            func(self,0)

    def Dispatch(self,obj):
        self.PushPos()
        if self.AtElement():
            etn = self.ElementTypeName
            if hasattr(obj,"handle_%s" % etn):
                getattr(obj,"handle_%s" % etn)(1)
            elif hasattr(obj,"default_handler"):
                obj.default_handler(1)
            self.PushPos()
            for c in self.Children():
                self.Seek(c)
                self.Dispatch(obj)
            self.PopPos()
            if hasattr(obj,"handle_%s" % etn):
```

```
                    getattr(obj,"handle_%s" % etn)(0)
            elif hasattr(obj,"default_handler"):
                    obj.default_handler(0)
        else:
            if hasattr(obj,"characters"):
                    getattr(obj,"characters")(1)
                    getattr(obj,"characters")(0)
        self.PopPos()
def PYX2xTree(self,f):
    """
    Build an xTree from a PYX source.
    """
    if self.RootNode:
            self.ZapTree()
    # Create a temporary root node -- will be zapped after
    # the build.
    self.RootNode = xElement("!TEMP")

    self.CurPos = self.RootNode
    # Start off, pasting nodes in a downward direction.
    PasteDown = 1
    while 1:
            L = f.readline()[:-1]
            if L=="":
                    raise IOError("PYX stream terminated
                        prematurely")
            if L[0] == '(':
                    # Start-tag, create an element node.
                    etn = L[1:]
                    element = xElement(etn)
                    # Attach the new node to the tree.
                    if PasteDown:
                            self.CurPos.Down = element
                            element.Up = self.CurPos
                            self.CurPos = element
                    else:
                            self.CurPos.Right = element
                            element.Left = self.CurPos
                            element.Up = self.CurPos.Up
                            self.CurPos = element
                            PasteDown = 1

            elif L[0] == ')':
                    # End-tag, next node will be pasted
                    # right rather
                    # than down.
```

```
                        if not PasteDown:
                            self.CurPos = self.CurPos.Up
                        PasteDown = 0
                        if self.CurPos == self.RootNode.Down:
                            # Back to root? If so, finished.
                            break

            elif L[0] == '_':
                        # Character data, create an xData
                        # node with the
                        # decoded data.
                        datum = xData(PYXDecoder(L[1:]))
                        if PasteDown:
                            self.CurPos.Down = datum
                            datum.Up = self.CurPos
                            self.CurPos = datum
                            PasteDown = 0
                        else:
                            self.CurPos.Right = datum
                            datum.Left = self.CurPos
                            datum.Up = self.CurPos.Up
                            self.CurPos = datum

            elif L[0] == 'A':
                        # An attribute. Up to the first
                        # space is the attribute name;
                        # the rest is the attribute value.
                        i = string.index (L," ")
                        aName = L[1:i]
                        aValue = L[i+1:]
                        self.CurPos.AttributeValues[aName] =
PYXDecoder(aValue)
            elif L[0] == '?':
                        # A processing instruction. These
                        # are stored in the tree as "?pi"
                        # pseudoelements with two attributes
                        # called "target" and "data".
                        # Up to first space is the PI target,
                        # rest is the PI data.
                        i = string.index (L," ")
                        target = L[1:i]
                        data = L[i+1:]
                        element = xElement("?pi")
                        element.AttributeValues["target"] =
                          target
```

```
                        element.AttributeValues["data"] = data
                        if PasteDown:
                                self.CurPos.Down = element
                                element.Up = self.CurPos
                                self.CurPos = element
                        else:
                                self.CurPos.Right = element
                                element.Left = self.CurPos
                                element.Up = self.CurPos.Up
                                self.CurPos = element

        # Get rid of temporary root node.
        temp = self.RootNode.Down
        self.RootNode.Down = None
        temp.Up = None
        self.RootNode = temp
        # After loading from PYX source, root node is
        # current position.
        self.CurPos = self.RootNode
        return self

def Cut(self):
    """
    Cut out tree rooted at current position and re-
    turn it as a new tree.
    New Current Position is set to parent of current node.
    """
    if self.CurPos.Up is None:
            return self
    l = self.CurPos.Left
    r = self.CurPos.Right
    if r:
            r.Left = l
    if l:
            l.Right = r
    self.CurPos.Right = self.CurPos.Left = None
    tree = xTree()
    tree.CurPos = tree.RootNode = self.CurPos
    t = self.CurPos.Up
    self.CurPos.Up = None
    if l is None:
            t.Down = r
    # New Current Position always becomes parent of
    # current node.
    self.CurPos = t
```

```
        return tree

    def PasteDown(self,l):
        """
        Paste the specified tree into this tree as first
        child of current position.
        """
        assert isinstance (l,xTree)
        b = self.CurPos.Down
        self.CurPos.Down = l.RootNode
        if b:
            b.Left = l.RootNode
        l.RootNode.Up = self.CurPos
        l.RootNode.Right = b
        l.RootNode.Left = None
        l.CurPos = l.root = None

    def PasteRight(self,l):
        """
        Paste the specified tree into this tree as next
        sibling of current position.
        """
        assert isinstance (l,xTree)
        e = self.CurPos.Right
        self.CurPos.Right = l.RootNode
        l.RootNode.Left = self.CurPos
        l.RootNode.Up = self.CurPos.Up
        if e:
            e.Left = l.RootNode
        l.RootNode.Right = e
        l.CurPos = l.RootNode = None

    def __repr__(self):
        """
        Return xml serialization of an xTree.
        """
        return '<?xml version="1.0"?>\n' + `self.CurPos`

    def Descendants1(self,res,n):
        """
        Add descendants of node "n" to the result list "res".
        This is an internal recursive method invoked from
        the Descendants method.
        """
        if n is None:
            return
```

```
        pos = n.Down
        if pos is None:
            return
        while pos:
            res.append (pos)
            self.Descendants1(res,pos)
            pos = pos.Right

def Descendants(self,n=None):
    """
    Create a list of the descendants of the current
    node or the specified node. Most of the work is
    done by the recursive Descendants1 method.
    """
    self.PushPos()
    if n==None:
        n = self.CurPos
    res = []
    self.Descendants1(res,n)
    self.PopPos()
    return res

def JoinData(self,sep,n=None):
    """
    Create a string by concatenating the data content
    of an element node. A separator string will be
    spliced between adjacent data items.
    """
    res = []
    if n == None:
        n = self.CurPos
    D = self.Descendants(n)
    for i in D:
        if isinstance(i,xData):
            res.append(i.Data)
    return string.join(res,sep)

def Children (self,n=None):
    """
    Create a list of the children of the current node
    or the specified node. Most of the work is done by
    the recursive Children1 method.
    """
    self.PushPos()
    if n is None:
        n = self.CurPos
```

```python
        res = []
        self.Children1(res,n)
        self.PopPos()
        return res

    def Children1(self,res,n):
        """
        Create a list of the children of node "n", adding
        the child nodes to the result list "res".
        """
        pos = n.Down
        if not pos:
            return res
        res.append(pos)
        while pos.Right:
            pos = pos.Right
            res.append(pos)
        return res

    def Ancestors1(self,res,n):
        """
        Create a list of the ancestors of node "n",
        adding the child nodes to the result list "res".
        """
        while n.Up:
            n = n.Up
            res.append(n)

    def Ancestors(self,n=None):
        """
        Create a list of the Ancestors of the current
        node or the specified node.
        """
        self.PushPos()
        res = []
        if n is None:
            n = self.CurPos
        while n.Up:
            n = n.Up
            res.append(n)
        self.PopPos()
        return res
# xDispatch: A class for event-driven XML processing
# _____
class xDispatch:
    """
```

```
xDispatch: a Class supporting event-driven XML processing
via callback methods

start_foo     : start of element foo
end_foo       : end of element foo
characters    : character data
default_start: start of element with no specified
                handler
default_end   : end of element with no specified handler
processinginstruction: processing instruction

Keeps track of ancestors and their descendants in the
Ancestors instance method.

Allows PYX events to be pushed back onto the
stream of events (used to support sparse tree building).

Can act as a data source for PYX2xTree.
"""
def __init__(self,fo=None):
    self.Ancestors = []
    self.PYXSource = fo
    self.PushedEvents = []

def Sanitize(self,s):
    """
    Replace periods with underscores so that an ele-
    ment called x.y will have  handler methods called
    start_x_y and end_x_y
    """
    s = string.replace(s,".","_")
    return s

def PushElement(self,etn,attrs):
    """
    Given an element type name and an attribute dic-
    tionary xElement, push the PYX events necessary
    to create it onto a stack of events. This is used
    to support sparse tree building.
    """
    avs = attrs.items()
    avs.sort()
    avs.reverse()
    for (a,v) in avs:
        self.PushedEvents.append ("A%s %s\n" % (a,v))
    self.PushedEvents.append ("(%s\n" % etn)
```

```
        self.Ancestors.pop()

def readline(self):
    """
    Return the next line of PYX. Any PYX pushed via
    previous PushElement() calls take precedence.
    """
    if self.PushedEvents:
        # At least 1 pushed event exists.
        Line = self.PushedEvents.pop()
        return Line
    # No pushed events
    Line = self.PYXSource.readline()
    return Line

def Dispatch(self,fo=None):
    """
    Process a PYX source calling any callback methods
    defined in this class.
    """
    if fo is not None:
        self.PYXSource = fo
    L = self.readline()[:-1]
    while 1:
        if L=="":
            raise IOError("PYX stream terminated
                prematurely")
        if L[0] == '(':
            etn = L[1:]
            attrs = {}
            # Accumulate attributes for this
            # element.
            L = self.readline()[:-1]
            while L[0] == "A":
                i = string.index (L," ")
                aName = L[1:i]
                aValue = L[i+1:]
                attrs[aName] = aValue
                L = self.readline()[:-1]
            # Push the event after the start-
            # tag+attributes back on the event
            # stream. This is important because
            # the handler we are about to call
            # may rely on everything being on the
            # event stream -- e.g., for sparse
            # tree building
```

```
        self.PushedEvents.append (L+"\n")
        StartMethod = "start_%s" % self.
          Sanitize(etn)
        # Does a handler exist for this element?
        if hasattr(self,StartMethod):
            getattr(self,StartMethod)
              (etn,attrs)
        elif hasattr(self,"default_start"):
            # call default start_tag handler
            self.default_start(etn,attrs)
        # Add current element to the list of
        # open elements.
        self.Ancestors.append((etn,attrs.
          copy()))
elif L[0] == ')':
        etn = L[1:]
        EndMethod = "end_%s" % self.
          Sanitize(etn)
        # Take most recently opened element
        # off the list of open elements.
        self.Ancestors.pop()
        # Does the element type have an
        # end_tag handler?
        if hasattr(self,EndMethod):
            getattr(self,EndMethod)(etn)
        elif hasattr(self,"default_end"):
            # Call the default end-tag
            # handler.
            self.default_end(etn)
        if len(self.Ancestors)==0:
            # Stop dispatching once end-tag
            # for root element is encountered.
            return
elif L[0] == '_':
        # Call character data handler if it
        # exists.
        if hasattr(self,"characters"):
            self.characters(L[1:])
elif L[0] == '?':
        # Call processing instruction handler
        # if it exists.
        if hasattr(self,"processing
          instruction"):
            target = L[1:i]
            data = L[i+1:]
            self.processinginstruction
```

```
                                    (target,data)
                    else:
                            raise PyxieException (
                                    "Unknown PYX event '%s'" % L[0])
                    L = self.readline()[:_1]


# xDispatchMultiplexor: A class for parallel dispatch of XML events
# _____
class xDispatchMultiplexor(xDispatch):
      def __init__(self,fo=None):
            xDispatch.__init__(self,fo)
            # Storage for the list of objects that wish to
              receive event notification
            self.Sinks=[]

      def RegisterSink (self,object):
            """
            Register a sink with the Multiplexor.
            """
            self.Sinks.append(object)

      def default_start(self,etn,attrs):
            """
            For each registered sink, see if it has a start
            handler specifically for this element type. Fail-
            ing that, see if it has a default start handler.
            """
            for s in self.Sinks:
                  if hasattr(s,"start--%s" % etn):
                        getattr(s,"start--%s" % etn)(etn,attrs)
                  elif hasattr(s,"default_start"):
                        getattr(s,"default_start")(etn,attrs)

      def default_end(self,etn):
            """
            For each registered sink, see if it has an end
            handler specifically for this element type. Fail-
            ing that, see if it has a default end handler.
            """
            for s in self.Sinks:
                  if hasattr(s,"end--%s" % etn):
                        getattr(s,"end_%s" % etn)(etn)
                  elif hasattr(s,"default_end"):
                        getattr(s,"default_end")(etn)

      def characters(self,data):
```

```
        """
        For each registered sink, see if it has a character
        handler.
        """
        for s in self.Sinks:
            if hasattr(s,"characters"):
                getattr(s,"characters")(data)

    def processinginstruction(self,target,data):
        """
        For each registered sink, see if it has a
        processing instruction handler.
        """
        for s in self.Sinks:
            if hasattr(s,"processinginstruction"):
                getattr(s,"processinginstruction")
                    (data)

# End of xDispatchMultiplexor Class

def Elements(nodelist,elist=[]):
    """
    Filter a node list to xElement nodes.
    """
    res = []
    for n in nodelist:
        if isinstance(n,xElement):
            if elist==[] or (n.ElementTypeName in
                elist):
                    res.append (n)
    return res

def ElementTypeNames(nodelist):
    """
    Filter a node list to the names of its xElement nodes.
    """
    res = []
    for n in nodelist:
        if isinstance(n,xElement):
            res.append (n.ElementTypeName)
    return res

def DataNodes(nodelist):
    """
    Filter a node list to the character data nodes.
    """
```

```
res = []
for n in nodelist:
        if isinstance(n,xData):
                res.append (n)
return res

def NormalizeWhiteSpaceSMG(t):
    """
    Normalize white space SMG (Sean McGrath style).

    A SGML-ish white space processing algorithm for xTree
      objects

    _ A line end immediately after a start-tag is ignored.
    _ A line end immediately before an end-tag is ignored.
    _ All other line ends are treated as spaces.
    _ No white space processing performed anywhere in an
      element,
    _ where xml:space=="preserve" anywhere in the ancestry of
    _ the element.
    """
    global PreserveWhiteSpace
    PreserveWhiteSpace = 0

    def NWS(t,StartOrEnd):
        global PreserveWhiteSpace
        if t.AtElement():
            if t.AttributeValues.has_key("xml:space"):
                sp = t.AttributeValues["xml:space"]
                if sp == "preserve":
                    if StartOrEnd:
                            PreserveWhiteSpace = \
                                    PreserveWhite
                                        Space + 1
                    else:
                            PreserveWhiteSpace = \
                                    PreserveWhite
                                        Space - 1

        elif t.AtData() and PreserveWhiteSpace == 0:
            if StartOrEnd:
                if not t.CurPos.Left and t.CurPos.
                    Data[0] == "\n":
                        t.CurPos.Data = t.CurPos.
                            Data[1:]
                if not t.CurPos.Right and (
```

```
                                    t.CurPos.Data[-1] == "\n"):
                                         t.CurPos.Data = t.CurPos.
                                             Data[:-1]
                            t.CurPos.Data = string.replace(
                                t.CurPos.Data,"\n"," ")
        t.PushPos()
        t.Home()
        t.Walk (NWS)
        t.Home()
        # Traverse tree for empty data nodes and remove them.
        for n in t:
                t.Seek(n)
                if t.AtData() and t.Data == "":
                        t.Cut()
        t.PopPos()
        return t

def PYXEncoder(s):
    """
    Replace any tab or newline characters with escaped forms.
    """
    s = string.replace(s,"\n","\\n")
    s = string.replace(s,"\t","\\t")
    return s

def PYXDecoder(s):
    """
    Replace any escaped tab or newline characters with
    literal tabs and newlines.
    """
    s = string.replace(s,"\\n","\n")
    s = string.replace(s,"\\t","\t")
    return s

def PYX2xTree(f):
    """
    Build an xTree from a file-like object.
    Input in PYX format            /
    returns xTree.
    Optionally, root the new tree at a specified root node.
    """
    return xTree().PYX2xTree(f)

def String2xTree (str):
    """
    Create an xTree from an XML instance provided in a string.
```

```
        Uses PyExpat as the XML parser.
        """
        return PYX2xTree (PYExpat2PYX(StringIO.StringIO(str)))

def String2PYX(str):
        """
        Return a PYX source from an XML instance provided in a string.
        Uses PyExpat as the XML parser.
        """
        return PYExpat2PYX(StringIO.StringIO(str))

def File2xTree(filename):
        """
        Return an xTree built from the XML in the specified file.
        Uses PyExpat as the XML parser.
        """
        return PYX2xTree (PYExpat2PYX(open(filename,"r")))
def File2PYX(filename):
        """
        Return a PYX source built from the XML in the specified file.
        Uses PyExpat as the XML parser.
        """
        return PYExpat2PYX(open(filename,"r"))

def PYExpat2PYX(fo):
        """
        Utility function to create PYX notation from a SAX
        parser
        """
        from xml.parsers import pyexpat
        import tempfile
        tempfilename = tempfile.mktemp()
        global tfo
        tfo = open (tempfilename,"w")

        def StartElementHandler(name,attrs):
                global tfo
                tfo.write ("(%s\n" % name)
                i = 0
                while i < len(attrs):
                        tfo.write ("A%s %s\n" % (attrs[i] , attrs
                          [i+1]))
                        i = i + 2

        def EndElementHandler(name):
                global tfo
```

```
                tfo.write (")%s\n" % name)

        def CharacterDataHandler(data):
            global tfo
        tfo.write ("-%s\n" % PYXEncoder(data))
        def ProcessingInstructionHandler(target,data):
            global tfo
            tfo.write ("?%s %s\n" % (target,data))

        Parser = pyexpat.ParserCreate()
        Parser.StartElementHandler = StartElementHandler
        Parser.EndElementHandler = EndElementHandler
        Parser.CharacterDataHandler = CharacterDataHandler
        Parser.ProcessingInstructionHandler = Processing
        InstructionHandler
        ParserStatus = Parser.Parse( fo.read(), 1)
        if ParserStatus == 0:
            raise PyxieException("Parse failed")
        tfo.close()
        tfo = open (tempfilename,"r")
        return tfo

def SAX2PYX(fo,ParserSelection=None):
    from xml.sax import saxexts, saxlib, saxutils
    import tempfile
    tempfilename = tempfile.mktemp()

    class myHandler (saxlib.HandlerBase):
        def __init__(self,tempfilename):
            self.fo = open (tempfilename,"w")

        def startElement(self,Element,Attributes):
            self.fo.write("(%s\n" % Element)
            for i in range (0,Attributes.getLength()):
                self.fo.write("A%s %s\n" % (
                    Attributes.getName(i),
                    PYXEncoder(Attributes.get
                      Value(i))))

        def characters(self,data,offset,length):
            self.fo.write("-%s\n" % (
                PYXEncoder(data[offset:offset+
                  length])))

        def processingInstruction (target, data):
            self.fo.write("?%s %s\n" % (target,data))
```

```python
            def endElement(self,Element):
                    self.fo.write(")%s\n"  % Element)

            def endDocument(self):
                    self.fo.close()

        h = myHandler(tempfilename)
        parser = saxexts.make_parser("xml.sax.drivers.drv_" +
            ParserSelection)
        parser.setDocumentHandler(h)
        parser.parse (fo)
        tfo = open (tempfilename,"r")
        return tfo

if __name__ == "__main__":
        """
        Test harness for Pyxie
        """
        import sys,StringIO,tempfile
        tables = """
<test a = "b">
Some data content in foo
<table>
<tr><td>Table 1 r1c1</td><td>Table 1 r1c2</td></tr>
<tr><td>Table 1 r2c1</td><td>Table 1 r2c2</td></tr>
</table>
<B x = "42">
Some data content in B
</B>
<table>
<tr><td>Table 2 r1c1</td><td>Table 2 r1c2</td></tr>
<tr><td>Table 2 r2c1</td><td>Table 2 r2c2</td></tr>
</table>
Some more content in foo
<G></G>
</test>
        """
        try:
                print "_____"
                print "Pyxie %s Test Harness output:" % __version__
                print "_____"

                t = String2xTree (tables)
                print "_____"
                print "Root element:"
                print t
```

```
        print "_____"
        print "Serialized tree:"
        print `t`

        print "_____"
        print "Element Type Names:"
        for n in t:
                if t.AtElement():
                        print t.ElementTypeName,
        print

        print "_____"
        print "Summarized Data content:"
        for n in t:
                if t.AtData():
                        print PYXEncoder(`t.CurPos`)+"...",
        print

        print "_____"
        print "Tree with normalized white space:"
        NormalizeWhiteSpaceSMG(t)
        print `t`

        print "_____"
        print "Example of PYX event dispatching:"
class myHandler (xDispatch):
        def __init__(self,fo):
                xDispatch.__init__(self,fo)
                self.Dispatch()
        def start_table(self,etn,attrs):
                print "starting ",etn
        def end_table(self,etn):
                print "ending ",etn
        def characters(self,data):
                print "data",data[:10],"...",
myHandler(String2PYX(tables))
print
print "_____"
print "Example of xTree event dispatching:"

t = String2xTree (tables)

class foo:
        def __init__(self,t):
                self.Tree = t
```

```
                  self.Tree.Dispatch(self)

          def handle_table(self,s):
                  if s:
                          print "table start"
                  else:
                          print "table end"

          def characters(self,s):
                  if s:
                          print PYXEncoder(self.Tree.Data[:5])

  foo (t)

  print "_____"
  print "Example of sparse tree building:"

  class myHandler (xDispatch):
          def __init__(self,fo):
                  xDispatch.__init__(self,fo)
                  self.Dispatch()
          def start_table(self,etn,attrs):
                  print "sparse tree build of table element"
                          # Push the table start-tag data back
                          # to be redispatched.
                          self.PushElement(etn,attrs)
                          t = PYX2xTree(self)
                          print `t`
                  def end_table(self,etn):
                          print "ending table"

                  def default_start(self,etn,attrs):
                          print "start",etn

                  def default_end(self,etn):
                          print "end",etn

          myHandler(String2PYX(tables))

          print "_____"
          print "Example of event multiplexing:"

          class Sink1(xDispatch):
                  def start_table(self,etn,attrs):
                          print "Sink 1 _ start table"
                  def end_table(self,etn):
```

```
                    print "Sink 1 _ end table"

        class Sink2(xDispatch):
              def start_table(self,etn,attrs):
                    print "Sink 2 _ start table"
              def end_table(self,etn):
                    print "Sink 2 _ end table"

        mux = xDispatchMultiplexor()
        mux.RegisterSink (Sink1())
        mux.RegisterSink (Sink2())
        mux.Dispatch(String2PYX(tables))

except PyxieException,e:
      print e.problem
```

xFS: Filesystem Information in XML

M ost filesystems allow users to create directories to organize file storage into hierarchies. These hierarchical structures map very easily to XML. In this chapter, we develop a Python utility for converting filesystem information into XML.

Having a facility to view a filesystem as an XML file is of more than just academic interest. Once in XML, we can contemplate:

- Displaying the XML in an XML-aware Web browser

- Transforming the XML to HTML, using XSL and related technologies

- Using the `xgrep` utility to search filesystem information

- Displaying or editing the filesystem information in the C3 utility

- Developing filesystem processing applications by using Pyxie or, indeed, any XML processing library

397

The goal in this chapter is a simple one: to illustrate how transforming a structured data source to XML leads to a maximum reuse of existing applications and knowledge. Of course, filesystem data is only one of a myriad of possible structured data sources. I'm sure you will find some lying around your own systems that could perhaps benefit from an XML interchange format.

13.1 | A Simple XML DTD for Filesystem Information

We will work with the following very simple representation of filesystem information.

```
CD-ROM reference=13001.txt
<!__
A simple DTD for filesystem information

A filesystem consists of a root xfs element that can contain
files and/or other directories.

Both directories and files have names and modification
dates.

Files have an associated size in bytes
-->

<!-- Root element type -->
< xfs (pattern,(dir|file)*)>

<!-- The wildcard pattern used to create the filesystem list-
     ing -->
< pattern (#PCDATA)>

<!-- A directory has a name, a modification time and 0 or
     more of either files or directories -->
< dir (name,mod,(dir|file)*)>

<!-- A file has a name, a size and a modification time -->
< file (name,size,mod)>
```

```
<!-- a directory or file name -->
< name (#PCDATA)>

<!-- A file size in bytes -->
< size (#PCDATA)>

<!-- a date e.g., Sat Jun 12 16:22:02 1999 -->
< mod (#PCDATA)>
```

Here is a simple file marked up to this DTD.

```
CD-ROM reference=13002.txt
<?xml version="1.0"?>
<!DOCTYPE xfs SYSTEM "xfs.dtd">
<xfs>
<pattern>.\*</pattern>
 <file>
  <name>.\xmln.c</name>
  <size>0000005181</size>
  <mod>Wed Jun 02 15:51:04 1999</mod>
 </file>
</xfs>
```

13.2 | Some Python Features Used in the xFS Application

Before we delve into the code of xFS, we will take a look at some Python features that we have not yet encountered.

13.2.1 Getting Filesystem Information with the os and stat Modules

The xFS application code makes use of a function in Python's standard os module called stat. Given a filename, the stat function returns a list containing 10 useful pieces of information about the file.

```
CD-ROM reference=13003.txt
```

```
>>> import os
>>> os.stat("xmlc.c")
(33206, 0, 2, 1, 0, 0, 4382, 934758000, 928768362, 928768947)
```

A quick way to find out what each of the numbers means is to print out the docstring for the stat function:

```
CD-ROM reference=13004.txt
>>> print os.stat.__doc__
stat(path) --> (mode,ino,dev,nlink,uid,gid,size,atime,mtime,
ctime)
Perform a stat system call on the given path.
```

Some of the numbers are only meaningful in Unix and will only make sense to you if you are familiar with Unix. The standard stat module provides useful mnemonics for each offset into the tuple structure returned by os.stat. These are tabulated in table 13.1.

Here is a program that prints the size of a file in bytes.

Table 13.1 Offsets returned by os.stat

Offset	Description
ST_MODE	inode protection mode (Unix)
ST_INODE	inode number (Unix)
ST_DEV	Device number (Unix)
ST_NLINK	Number of links (Unix)
ST_UID	User ID of the owner (Unix)
ST_GID	Group ID of the owner (Unix)
ST_SIZE	File size in bytes
ST_ATIME	Last access time
ST_MTIME	Last modification time
ST_CTIME	Time of last status change

```
CD-ROM reference=13005.txt
C>type filesize.py

"""
Print the size of the specifed file in bytes.

"""
import os,stat

def filesize(f):
        return os.stat (f) [stat.ST_SIZE]

if __name__ == "__main__":
        import sys
        print filesize(sys.argv[1])
C>python filesize.py xmln.c
5181


C>dir xmln.c
02/06/99  15:40                        5,181 xmln.c
```

13.2.2   *The Repetition Operator*

The xFS application indents its output to make it easier to read. Depending on the depth of the directory hierarchy, xFS may require one or perhaps dozens of spaces to precede each line of output.

Python provides a very useful way of repeating any string a specified number of times. The repetition operator is *. In the following example, we cause the string "Hello" to be repeated four times by applying the repetition operator.

```
CD-ROM reference=13006.txt
>>> print "Hello" * 4
HelloHelloHelloHello
```

In the example below, the string "9" is repeated three times and then interpolated into another string.

```
CD-ROM reference=13007.txt
>>> print "Nine three times:%s" % ("9" * 3)
Nine three times 999
```

Note that in the last example, the parentheses are required in order to associate the repetition with the string "9" rather than the string "Nine three times:9". To see the difference, leave out the parentheses.

```
CD-ROM reference=13008.txt
>>> print "Nine three times %s" % "9" * 3
Nine three times 9Nine three times 9Nine three times 9
```

The repetition operator can in fact be used with any sequence type. It is equally at home with lists and tuples.

```
CD-ROM reference=13009.txt
>>>[1,2,3] * 2
[1,2,3,1,2,3]

>>> (1,2,3) * 2
(1,2,3,1,2,3)
```

13.2.3 *The Time Module*

Python's standard `time` module supports the manipulation of date and time values. Time is measured in terms of elapsed seconds since the *epoch,* which is midnight January 1, 1970, on Unix and Windows platforms. The `stat` function returns times in this form. The `ctime` function provided in the `time` module converts these times to English strings. The following program prints the time a file was last changed.

```
CD-ROM reference=13010.txt
C>type filechanged.py

" " "
Print the time a file was last changed.

" " "
import os,stat,time
def filechanged(f):
        o = os.stat(f)
        t = o[stat.ST_CTIME]
        return time.ctime(t)

if __name__ == "__main__":
```

```
import sys
print filechanged(sys.argv[1])
```

`C>python filechanged.py xmln.c`
```
Wed Jun 02 15:51:04 1999
```

13.3 | Viewing xFS Data with the C3 XML Editor/Viewer

It will come as little surprise that the XML produced by xFS can be pumped into other XML applications such as the C3 XML editor/viewer. The following sequence of commands creates an XML file conforming to the xFS DTD, parses it, and then displays the file in C3. (See figure 13–1.)

```
CD-ROM reference=13011.txt
```
`C>python xFS.py > res.xml`
`C>xmlv res.xml >nul`
`C>python c3.py res.xml`

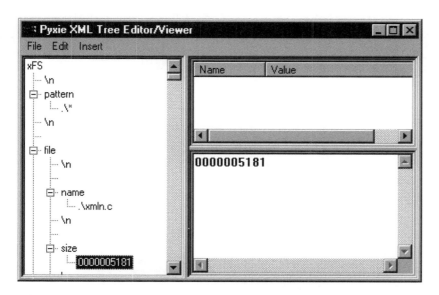

Figure 13–1 Filesystem information displayed in the C3 XML editor/viewer

13.4 | Performing Filesystem Queries with xgrep

The xFS utility purposely outputs file sizes, using a fixed number of digits, like this:

```
CD-ROM reference=13012.txt
  <size>0000005181</size>
```

We have a tool, (xgrep), that enables us to match patterns within size elements only. With xgrep, it is straightforward to find all files occupying more than a given number of bytes. In this example, the sizes of files in excess of 500,000 bytes are printed. First, we create an xFS file from the contents of the current directory.

```
CD-ROM reference=13013.txt
C>python xdir.py > fs.xml
```

The first few lines of the generated XML file are shown below.

```
CD-ROM reference=13014.txt
C>type fs.xml

<?xml version="1.0"?>
<!DOCTYPE xFS SYSTEM "xFS.dtd">
<xFS>
<pattern>.\*</pattern>
 <file>
  <name>.\xmln.c</name>
  <size>0000005181</size>
  <mod>Wed Jun 02 15:51:04 1999</mod>
 </file>
 <file>
  <name>.\hamlet.xml</name>
  <size>0000288816</size>
  <mod>Thu Jun 03 15:55:19 1999</mod>
 </file>
...
</xFS>
```

The following command searches the file `fs.xml`, looking for file sizes in excess of 500,000 bytes. The `\d` in the pattern means "match exactly 1 digit."

```
CD-ROM reference=13015.txt
C>python xgrep.py _m _p 5\d\d\d\d\d --parent size fs.xml

foo.xml{Character Data}:000[563902]
foo.xml{Character Data}:00[502833]9
foo.xml{Character Data}:000[546074]
foo.xml{Character Data}:00[502817]5
foo.xml{Character Data}:001[560288]
foo.xml{Character Data}:002[533053]
```

13.5 | Source Code for xFS

```
CD-ROM reference=13016.txt
"""
Convert the information about a filesystem or partial
filesystem to XML conforming to the xFS DTD.

XML Processing with Python
Sean Mc Grath
http://www.digitome.com
"""

import os,sys,glob,stat,time,copy
import string

def escape (s):
    """
    Convert XML special characters to
    their entity reference representations.
    """
    s = string.join (string.split (s,"<"),"&lt;")
    s = string.join (string.split (s,"&"),"&amp;")
    return s

    def xFS (spec,indent=1):
    """
```

```
    Given a directory specification, generate XML from file
    information.
    Recursively process subdirectories.
    """
    for f in glob.glob (spec):
        # Pick up information about the file.
        o = os.stat(f)
        # The mode value can be used to determine if this
        # is a directory.
        mode = o[stat.ST_MODE]
        if stat.S_ISDIR(mode):
            # Output dir start-tag indented.
            print "%s<dir>" % (" "*indent,)
        else:
            # Output file start-tag indented.
            print "%s<file>" % (" "*indent,)
        # Output file/directory name.
        print "%s <name>%s</name>" % (" "*indent,
        escape(f))
        if not stat.S_ISDIR(mode):
            # print size(in bytes) only for files.
            print "%s <size>%010d</size>" % (
                " " *indent, o[stat.ST_SIZE])
        # Print modification time.
        print "%s <mod>%s</mod>" % (
            " "*indent,
            time.ctime(o[stat.ST_CTIME]))
        if stat.S_ISDIR(mode):
            # Recurse for subdirectories.
            xFS (f+"\*",indent+2)
        if stat.S_ISDIR(mode):
            # Output dir end-tag indented.
            print "%s</dir>" % (" "*indent,)
        else:
            # Output file end-tag indented.
            print "%s</file>" % (" "*indent,)

if __name__ == "__main__":
    if len(sys.argv)==1:
        # Default to current directory.
        print '<?xml version="1.0"?>'
        print '<!DOCTYPE xFS SYSTEM "xFS.dtd">'
        print "<xFS>\n<pattern>.\*</pattern>"
        xFS (".\*")
        print "</xFS>"
    else:
```

```
# Process path specified on command line.
print '<?xml version="1.0"?>'
print '<!DOCTYPE xFS SYSTEM "xFS.dtd">'
print "<xFS>\n<pattern>%s</pattern>" % (
sys.argv[1],)
xFS (sys.argv[1])
print "</xFS>"
```

xMail: E-mail as XML

E- mail is a good example of a structured text format that can usefully be converted to XML for processing, archiving, and searching. In this chapter, we develop `xMail`–a Python application to convert e-mail to XML.

It is an unfortunate fact of life that e-mail systems differ in the way they store e-mail. Some store it in proprietary binary formats. The two e-mail notations we deal with in this chapter (Unix mbox and Eudora) are, thankfully, text based. On Linux, e-mail messages are stored so that each message begins with `From:`. If that sequence of characters happens to occur within the body of a message, it is escaped by being prefixed with a > character. The Eudora e-mail client begins each message with a sentinel string of the form `From ???@???`.

Although there are differences in the way Linux and Eudora store e-mail messages, there is a lot of commonality we can exploit in the conversion code. In particular, we can take advantage of the Python standard `rfc822` module to do most of the work in parsing e-mail headers.

14.1 | The rfc822 Module

The term rfc822 refers to the standard for the header information used in Internet e-mail messages. The full specification can be found at http://www.ietf.org/rfcs/rfc0822.txt. The bulk of rfc822 is concerned with specifying the syntax for the headers that accompany the body of e-mail messages; headers such as from, to, subject, and so on. Python's rfc822 module takes a file object and puts as much of the content as it can parse into headers, according to the rules of rfc822.

The following program illustrates how the rfc822 module is used.

```
CD-ROM reference=14001.txt
"""
Simple program to illustrate use of Python's rfc822 module

"""

import rfc822,StringIO

email = """To: sean@digitome.com
From: paul@digitome.com
Subject: Parsing e-mail headers
Reply-To: Majordomo@allrealgood.com
Message-Id: <199902051120.EAA14648@digitome.com>

Sean,

Can Python parse this?

regards,
Paul
"""
fo =StringIO.StringIO(email)
m = rfc822.Message (fo)
print "<headers>"
for (k,v) in m.items():
      print "<%s>%s</%s>" % (k,v,k)
print "</headers>"
print "<body>"
print fo.read()
print "</body>"
```

The result of running this program is shown below.

```
CD-ROM reference=14002.txt
<headers>
<subject>Parsing e-mail headers</subject>
<from>paul@digitome.com</from>
<message-id><199902051120.EAA14648@digitome.com></message-id>
<reply-to>paul@digitome.com</reply-to>
<to>sean@digitome.com</to>
</headers>
<body>
Sean,

Can Python parse this?

regards,
Paul

</body>
```

14.2 | A Simple DTD for E-mail

Before going any further with parsing Linux or Eudora mailboxes, we need to settle on an XML representation of a mailbox. We will use the following simple DTD.

```
CD-ROM reference=14003.txt
<!--
XMail = A simple DTD for a collection of e-mail messages

An xMail file consists of zero or more message elements.

A message has a headers element that contains fields such as
from, to, subject, and so on. The body element houses
the text of the e-mail
-->

<!ELEMENT xmail    (message)*>
<!ELEMENT message (headers,body)>
<!ELEMENT headers (field)+>
```

```
<!ELEMENT field     (name,value)>
<!ELEMENT name      (#PCDATA)>
<!ELEMENT value     (#PCDATA)>
<!ELEMENT body      (#PCDATA)>
```

14.3 | An Example of an E-mail Message in XML

Here is an example of an e-mail message that conforms to the xMail DTD.

```
CD-ROM reference=14004.txt
<?xml version="1.0"?>
<!DOCTYPE xmail SYSTEM "xmail.dtd">
<xmail>
<message>
<headers>
<field>
<name>subject</name>
<value>Greetings</value>
</field>
</headers>
<body>
Hello World
</body>
</message>
</xmail>
```

14.4 | Processing a Eudora Mailbox

The following code fragment shows the control structure required to process a Eudora mailbox into individual e-mail messages. The processing of each message has been delegated to the ProcessMessage function. This function is used by both the Linux and Eudora converters. Note how the sentinel string "From ???@???" is used to chop the contents of the mailbox into individual messages.

```
CD-ROM reference=14005.txt
def DoEudoraMailbox(f):
     # f is a file object.
     # Chop the contents of a Eudora mailbox
     # into individual messages for processing
     # by the ProcessMessage subroutine.
     Message = []
     L = f.readline()
     while L:
          if string.find(L,"From ???@???")!=-1:
               # Full message accumulated in the Message
               # list, so process it to XML.
               ProcessMessage(Message,out)
               Message = []
          else:
               # Accumulate e-mail contents line by line in
               # Message list.
               Message.append (L)
          L = f.readline()
     if Message:
          # Last message in the mailbox
          ProcessMessage(Message,out)
```

14.5 | Processing a Linux Mailbox

To process a Linux-style mailbox into individual messages, a different control structure is required. Note, however, that the processing of each individual e-mail is handled by ProcessMessage, which is common to both Linux and Eudora converters.

```
CD-ROM reference=14006.txt
DoLinuxMailBox(f):
     # f is a file object.
     L = f.readline()[:-1]
     if string.find(L,"From ")!=0:
          print 'Expected mailbox "%s" to start with "From
          "' % MailBox
          return
     Message = []
     L = f.readline()
     while L:
```

```
            if string.find(L,"From ")==0:
                # Full message accumulated in the Message
                # list, so process it to XML
                ProcessMessage(Message,out)
                Message = []
        else:
                # Accumulate e-mail contents line by line in
                # Message list.
                Message.append (L)
        L = f.readline()
    if Message:
        # Last message in the mailbox
        ProcessMessage(Message,out)
```

14.6 | Processing an E-mail Message by Using the rfc822 Module

The two functions DoLinuxMailBox and DoEudoraMailBox chop up mailboxes into individual messages that are processed by the ProcessMessage function. This function uses the rfc822 module to separate the headers from the body of the message.

```
CD-ROM reference=14007.txt
def ProcessMessage(lines,out):
    """

    Given the lines that make up an e-mail message,
    create an XML message element. Uses the rfc822
    module to parse the e-mail headers.
    """
    out.write("<message>\n")
    # Create a single string from these lines.
    MessageString = string.joinfields(lines,"")
    # Create a file object from the string for use
    # by the rfc822 module.
    fo = StringIO.StringIO(MessageString)
    m = rfc822.Message (fo)
    # The m object now contains all the headers.
    # The headers can be accessed as a Python dictionary.
    out.write("<headers>\n")
    for (h,v) in m.items():
```

```
            out.write("<field>\n")
            out.write("<name>%s</name>\n" % XMLEscape(h))
            out.write("<value>%s</value>\n" % XMLEscape(v))
            out.write("</field>\n")
        out.write("</headers>\n")
        out.write("<body>\n")
        out.write(XMLEscape(fo.read()))
        out.write("</body>\n")
        out.write("</message>\n")
```

Time to illustrate the program in action. The -l (Linux) or -e (Eudora) command-line switch tells the program what type of mailbox to process.

Here is a small Eudora mailbox.

```
CD-ROM reference=14008.txt
```

C>**type test.mbx**

```
From ???@??? Mon Sep 06 14:07:14 1999
To: sean@p13
From: Sean Mc Grath <sean@digitome.com>
Subject: Hello
Cc:
Bcc:
X-Attachments:
In-Reply-To:
References:
X-Eudora-Signature: <Standard>

World

From ???@??? Mon Sep 06 14:07:31 1999
To: sean@p13
From: Sean Mc Grath <sean@digitome.com>
Subject: Message 2
Cc:
Bcc:
X_Attachments:
In-Reply-To:
References:
X-Eudora-Signature: <Standard>
```

```
Hello

From ???@??? Mon Sep 06 14:13:41 1999
To: sean@p13
From: Sean Mc Grath <sean@digitome.com>
Subject: Message 2
Cc:
Bcc:
X-Attachments:
In-Reply-To:
References:
X-Eudora-Signature: <Standard>

From sean@digitome.com

Hello
```

The file can be converted to XML as follows.

CD-ROM reference=14009.txt

C>**python xmail.py -e test.mbx**

```
<?xml version="1.0"?>
<!DOCTYPE xmail SYSTEM "xmail.dtd">
<xmail>
<message>
<headers>
<field>
<name>subject</name>
<value>Hello</value>
</field>
<field>
<name>references</name>
<value></value>
</field>
<field>
<name>bcc</name>
<value></value>
</field>
<field>
<name>x-attachments</name>
<value></value>
</field>
<field>
```

```xml
<name>cc</name>
<value></value>
</field>
<field>
<name>in-reply-to</name>
<value></value>
</field>
<field>
<name>x-eudora-signature</name>
<value>&lt;Standard></value>
</field>
<field>
<name>from</name>
<value>Sean Mc Grath &lt;sean@digitome.com></value>
</field>
<field>
<name>to</name>
<value>sean@p13</value>
</field>
</headers>
<body>
World

</body>
</message>
<message>
<headers>
<field>
<name>subject</name>
<value>Message 2</value>
</field>
<field>
<name>references</name>
<value></value>
</field>
<field>
<name>bcc</name>
<value></value>
</field>
<field>
<name>x-attachments</name>
<value></value>
</field>
<field>
<name>cc</name>
<value></value>
```

```
</field>
<field>
<name>in-reply-to</name>
<value></value>
</field>
<field>
<name>x-eudora-signature</name>
<value>&lt;Standard></value>
</field>
<field>
<name>from</name>
<value>Sean Mc Grath &lt;sean@digitome.com></value>
</field>
<field>
<name>to</name>
<value>sean@p13</value>
</field>
</headers>
<body>
Hello

</body>
</message>
<message>
<headers>
<field>
<name>subject</name>
<value>Message 2</value>
</field>
<field>
<name>references</name>
<value></value>
</field>
<field>
<name>bcc</name>
<value></value>
</field>
<field>
<name>x-attachments</name>
<value></value>
</field>
<field>
<name>cc</name>
<value></value>
</field>
<field>
```

```
<name>in-reply-to</name>
<value></value>
</field>
<field>
<name>x-eudora-signature</name>
<value>&lt;Standard></value>
</field>
<field>
<name>from</name>
<value>Sean Mc Grath &lt;sean@digitome.com></value>
</field>
<field>
<name>to</name>
<value>sean@p13</value>
</field>
</headers>
<body>
From sean@digitome.com

Hello

</body>
</message>
</xmail>
```

   Notice how the & character has been escaped to & whenever it occurs in a header or the body of an e-mail message.
   Here is a small, Linux-style mailbox.

```
CD-ROM reference=14010.txt
```

$cat test

```
From sean@digitome.com  Mon Sep  6 13:58:36 1999
Return-Path: <sean@digitome.com>
Received: from gateway ([100.100.100.105])
        by p13.digitome.com (8.9.3/8.8.7) with SMTP id NAA07403
        for <sean@p13>; Mon, 6 Sep 1999 13:58:36 GMT
Message-Id: <3.0.6.32.19990906140714.009b0ac0@p13>
X-Sender: sean@p13
X-Mailer: QUALCOMM Windows Eudora Light Version 3.0.6 (32)
Date: Mon, 06 Sep 1999 14:07:14 +0100
To: sean@p13.digitome.com
From: Sean Mc Grath <sean@digitome.com>
Subject: Hello
```

```
Mime-Version: 1.0
Content-Type: text/plain; charset="us-ascii"

World

From sean@digitome.com  Mon Sep  6 13:58:53 1999
Return-Path: <sean@digitome.com>
Received: from gateway ([100.100.100.105])
        by p13.digitome.com (8.9.3/8.8.7) with SMTP id NAA07407
        for <sean@p13>; Mon, 6 Sep 1999 13:58:52 GMT
Message-Id: <3.0.6.32.19990906140731.009b6a40@p13>
X-Sender: sean@p13
X-Mailer: QUALCOMM Windows Eudora Light Version 3.0.6 (32)
Date: Mon, 06 Sep 1999 14:07:31 +0100
To: sean@p13.digitome.com
From: Sean Mc Grath <sean@digitome.com>
Subject: Message 2
Mime-Version: 1.0
Content-Type: text/plain; charset="us-ascii"

Hello
```

It can be converted to XML with the following command.

```
CD-ROM reference=14011.txt
```

$**python xmail.py -l test**

```
<?xml version="1.0"?>
<!DOCTYPE xmail SYSTEM "xmail.dtd">
<xmail>
<message>
<headers>
<field>
<name>subject</name>
<value>Hello</value>
</field>
<field>
<name>x-sender</name>
<value>sean@p13</value>
</field>
<field>
<name>x-mailer</name>
<value>QUALCOMM Windows Eudora Light Version 3.0.6 (32)</value>
</field>
<field>
<name>content-type</name>
```

```
<value>text/plain; charset="us-ascii"</value>
</field>
<field>
<name>message-id</name>
<value>&lt;3.0.6.32.19990906140714.009b0ac0@p13></value>
</field>
<field>
<name>to</name>
<value>sean@p13.digitome.com</value>
</field>
<field>
<name>date</name>
<value>Mon, 06 Sep 1999 14:07:14 +0100</value>
</field>
<field>
<name>mime-version</name>
<value>1.0</value>
</field>
<field>
<name>return-path</name>
<value>&lt;sean@digitome.com></value>
</field>
<field>
<name>from</name>
<value>Sean Mc Grath &lt;sean@digitome.com></value>
</field>
<field>
<name>received</name>
<value>from gateway ([100.100.100.105])
 by p13.digitome.com (8.9.3/8.8.7) with SMTP id NAA07403
 for &lt;sean@p13>; Mon, 6 Sep 1999 13:58:36 GMT</value>
</field>
</headers>
<body>
World

</body>
</message>
<message>
<headers>
<field>
<name>subject</name>
<value>Message 2</value>
</field>
<field>
<name>x-sender</name>
<value>sean@p13</value>
```

```
</field>
<field>
<name>x-mailer</name>
<value>QUALCOMM Windows Eudora Light Version 3.0.6 (32)</value>
</field>
<field>
<name>content-type</name>
<value>text/plain; charset="us-ascii"</value>
</field>
<field>
<name>message-id</name>
<value>&lt;3.0.6.32.19990906140731.009b6a40@p13></value>
</field>
<field>
<name>to</name>
<value>sean@p13.digitome.com</value>
</field>
<field>
<name>date</name>
<value>Mon, 06 Sep 1999 14:07:31 +0100</value>
</field>
<field>
<name>mime-version</name>
<value>1.0</value>
</field>
<field>
<name>return-path</name>
<value>&lt;sean@digitome.com></value>
</field>
<field>
<name>from</name>
<value>Sean Mc Grath &lt;sean@digitome.com></value>
</field>
<field>
<name>received</name>
<value>from gateway ([100.100.100.105])
 by p13.digitome.com (8.9.3/8.8.7) with SMTP id NAA07407
 for &lt;sean@p13>; Mon, 6 Sep 1999 13:58:52 GMT</value>
</field>
</headers>
<body>
Hello

</body>
</message>
</xmail>
```

14.7 | Sending E-mail by Using xMail

Having converted the e-mail to XML, we can process it in a variety of ways by using any XML-aware databases, editors, search engines, and so on. We can contemplate processing them with Python by using Pyxie or SAX- or DOM-style processing. One useful form of processing would be to send e-mail from this XML notation. In this section, we develop a Pyxie application, `sendxMail`, to do that.

Sending e-mail to a group of people at the same time is common, so we start by defining an XML notation for a mailing list. Here is a sample document conforming to a `contacts` DTD.

```
CD-ROM reference=14012.txt
<!DOCTYPE contacts SYSTEM "contacts.dtd">
<contacts>
<contact>
<name>Neville Bagnall</name>
<email>neville@digitome.com</email>
</contact>
<contact>
<name>Noel Duffy</name>
<email>noel@digitome.com</email>
</contact>
<contact>
<name>Sean Mc Grath</name>
<email>sean@digitome.com</email>
</contact>
</contacts>
```

The DTD for this is, of course, trivial.

```
CD-ROM reference=14013.txt

C>type contacts.dtd

<!--

Trivial DTD for a mailing list

-->
```

```
<!ELEMENT contacts (contact)*>
<!ELEMENT contact (name,email)>
<!ELEMENT name (#PCDATA)>
<!ELEMENT email (#PCDATA)>
```

The full source code for sendxMail is given at the end of this chapter. The program uses the smtplib Python standard library. This library allows Python programs to send e-mail messages by talking to an SMTP server. Here is a small test program that illustrates how the smtplib module works.

```
CD-ROM reference=14014.txt
"""
Small test program to illustrate Python's standard smtplib library
"""
import smtplib

SMTPServer = "gpo.iol.ie"

#Create an SMTP server object.
server = smtplib.SMTP (SMTPServer)

#Turn debugging on.
server.set_debuglevel(1)

# Send an e-mail. First argument is the sender. Second argument
# is a list of recepients. Third argument is the text of the
# message.
server.sendmail (
  "From:sean@digitome.com",
  ["paul@digitome.com"],
  "Hello World")
```

To execute this program, change SMPTServer to point to a suitable SMTP server. The program will produce a lot of output because debugging has been turned on. The abridged output from an execution of this program is shown here.

```
CD-ROM reference=14015.txt

send: 'ehlo GATEWAY\015\012'
reply: '250-gpo2.mail.iol.ie Hello dialup-024.ballina.iol.ie
```

```
[194.125.48.152], pleased to meet you\015\012'
reply: retcode (250); Msg: gpo2.mail.iol.ie Hello dialup_
  024.ballina.iol.ie
[194.125.48.152], pleased to meet you
send: 'mail FROM:<sean@digitome.com> size=11\015\012'
reply: '250 <sean@digitome.com>... Sender ok\015\012'
reply: retcode (250); Msg: <sean@digitome.com>... Sender ok
send: 'rcpt TO:<paul@digitome.com>\015\012'
reply: '250 <paul@digitome.com>... Recipient ok\015\012'
reply: retcode (250); Msg: <paul@digitome.com>... Recipient ok
send: 'data \015\012'
reply: '354 Enter mail, end with "." on a line by itself\
  015\012'
reply: retcode (354); Msg: Enter mail, end with "." on a line
  by itself
data: (354, 'Enter mail, end with "." on a line by itself')
send: 'Hello World'
send: '\015\012.\015\012'
reply: '250 QAA03299 Message accepted for delivery\015\012'
reply: retcode (250); Msg: QAA03299 Message accepted for
  delivery
data: (250, 'QAA03299 Message accepted for delivery')
```

To execute `sendxMail`, you provide it with four parameters:

- The e-mail address of the sender.

- The XML document containing the list of recepients. This file should conform to the contacts DTD.

- The e-mail message document. This document should conform to the xMail DTD.

- The name of the SMTP server to use.

A sample invocation is shown below.

```
CD-ROM reference=14016.txt
C>python sendxMail.py sean@digitome.com PyxieList.xml
  Welcome.xml gpo.iol.ie
```

14.8 | Source Code for the SendxMail Application

```
CD-ROM reference=14017.txt
"""
sendxMail
XML Processing with Python
Sean Mc Grath

Send e-mail over the Internet to a group of e-mail accounts,
using the xmail XML representation.

The program connects to the specified SMTP server and uses
Python's smtplib library.

The list of addresses in also in XML.

A simple message file looks like this:

<xmail>
<message>
<headers>
 <field><name>subject</name><value>Greetings</value></field>
</headers>
<body>
Hello World
</body>
</message>
</xmail>


A simple address file looks like this:

<contacts>
 <contact>
  <name>Neville Bagnall</name>
  <email>neville@digitome.com</email>
 </contact>
</contacts>


Sample invocation:
      python sendxmail.py sean@digitome.com contacts.xml
        email.xml
gpo.iol.ie
"""
```

```python
import smtplib
from pyxie import *

# Class uses event-driven XML processing style to send messages
# one at a time and so inherits from xDispatch.
class xMailSender(xDispatch):
    def __init__(self,Sender,MailingListFile,MessageFile,
      SMTPServer):
        # PYX source for later event dispatching is the
        # message file
        xDispatch.__init__(self,File2PYX(MessageFile)).
        # The Gathered variable is used to gather characters
        # arriving in the data handler method between certain
        # start- and end-tags.
        self.Gathered = []
        self.Sender = Sender
        self.Addresses = []
        self.MessageFile = MessageFile
        # Accumulated message header
        self.MessageHeader = ""
        # Accumulated message body
        self.MessageText = ""

        self.Recepients = []
        self.server = smtplib.SMTP( SMTPServer )
        self.server.set_debuglevel(1)

        # Use tree-processing style to assemble list of
        # recipients.
        T = File2Tree(self.MessageListFile)
        for n in T:
            T.Seek(n)
            if T.AtElement("email"):
                email = T.JoinData(" ")
                self.Addresses.append(email)

            # Invoke event dispatching to handler methods
            # PYX source is the message file.
            self.Dispatch()

    def start_body(self,etn,attrs):
        # Reset gathered data for each message body.
        self.Gathered = []
    def end_body(self,etn,attrs):
        # Save gathered data as message body.
        self.messageText = string.join(self.Gathered)
```

```python
    def start_name(self,etn,attrs):
        # Reset gathered data for each name element.
        self.Gathered = []
    def start_value(self,etn,attrs):
        # Reset gathered data for each value element.
        self.Gathered = []
    def end_name(self,etn):
        # Save gathered data as header field
        # recipient name.
        self.fieldname = string.join(self.Gathered)

    def end_value(self,etn):
        # Save gathered data as header field value.
        self.fieldvalue = string.join(self.
          Gathered)
        # Add the new name/value pair to the end of
        # the message header.
        self.MessageHeader = self.MessageHeader +
        self.fieldname + ": " + self.fieldvalue + "\n"
    def characters(self,str):
        # Handler for character data. Accumulate
        # data in the Gathered variable. Various
        # end-tag handlers copy out the accumulated
        # contents as needed.
        self.Gathered.append (PYXDecoder(str))
    def end_body(self,etn):
        # At this point, we have everything we need
        # to send e-mail.
        self.MessageText = string.join (self
          .Gathered)
        self.server.sendmail (self.Sender,
        self.Addresses, self.MessageHeader+"\n"+
          self.MessageText )
        # Close down the SMTP connection.
        self.server.quit()


if __name__ == '__main__':
    import sys
    if len(sys.argv)==1:
        xMailSender ("sean@digitome.com",
                     "contacts.xml",
                     "email.xml",
                     "gpo.iol.ie")
    else:
        xMailSender (sys.argv[1],
                     sys.argv[2],
```

```
                    sys.argv[3],
                    sys.argv[4])
```

14.9 | Source Code for the xMail Application

CD-ROM reference=14018.txt

```
"""
xMail
Convert mailboxes to a simple XML form for
e-mail messages.

XML Processing with Python
Sean Mc Grath

The Eudora e-mail client stores e-mail messages in mailboxes.
The file format is plain text. Individual messages are sepa-
rated by the string "From ???@???".

This program processes a mailbox creating an XML file
that conforms to the xmail DTD.

"""
# Import some standard modules
# rfc822 is the module for e_mail header parsing
import string,rfc822,StringIO

LINUX  = 0
EUDORA = 1
def XMLEscape(s):
        """
        Escape XMLs two special characters which may
        occur within an e-mail message.
        """

        s = string.replace(s,"&","&amp;")
        s = string.replace(s,"<","&lt;")
        return s

def ProcessMessage(lines,out):
```

```
    """
    Given the lines that make up an e-mail message,
    create an XML message element. Uses the rfc822
    module to parse the e_mail headers.
    """
    out.write("<message>\n")
    # Create a single string from these lines.
    MessageString = string.joinfields(lines,"")
    # Create a file object from the string for use
    # by the rfc822 module.
    fo = StringIO.StringIO(MessageString)
    m = rfc822.Message (fo)
    # The m object now contains all the headers.
    # The headers can be accessed as a Python dictionary.
    out.write("<headers>\n")
    for (h,v) in m.items():
        out.write("<field>\n")
        out.write("<name>%s</name>\n" % XMLEscape(h))
        out.write("<value>%s</value>\n" % XMLEscape(v))
        out.write("</field>\n")
    out.write("</headers>\n")
    out.write("<body>\n")
    out.write(XMLEscape(fo.read()))
    out.write("</body>\n")
    out.write("</message>\n")

def DoEudoraMailBox(MailBox):
    """
    Given a Eudora mailbox, convert its contents to XML
    conforming to the xmail DTD.
    """
    f = open (MailBox,"r")
    l = f.readline()[:_1]
    if string.find(l,"From ???@???")==_1:
        # Sentinel that separates e-mail messages in the
        # Eudora mbx notation.
        print 'Expected mailbox "%s"' % MailBox,
        Print 'to start with "From ???@???"'

        return
    if MailBox[-4:] != ".mbx":
        print "Expected mailbox to have .mbx file
            extension", MailBox
        return
    # Output file has same base name but .xml extension.
    out = open(MailBox[:-3]+"xml","w")
```

```python
    out.write ('<?xml version="1.0"?>\n')
    out.write ('<!DOCTYPE xmail SYSTEM "xmail.dtd">\n')
    out.write ('<xmail>\n')
    Message = []
    l = f.readline()
    while l:
        if string.find(l,"From ???@???")!=-1:
            # Full message accumulated in the Message list,
            # so process it to XML.
            ProcessMessage(Message,out)
            Message = []
        else:
            # Accumulate e-mail contents line by line in
            # Message list.
            Message.append (l)
        l = f.readline()
    if Message:
        # Last message in the mailbox
        ProcessMessage(Message,out)
    out.write ('</xmail>\n')
    f.close()
    out.close()

def DoLinuxMailBox(MailBox):
    """
    Given a Unix mbox style mailbox, convert its contents
    to XML conforming to the xmail DTD.
    """
    f = open (MailBox,"r")
    l = f.readline()[:_1]
    if string.find(l,"From ")!=0:
        print 'Expected mailbox "%s" to start with "From
        "' % MailBox
        return
    # Output file has same name as mailbox but with ".xml" added.
    out = open(MailBox+".xml","w")
    out.write ('<?xml version="1.0"?>\n')
    out.write ('<!DOCTYPE xmail SYSTEM "xmail.dtd">\n')
    out.write ('<xmail>\n')
    Message = []
    l = f.readline()
    while l:
        if string.find(l,"From ")==0:
            # Full message accumulated in the Message list,
            # so process it to XML.
            ProcessMessage(Message,out)
```

```
                    Message = []
            else:
                    # Accumulate e_mail contents line by line in
                    # Message list.
                    Message.append (l)
            l = f.readline()
    if Message:
            # Last message in the mailbox
            ProcessMessage(Message,out)
    out.write ('</xmail>\n')
    f.close()
    out.close()

if __name__=="__main__":
    import sys,getopt
    format = LINUX
    (options,remainder) = getopt.getopt (sys.argv[1:],"le")
    for (option,value) in options:
            if option == "-l":
                    format = LINUX
            elif option == "-e":
                    format = EUDORA
    if len(remainder)!=1:
            print "Usage: %s -l|-e mailbox" % sys.argv[0]
            sys.exit()
    if format==EUDORA:
            DoEudoraMailBox(remainder[0])
    elif format==LINUX:
            DoLinuxMailBox(remainder[0])
```

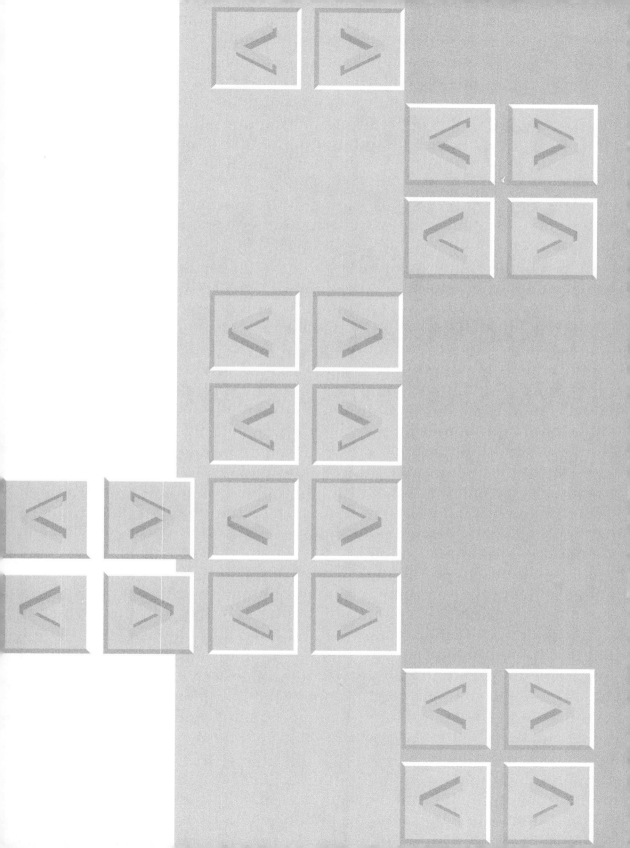

xMySQL: Relational Database Harvesting with Python SAX

Relational database technology is a well-established, proven technique for dealing with large volumes of rigidly structured data. In this chapter, we develop a simple but powerful, general-purpose database-harvesting utility, using Python SAX.

Python has interfaces to many database systems and APIs such as Oracle®, ODBC, DBM, and so on. In this chapter, we will use a relational database system known as MySQL.

15.1 | Installing MySQL

MySQL is a powerful, Internet-based, multiuser, relational database system with SQL support, developed by T.c.X AB in Sweden. It is freely available for Unix platforms. For Microsoft platforms, a nominal license is payable after a 30-day evaluation period. For your convenience, MySQL distributions for Linux and Windows are available on the CD-ROM. For the latest information and licensing details, please consult `http://www.mysql.com`.

Windows On the CD-ROM, you will find `mysql-shareware-win32-1-1.zip`. Unzip the contents of this zip file into a temporary directory, and then execute `setup.exe`. The software is always installed in the directory `\mysql`. All the executable programs live in the directory `\mysql\bin`. You might like to add this directory to your path. ■

Linux On the CD-ROM you will find `MySQL-3.22.25-1.i386.rpm` and `MySQL-client-3.22.25-1.i386.rpm`. These are the server and client parts of MySQL. Install these RPMs in the normal fashion. Non-Linux users will find MySQL distributions for many Unix platforms on `http://www.mysql.com` and its mirror sites. ■

15.2 | Testing the MySQL Installation

MySQL is a client/server system. The server side is called `mysqld`. This application must be running in order for the client side program `mysql` to work. On Linux, you can simply type `mysqld` to start the server process. On Windows, the simplest way to run the server is to type `mysqld --standalone` from a command window. On NT, the server can be installed as a service by typing `mysqld --install`.

From a command window, execute the command `mysql`. You should see something like the following.

```
CD-ROM reference=15001.txt
Welcome to the MySQL monitor.  Commands end with ; or \g.
Your MySQL connection id is 1 to server version:
3.21.29a_gamma_debug

Type 'help' for help.

mysql>
```

If you see the message, you have succesfully connected to the MySQL server. If not, please consult the installation guides available on `http://www.mysql.com` and mirror sites. Troubleshooting information is also available on `http://www.pyxie.org`.

The server can be shut down as follows:

```
CD-ROM reference=15002.txt
C>mysqladmin shutdown
```

If you are using Windows NT and have installed `mysqld` as a service, it will automatically load whenever you reboot the machine.

15.3 | Installing the Python Interface to MySQL

On the CD-ROM, you will find `MySQL.pyd` and windows `lib-mySQL.dll`. Copy these into some suitable location. I keep `MySQL.pyd` in my `python\lib` directory and `libmySQL.dll` in my `python\DLLS` directory. **Windows**

On the CD-ROM, you will find `MySQLdb-0.0.3.tar.gz`. This Python interface to MySQL is the work of Andy Dustman (`http://starship.python.net/crew/adustman/MySQLdb .html`). Extract the contents of the archive and execute the `build.py` script. **Linux**

15.4 | Testing the Python Interface to MySQL

We use the following simple MySQL program to prove that the Python MySQL interface is up and running.

```
CD-ROM reference=15003.txt
C>type testmysql.py


"""
Program to test Python interface to MySQL
"""
```

```
import MySQL

# Connect to MySQL.
db=MySQL.connect('','')

# Select the mysql database. This database is
# always available in a MySQL system.
db.selectdb("mysql")

# Retrieve a list of tables in that database.
query = db.query("show tables")

# Retrieve the rows that make up the query result.
rows=query.fetchrows()

# Print them out.
print rows
```

The result of executing the program is shown below.

```
CD-ROM reference=15004.txt
C>python testmysql.py
[['db'], ['host'], ['user']]
```

15.5 | Mapping Relational Data to XML

Relational databases are made up of tables of data. Each table row is known as a record. A record is made up of a fixed set of fields that can be of various types such as string, date, integer, and so on.

It is straightforward to map the tabular structure of relational database tables into XML. The simplest mapping is achieved when a table maps to a `table` element that can contain zero or more `record` elements. Each `record` element will contain zero or more `field` elements.

Let us create a simple database in MySQL. We will then develop a simple mapping to XML for arbitrary MySQL tables.

Create a new database called `shoeinfo` as follows.

```
CD-ROM reference=15005.txt
mysql> create database shoeinfo;
Query OK, 1 row affected (0.03 sec)
mysql> use shoeinfo
Database changed
```

The next thing to do is to create a table. We will create three fields: FirstName, LastName, and ShoeSize. Both FirstName and LastName will be strings of length 30. ShoeSize will be an integer. Here is the statement that creates this table with mySQL.

```
CD-ROM reference=15006.txt
mysql> create table people (FirstName CHAR(20),
 LastName CHAR(20),
 ShoeSize INT);

Query OK, 0 rows affected (0.05 sec)

mysql> describe people;
+------------+----------+------+-----+---------+-------+
| Field      | Type     | Null | Key | Default | Extra |
+------------+----------+------+-----+---------+-------+
| FirstName  | char(20) | YES  |     | NULL    |       |
| LastName   | char(20) | YES  |     | NULL    |       |
| ShoeSize   | int(11)  | YES  |     | NULL    |       |
+------------+----------+------+-----+---------+-------+
3 rows in set (0.01 sec)
```

Now, we need to add some records to the database. We can do this interactively as follows.

```
CD-ROM reference=15007.txt
mysql>  insert into people VALUES ("Sean","Mc Grath",14);
Query OK, 1 row affected (0.02 sec)

mysql> insert into people VALUES ("Noel","Duffy",9);
Query OK, 1 row affected (0.01 sec)

mysql> insert into people VALUES ("Neville","Bagnall",10);
Query OK, 1 row affected (0.01 sec)
```

Here is how to get a listing of the records in the people table.

```
CD-ROM reference=15008.txt
mysql> select * from people;
+-------------+-------------+-------------+
| FirstName   | LastName    | ShoeSize    |
+-------------+-------------+-------------+
| Sean        | Mc Grath    |         14  |
| Noel        | Duffy       |          9  |
| Neville     | Bagnall     |         10  |
+-------------+-------------+-------------+
3 rows in set (0.01 sec)
```

Viewing the data in different sort orders is trivial. Here are the records from the people table sorted in order of descending shoe size.

```
CD-ROM reference=15009.txt
mysql> select * from people order by ShoeSize DESC;
+-------------+-------------+-------------+
| FirstName   | LastName    | ShoeSize    |
+-------------+-------------+-------------+
| Sean        | Mc Grath    |         14  |
| Neville     | Bagnall     |         10  |
| Noel        | Duffy       |          9  |
+-------------+-------------+-------------+
3 rows in set (0.01 sec)
```

Selecting particular columns is also easy. Here is a list of first names, in ascending alphabetical order.

```
CD-ROM reference=15010.txt
mysql> select (FirstName) from people order by FirstName ASC;
+-------------+
| FirstName   |
+-------------+
| Neville     |
| Noel        |
| Sean        |
+-------------+
3 rows in set (0.01 sec)
```

The most straightforward way to map the outputs from these SQL select statements into XML is to treat the result as a series of rows containing one or more fields. Given the following query result,

```
CD-ROM reference=15011.txt
+_____+_____+_____+
| FirstName   | LastName   | ShoeSize   |
+_____+_____+_____+
| Sean        | Mc Grath   |         14 |
| Neville     | Bagnall    |         10 |
| Noel        | Duffy      |          9 |
+_____+_____+_____+
```

we can easily map it to the following XML form,

```
CD-ROM reference=15012.txt
<mysql>
 <row>
 <FirstName>Sean</FirstName>
 <LastName>Mc Grath</LastName>
 <ShowSize>14</ShowSize>
 </row>
 <row>
 <FirstName>Neville</FirstName>
 <LastName>Bagnall</LastName>
 <ShowSize>10</ShowSize>
 </row>
 <row>
 <FirstName>Noel</FirstName>
 <LastName>Duffy</LastName>
 <ShowSize>9</ShowSize>
 </row>
 </mysql>
```

and the DTD for this mapping is trivial, as you would expect:

```
CD-ROM reference=15013.txt
<!ELEMENT mysql (row)*>
<!ELEMENT row (FirstName,LastName,ShowSize)>
<!ELEMENT FirstName (#PCDATA)>
<!ELEMENT LastName (#PCDATA)>
<!ELEMENT ShowSize (#PCDATA)>
```

What we need now is a flexible way of converting the results of arbitrary SQL queries into an XML form such as this. One good way to do it is to make MySQL look like an XML parser as far as the SAX API is concerned.

15.6 | The Python SAX Driver Interface

In chapter 10, "Just Enough SAX," I mentioned that the SAX API caters to the needs of parser writers as well as application developers. One powerful and flexible way to map relational database data, such as MySQL to XML, is to use a driver program that makes MySQL look like just another XML parser from an application developer's perspective.

The idea is that a SAX application developer working with the DTD above should not know or care if the data is coming from MySQL or coming from a "real" XML document. The SAX driver concept gives us a natural point at which to plug MySQL into Python SAX. After all, a central design criterion for SAX was that it should be possible to swap parsers without any source changes at the application level.

To prove that we have achieved this goal of no changes at the application level, we will use the saxdemo.py application that ships with the Python XML package. Given a filename and a SAX driver to use, the program re-creates XML from the generated SAX events.

```
CD-ROM reference=15014.txt
C>type hello.xml


<?xml version="1.0"?>
<greeting>
Hello <b>World</b>
</greeting>


C>python saxdemo.py -dpyexpat hello.xml


Parser: pyexpat (Unknown, 0.10)


<greeting>&#10;Hello <b>World</b>&#10;</greeting>
```

If we specify the name of another XML parser with the -d switch, the application will use the named parser.

```
CD-ROM reference=15015.txt
C>python saxdemo.py -dxmlproc  \xpp\cdrom\hello.xml
<greeting>&#10;Hello <b>World</b>&#10;</greeting>
```

```
Parser: xmlproc (0.60, 0.93)

<greeting>&#10;Hello <b>World</b>&#10;</greeting>
```

15.7 | Implementing a SAX Driver for MySQL

A SAX driver must, at a minimum, provide an implementation of the `Parser` interface. It must also provide a function called `create _parser()` that returns an object that implements this interface.

The most important method that needs to be implemented is called `parse`. Given a system identifier as a parameter, the `parse` method should process the contents of the system identifier, calling the methods in the `Document` interface, such as `startDocument`, `startElement`, `characters`, and so on.

15.8 | A Template for SAX Drivers

In this section, we develop a template Python SAX driver called `template` that will illustrate the overall structure of a Python SAX driver. Once this template works, we will customize it for MySQL.

```
CD-ROM reference=15016.txt
C>type drv_template.py

"""
Python SAX template driver

"""

import sys,os,string
from xml.sax import saxlib,saxutils


# SAX_template
#_____
class SAX_template(saxlib.Parser):
```

```python
"""
Template implementation of a SAX parser driver
"""
def __init__(self):
    saxlib.Parser.__init__(self)

def parse(self,sysID):
    # Call the start of document handler.
    self.doc_handler.startDocument()

    # Start an element called template with no
    # attributes.
    self.doc_handler.startElement (
        "template",
        saxutils.AttributeMap({}))

    # Create some character introducing the
    # name of the system identifier.
    self.doc_handler.characters (
        "System identifier",
        0,
        len("System identifier"))

    # Start an element called sysid.
    self.doc_handler.startElement ("sysid",
                        saxutils.AttributeMap({}))

    # Character data for the system identifier
    self.doc_handler.characters (
        sysID,
        0,
        len(sysID))

    # End the open elements.
    self.doc_handler.endElement('sysid')
    self.doc_handler.endElement('template')

    # Call handler for end of document.
    self.doc_handler.endDocument()

def get_parser_name(self):
    # The name of this parser
    return "template"
```

```
    def get_parser_version(self):
        # The version of the parser
        return "1.0"

    def get_driver_version(self):
        # The version of the driver
        return "1.0"

    def is_validating(self):
        # This is not a validating driver.
        return 0

    def is_dtd_reading(self):
        # This does not read the DTD.
        return 0

# The create_parser method is called by the make_parser utility
# function in saxexts.
def create_parser():
    return SAX_template()
```

To use this driver, simply copy it into the `drivers` subdirectory of the SAX directory in the XML package.

The `saxdemo.py` application can now be used with this driver as shown here.

```
CD-ROM reference=15017.txt
```

```
C>python saxdemo.py -dtemplate foo.xml
Parser: template (1.0, 1.0)

<template>System identifier<sysid>foo.xml</sysid></template>
```

15.9 | The MySQL SAX Driver

Now that we have the overall structure of a working driver, we can flesh out the template to make it work with MySQL.

```
CD-ROM reference=15018.txt
C>type drv_mysql.py
```

```
" " "
```

```
MySQL SAX driver

Sean Mc Grath and Noel Duffy
XML Processing with Python
"""

import sys,os,string
import MySQL

from xml.sax import saxlib,saxutils

# SAX_MySQL
#_____
class SAX_MySQL(saxlib.Parser):
    """
    Implements the SAX parser interface for the MySQL
      relational database
    """
    def __init__(self):
        saxlib.Parser.__init__(self)
        self.db = None
        self.DatabaseName = None
        self.QueryExpression = None

    def parse(self,sysID):
        # User specifies a database and an SQL
        # expression separated by a space.
        if string.count (sysID," ") >= 1:
            first = string.find(sysID," ")
            self.DatabaseName = sysID[:first]
            self.QueryExpression = sysID[first+1:]
        else:
            raise SAXException ("
            Expected database name and SQL expression")

        # Connect to MySQL (default username and password).
        self.db=MySQL.connect('','')

        # Use the required database.
        self.db.selectdb(self.DatabaseName)

        # Call the startDocument SAX handler.
        self.doc_handler.startDocument()

        # Perform the query.
        qry = self.db.query(self.QueryExpression)
```

```
    # fields is a list of fields in each row.
    self.fields=qry.fields()
    # rows is a list of result rows
    rows=qry.fetchrows()
    # Start an element for "mysql" (no attributes).
    self.doc_handler.startElement (
        "mysql",
        saxutils.AttributeMap({}))
    for row in rows:
        # Start an element for each "row" (no attributes).
        self.doc_handler.startElement('row',saxutils.
          AttributeMap({}))
        for c in range(len(row)):
            # Start an element for each field.
            self.doc_handler.startElement(
                self.fields[c][0],
                saxutils.AttributeMap({}))
            # If the field type is not a string,
            # convert it to a string,
            # then call the characters SAX handler
            # with the string, offset (0)
            # and string length.
            if type(row[c]) != type(''):
                self.doc_handler.characters(
                    'row[c]',
                    0,
                    len('row[c]'))
            else:
                self.doc_handler.characters(
                    row[c],
                    0,
                    len(row[c]))
            self.doc_handler.endElement(
                self.fields[c][0])
        # Call SAX handler for end of element 'row'.
        self.doc_handler.endElement('row')

        # Call SAX handler for end of element 'mysql'.
    self.doc_handler.endElement("mysql")
    self.doc_handler.endDocument()

def get_parser_name(self):
    return "pyMySQL"

def get_parser_version(self):
    return "0.5"
```

```
    def get_driver_version(self):
        return "0.5"

    def is_validating(self):
        return 0

    def is_dtd_reading(self):
        return 0

# The create_parser method is called by the make_parser
# utility function in saxexts.
def create_parser():
    return SAX_MySQL()
```

To install this driver, simply copy it into the `drivers` subdirectory of the SAX directory in the XML package.

15.10 | Some Examples

To use the driver, we take some liberties with the parameter to `saxdemo.py`. Instead of a filename (system identifier), we provide it with the name of a MySQL database and a `select` statement.

Here is an example of a simple `select` statement operating against the `shoeinfo` database.

```
CD-ROM reference=15019.txt
```

```
C>python saxdemo.py -dmysql "shoeinfo select * from people"
Parser: pyMySQL (0.5, 0.5)

<mysql>
 <row>
  <FirstName>Sean</FirstName>
  <LastName>Mc Grath</LastName>
  <ShoeSize>14</ShoeSize>
 </row>
 <row>
  <FirstName>Noel</FirstName>
  <LastName>Duffy</LastName>
  <ShoeSize>9</ShoeSize>
```

```
 </row>
 <row>
  <FirstName>Neville</FirstName>
  <LastName>Bagnall</LastName>
  <ShoeSize>10</ShoeSize>
 </row>
</mysql>
```

With the full expressive power of SQL behind us, we can harvest information now from any MySQL database in a variety of sort orders. To create an XML file with the same information as above but sorted in ascending order of shoe size, we simply need to use a modified SQL select as shown here.

```
CD-ROM reference=15020.txt
C>python saxdemo.py -dmysql "shoeinfo select * from people
order by ShoeSize ASC"
Parser: pyMySQL (0.5, 0.5)

<mysql>
 <row>
  <FirstName>Noel</FirstName>
  <LastName>Duffy</LastName>
  <ShoeSize>9</ShoeSize>
 </row>
 <row>
  <FirstName>Neville</FirstName>
  <LastName>Bagnall</LastName>
  <ShoeSize>10</ShoeSize>
 </row>
 <row>
  <FirstName>Sean</FirstName>
  <LastName>Mc Grath</LastName>
  <ShoeSize>14</ShoeSize>
 </row>
</mysql>
```

Finally, here is an invocation that lists all people with shoe size greater than 9 in descending order by first name.

```
CD-ROM reference=15021.txt
C>python saxdemo.py -dmysql \
 "shoeinfo select * from people
```

```
    where ShoeSize > 9
    order by FirstName DESC"

Parser: pyMySQL (0.5, 0.5)

<mysql>
 <row>
  <FirstName>Sean</FirstName>
  <LastName>Mc Grath</LastName>
  <ShoeSize>14</ShoeSize>
 </row>
 <row>
  <FirstName>Neville</FirstName>
  <LastName>Bagnall</LastName>
  <ShoeSize>10</ShoeSize>
 </row>
</mysql>
```

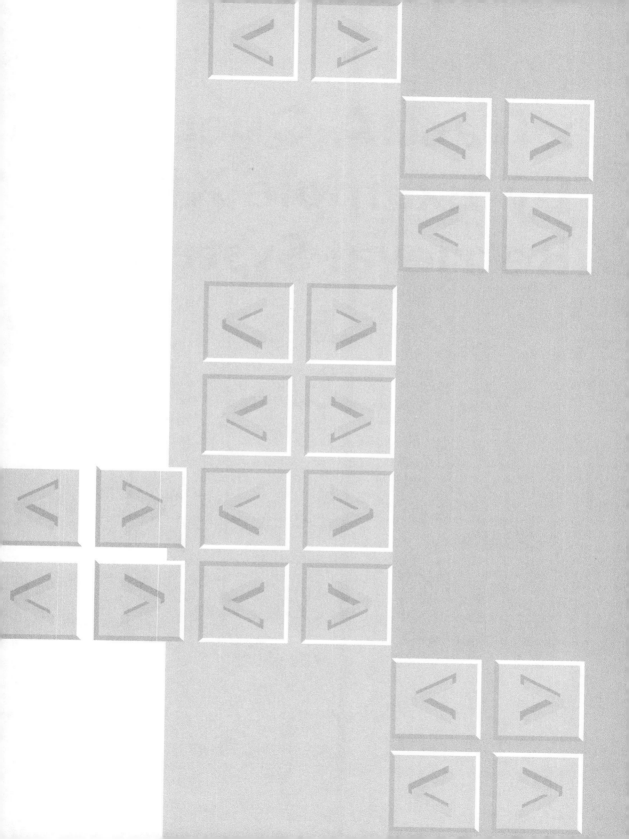

xTract: A Query-By-Example XML Retrieval System

I n this chapter, we develop xTract—a utility for retrieving fragments of XML files matching particular search criteria on the Web.

The user specifies a search *template* in a manner similar to Query-By-Example systems often used with relational databases.

An example will help make this clear. The web site http://www.slashdot.org publishes an XML file on their site that lists the main stories of the day. The geturl utility developed earlier can be used to retrieve this file.

```
CD-ROM reference=16001.txt
C>python geturl.py http://www.slashdot.org/slashdot.xml

<?xml version="1.0"?><backslash
xmlns:backslash="http://slashdot.org/backslash.dtd">

<story>
    <title>Doubleclick's Banner Ad Patent</title>
    <url>http://slashdot.org/articles/99/09/13/1950207
      .shtml</url>
    <time>1999_09_13 23:51:38</time>
    <author>CmdrTaco</author>
```

```
    <department>you_gotta_be_kidding_me</department>
    <topic>internet</topic>
    <comments>123</comments>
    <section>articles</section>
    <image>topicinternet.jpg</image>
  </story>
<story>
    <title>KDE 1.1.2 is out</title>
    <url>http://slashdot.org/articles/99/09/13/1928243
      .shtml</url>
    <time>1999_09_13 23:27:29</time>
    <author>HeUnique</author>
    <department>KDE_updates</department>
    <topic>kde</topic>
    <comments>169</comments>
    <section>articles</section>
    <image>topickde.gif</image>
  </story>
<story>
    <title>Talking with Matt Welsh</title>
    <url>http://slashdot.org/articles/99/09/13/1559245
      .shtml</url>
    <time>1999_09_13 22:01:51</time>
    <author>Hemos</author>
    <department>smart_smart_man</department>
    <topic>linux</topic>
    <comments>41</comments>
    <section>articles</section>
    <image>topiclinux.gif</image>
  </story>
<story>
    <title>Lego Mindstorms Controlled by Pilot Via JINI</title>
    <url>http://slashdot.org/articles/99/09/13/170257
      .shtml</url>
    <time>1999_09_13 21:04:14</time>
    <author>CmdrTaco</author>
    <department>stupid_pda_tricks</department>
    <topic>pilot</topic>
    <comments>121</comments>
    <section>articles</section>
    <image>topicpilot.gif</image>
  </story>
<story>
    <title>LinuxPPC unleashes LinuxPPC 1999 Q3</title>
    <url>http://slashdot.org/articles/99/09/13/1240212
      .shtml</url>
```

```
    <time>1999_09_13 20:43:11</time>
    <author>Hemos</author>
    <department>rolling_out_the_new</department>
    <topic>linux</topic>
    <comments>69</comments>
    <section>articles</section>
    <image>topiclinux.gif</image>
  </story>
<story>
    <title>On eBay Addiction</title>
    <url>http://slashdot.org/articles/99/09/13/1526243
       .shtml</url>
    <time>1999_09_13 19:31:09</time>
    <author>CmdrTaco</author>
    <department>stuff_to_read</department>
    <topic>humor</topic>
    <comments>84</comments>
    <section>articles</section>
    <image>topichumor.gif</image>
  </story>
<story>
    <title>Linux Lite?</title>
    <url>http://slashdot.org/articles/99/09/13/1019228
       .shtml</url>
    <time>1999_09_13 19:22:37</time>
    <author>Hemos</author>
    <department>security_issues_galore</department>
    <topic>linux</topic>
    <comments>142</comments>
    <section>articles</section>
    <image>topiclinux.gif</image>
  </story>
<story>
    <title>Why geek geniuses may lack social graces</title>
    <url>http://slashdot.org/articles/99/09/13/1223215
       .shtml</url>
    <time>1999_09_13 17:27:21</time>
    <author>Hemos</author>
    <department>it's_all_in_the_mind_if_you_wanna_test_me_i'm
       </department>
    <topic>science</topic>
    <comments>451</comments>
    <section>articles</section>
    <image>topicscience.gif</image>
  </story>
```

```
<story>
   <title>Kermit the Frog to promote V_Chip</title>
   <url>http://slashdot.org/articles/99/09/13/1210220
     .shtml</url>
   <time>1999_09_13 17:04:11</time>
   <author>Hemos</author>
   <department>no_destruction_of_an_icon</department>
   <topic>tv</topic>
   <comments>191</comments>
   <section>articles</section>
   <image>topictv.jpg</image>
  </story>
 <story>
   <title>Nokia brings out Linux Cellphone/TV/Browser</title>
   <url>http://slashdot.org/articles/99/09/13/1118246
     .shtml</url>
   <time>1999_09_13 16:08:18</time>
   <author>Hemos</author>
   <department>fun_with_new_technology</department>
   <topic>hardware</topic>
   <comments>129</comments>
   <section>articles</section>
   <image>topichardware.gif</image>
  </story>
</backslash>
```

16.1 | Expressing XML Queries

We would like to be able to batch-automate the retrieval of interesting stories from sites such as `http://www.slashdot.org`. We need some way of crisply expressing what fragments of an XML resource, such as the one above, are of interest to us.

Here is an example query expressed in English.

Find all stories in `http://www.slashdot.org/slashdot.xml` where:

- the title contains the word "Unix" or the word "Linux," and

- the story was published in 1999, and

- the story is in the "articles" section.

Here is an XML Query-By-Example search template, `interesting.xml`, that expresses this query. The idea is to use an XML fragment in which the element type names correspond to the element type names in the searched resource. The contents of these elements are interpreted as Python regular expressions. In the `title` element, the special | character has been used to express the query "Linux or Unix." In the `time` element, the special ^ character has been used to restrict matches of the string "1999" to those beginning at the start of a line.

```
CD-ROM reference=16002.txt
C>type interesting.xml

<story>
    <title>Linux|Unix</title>
    <time>^1999</time>
    <section>articles</section>
</story>
```

16.2 | The xTract.py Utility in Action

Here is an example execution of the `xTract` utility using the above XML file from `http://www.slashdot.com` and the above query template. Note how the three stories returned match the search criteria expressed in the `interesting.xml` file.

```
CD-ROM reference=16003.txt
C>python xTract.py http://www.slashdot.org/slashdot.xml
  interesting.xml

3 fragment(s) match.
<?xml version="1.0"?>
<story>
    <title>LinuxPPC unleashes LinuxPPC 1999 Q3</title>
    <url>http://slashdot.org/articles/99/09/13/1240212
      .shtml</url>
    <time>1999_09_13 20:43:11</time>
    <author>Hemos</author>
    <department>rolling_out_the_new</department>
    <topic>linux</topic>
```

```
        <comments>69</comments>
        <section>articles</section>
        <image>topiclinux.gif</image>
    </story>
 <?xml version="1.0"?>
 <story>
        <title>Linux Lite?</title>
        <url>http://slashdot.org/articles/99/09/13/1019228
          .shtml</url>
        <time>1999_09_13 19:22:37</time>
        <author>Hemos</author>
        <department>security_issues_galore</department>
        <topic>linux</topic>
        <comments>142</comments>
        <section>articles</section>
        <image>topiclinux.gif</image>
    </story>
 <?xml version="1.0"?>
 <story>
        <title>Nokia brings out Linux Cellphone/TV/Browser
          </title>
        <url>http://slashdot.org/articles/99/09/13/1118246
          .shtml</url>
        <time>1999_09_13 16:08:18</time>
        <author>Hemos</author>
        <department>fun_with_new_technology</department>
        <topic>hardware</topic>
        <comments>129</comments>
        <section>articles</section>
        <image>topichardware.gif</image>
    </story>
```

Here is an example that uses the `staff.xml` file we have used numerous times in this book. A fragment of the file is reproduced below.

```
CD-ROM reference=16004.txt
C>type staff.xml

<staff>
<department name="Technical">
<person>
<title>Technical Director</title>
<name>
<given>Sean</given>
```

```
<family>McGrath</family>
</name>
<email>Sean@digitome.com</email>
<web>http://www.digitome.com/Sean.html</web>
</person>
<person>
<title>Senior Software Engineer</title>
<name>
<given>Neville</given>
<family>Bagnall</family>
</name>
<email>neville@digitome.com</email>
<web>http://www.digitome.com/neville.html</web>
</person>
...
```

Here is a simple query template that will search this file. In English, the query says "find all staff with the word 'Technical' in their titles whose given name starts with 'S.'"

```
CD-ROM reference=16005.txt
C>type interesting.xml

<person>
<title>Technical</title>
<given>^S</given>
</person>
```

The result of executing this query against staff.xml is shown below.

```
CD-ROM reference=16006.txt
C>python xTract.py staff.xml interesting.xml
1 fragment(s) match.

<?xml version="1.0"?>
<person>
<title>Technical Director</title>
<name>
<given>Sean</given>
<family>McGrath</family>
</name>
<email>Sean@digitome.com</email>
<web>http://www.digitome.com/Sean.html</web>
</person>
```

A first cut implementation of xTract is shown below. The principal thing to watch for in the source code is how the tree-driven approach facilitated by Pyxie makes processing both the searched XML and the Query-By-Example XML quite straightforward. This simplicity has an associated cost in the current implementation. We discuss and then rectify this problem in a second implementation later on.

16.3 | xTract Version 1 Source Code

Here is the source code for version 1 of xTract.

```
CD-ROM reference=16007.txt
"""
xTract -- First Steps Toward an XML-Based
Query-by-Example System for Web Resource Retrieval

Given:
      A URL referencing an XML file
      An XML fragment to treat as a Query By Example
      template (containing Python regular expressions)

      Return list of matching XML fragments.

XML Processing with Python
Sean Mc Grath


"""


from geturl import geturl
from pyxie import *
import re,sys

# Set this to 1 to get a trace view of what is
# happening.
debug = 1

def xTract(ResourceXML,QueryByExampleXML):
      """
      Search an XML file, using another XML file
      as a query template.
      Return a list of matching XML fragments.
```

```
"""

# Initialize result.
ResultFragments = []

# Load the XML to be searched.
ResourceTree = String2xTree(geturl (ResourceXML))

# Load the Query By Example XML Template.
QBETree = File2xTree(QueryByExampleXML)

# Root element of the template to be matched
RootElementTypeName = QBETree.ElementTypeName

if debug:
      print "Fragment Root is",RootElementTypeName

# Gather the regular expressions to be matched
# into a dictionary, mapping element type name
# to regular expression.
Expressions = {}
for n in Elements(QBETree.Descendants()):
      QBETree.Seek(n)
      etn = QBETree.ElementTypeName
      regexp = QBETree.JoinData("")
      if regexp:
            Expressions[etn] = re.compile (regexp)

if debug:
      for (k,v) in Expressions.items():
            print "Element '%s'"%k,"must match '%s'"
              %v.pattern

for n in Elements(ResourceTree.Descendants()):
      ResourceTree.Seek(n)
      if ResourceTree.AtElement(RootElementTypeName):
            # Every fragment matches until the template
            # proves otherwise.
            ThisFragmentMatches = 1
            ResourceTree.PushPos()
            for n in Elements(ResourceTree.Descendants()):
                  ResourceTree.Seek(n)
                  etn = ResourceTree.ElementTypeName
                  if Expressions.has_key(etn):
                        Expression = Expressions[etn]
                        Text = ResourceTree.JoinData("")
                        if debug:
```

```
                                        print "Testing '%s'" %
                                            Text,
                                        print "against pattern
                                            '%s'" % (
                                                Expression.pattern)
                            mo = Expression.search(Text)
                            if mo is None:
                                if debug:
                                        print "failed"
                                    ThisFragmentMatches = 0
                    ResourceTree.PopPos()
                    if ThisFragmentMatches:
                            ResultFragments.append (Resource
                                Tree.Cut())
            return ResultFragments

if __name__ == "__main__":
        import sys
        if len(sys.argv)!=3:
                print "Usage:%s URL QBE" % sys.argv[0]
                sys.exit()
        matches = xTract(sys.argv[1],sys.argv[2])
        print "%d fragment(s) match" % len(matches)
        for fragment in matches:
                print 'fragment'
```

16.4 | Handling Large XML Files with xTract

The above implementation of xTract has the virtue that it is small and easy to understand. Unfortunately, it does not *scale* well. That is, if you were to use it to search a 30-Mbyte XML file, you would be in for long wait. The crux of the problem is that xTract as coded above is *memory bound*. It reads the entire XML file to be searched into memory.

It would be possible to rewrite xTract to use a complete event-driven approach. However, it is not an inviting prospect. Finding, say, `title` elements whose contents match the regular expression `"P*.?n"` can only be done once the entire content of the `title` element has been seen, that is, until after its end-tag event has been dispatched. A default start of the element handler would be needed to start accumulating data for each of the elements that occurs in the Query-By-Example template. A default end of element handler would need to perform the regular-expression matches. In short, the simple algorithm above needs to be bent out of shape to deal with the structure of the event stream.

There is an alternative that preserves the inherent simplicty of the `xTract` algorithm yet allows it to scale well. The solution lies in Pyxie's sparse tree support. In this new version, `xTract1`, we also use SAX as a source of PYX rather than using the `geturl` utility.

As long as we use a SAX driver that supports URLs, we still have the ability to search arbitrary Web-hosted XML with `xtract1`. The most important difference in basing `xTract1` on SAX is that we can use the `MySQL` SAX driver developed in chapter 15. The result is a search-and-retrieval utility that can handle huge XML files generated on-the-fly from a relational database in a memory-efficient way.

In chapter 15, we used a database known as `staff` as an example database. Here is sample XML generated from this database by the `saxdemo.py` application from the Python/XML distribution.

```
CD-ROM reference=16008.txt
C>python saxdemo.py -dmysql "staff select * from people"

<mysql>
 <row>
  <FamilyName>Mc Grath</FamilyName>
  <GivenName>Sean</GivenName>
  <ShoeSize>10</ShoeSize>
 </row>
 <row>
  <FamilyName>Duffy</FamilyName>
  <GivenName>Noel</GivenName>
  <ShoeSize>9</ShoeSize>
 </row>
 <row>
  <FamilyName>Bagnall</FamilyName>
```

```
   <GivenName>Neville</GivenName>
   <ShoeSize>8</ShoeSize>
  </row>
 </mysql>
```

Here is a template XML file we will use to query this data.

```
CD-ROM reference=16009.txt
<!--
Match any staff member whose name begins with "M" and
ends in "h" with a shoe size in the range 10 to 19.
-->
<row>
<FamilyName>M.*h</FamilyName>
<ShoeSize>^1\d$</ShoeSize>
</row>
```

The above query is rooted at an element called row. The new memory-efficient xTract1 loads each row in turn into an xTree structure. Only one row is ever in memory at any one time, and so the algorithm can happily process millions of rows. The syntax for invoking the new xTract1 utility to perform this query is shown below.

```
CD-ROM reference=16010.txt
C>python xTract1.py -dmysql "foo select * from people" inter-
esting.xml
```

Note the -d switch that has been introduced to allow the user to select which SAX driver to use to create the PYX data stream. The result of executing this command is shown below.

```
CD-ROM reference=16011.txt
1 fragment(s) match
<?xml version="1.0"?>
<row>
 <FamilyName>Mc Grath</FamilyName>
 <GivenName>Sean</GivenName>
 <ShoeSize>10</ShoeSize>
</row>
</code>
```

16.5 | Source Code for the xTract1 Utility

We end this chapter with the full source code for xTract1. The main thing to watch for in the code is how the XML to be searched is processed in an event-driven style. Once a start-tag occurs that matches the root element of the Query-By-Example template, processing switches to tree-driven style. A debug variable has been provided in this code. Set the variable to 1 to get logging information about what is going on as the algorithm executes.

```
CD-ROM reference=16012.txt
"""
xTract1 -- An XML-Based
Query-By-Example system for Web Resource Retrieval

Given:
        A URL referencing an XML file
        An XML fragment to treat as a Query-By-Example
        template (containing Python regular expressions)

        Return list of matching XML fragments.

Processing of target XML file is performed,
using a sparse tree builder, so this
program should be able to handle
very large XML files, e.g., XML generated
from a relational database driver such
as the MySQL SAX driver.

XML Processing with Python
Sean Mc Grath

"""

from geturl import geturl
from pyxie import *
import re,sys
```

```
# Set this to 1 to get a trace view of what is
# happening.
debug = 0

def xTract(SAXDriver,ResourceXML,QueryByExampleXML):
    """
    Search an XML file, using another XML file
    as a query template.
    Return a list of matching XML fragments.
    """

    class myHandler(xDispatch):
        """
        Event-driven class to field start-tags watching
        for the tag that will trigger the tree
        building process
        """
        def __init__(self,QBETree,fo,trigger):
            xDispatch.__init__(self,fo)
            self.trigger = trigger
            # Initialize list of matching fragments.
            self.ResultFragments = []
            # Initialize dictionary of regular expressions.
            # This dictionary maps element type name
            # to regular expression.
            self.Expressions = {}

            # Gather the regular expressions to be matched
            # into a dictionary, mapping element type name
            # to regular expressions.

            for n in Elements(QBETree.Descendants()):
                QBETree.Seek(n)
                etn = QBETree.ElementTypeName
                regexp = QBETree.JoinData("")
                if regexp:
                    self.Expressions[etn] = \
                        re.compile (regexp)

            if debug:
                for (k,v) in self.Expressions.items():
                    print "Element '%s'"%k,
                    Print "must match '%s'" %v.pattern
            self.Dispatch()
```

```
def default_start(self,etn,attrs):
    # Handler for all start-tags
    # Do nothing until the trigger
    # start-tag appears.
    if etn==self.trigger:
        # Push the start-tag back onto
        # the event stream for subsequent
        # tree building.
        self.PushElement(etn,attrs)
        t = PYX2xTree(self)

        # Every fragment matches until the
        # template proves
        # otherwise.
        ThisFragmentMatches = 1
        for n in Elements(t.Descendants()):
            t.Seek(n)
            etn = t.ElementTypeName
            if self.Expressions.has
              _key(etn):
                # Is there a regular
                # expression
                # for this element?
                Expression = self.\
                  Expressions[etn]
                Text = t.JoinData("")
                if debug:
                    print "Testing\
                      '%s'" % Text
                    print "against\
                      pattern '%s'" % (
                        Text,Expres\
                        sion.pattern)
                mo = Expression.search\
                  (Text)
                if mo is None:
                    if debug:
                        print "Match\
                          failed"
                    ThisFragmentMatches\
                      = 0
        if ThisFragmentMatches:
            # A match - store the fragment.
            self.ResultFragments.append\
              (t.Home())
```

```python
    # Load the Query-By-Example XML Template.
    QBETree = File2xTree(QueryByExampleXML)

    # Root element of the template to be matched
    RootElementTypeName = QBETree.ElementTypeName

    if debug:
        print "Fragment Root is",RootElementTypeName

    # Create an instance of myHandler.
    # Pass in:
    #  - The template XML query
    #  - The PYX source created from the user-specified
    #    SAX driver
    #  - The "trigger" element for matching fragments
    #
    # Creating a myHandler object causes the dispatching
    # of events. Afterwards, the ResultFragments
    # instance variable has a list of the matching
    # fragments, which is what is returned to the
    # caller.
    return myHandler(QBETree,
                SAX2PYX(ResourceXML,
                    SAXDriver),
                RootElementTypeName).ResultFragments

if __name__ == "__main__":
    import sys,getopt
    (options,remainder) = getopt.getopt (sys.argv[1:],"d:")
    # SAX driver defaults to pyexpat.
    SAXDriver = "pyexpat"
    for (option,value) in options:
        if option == "-d":
            SAXDriver = value
    if len(remainder)!=2:
        print "Usage:%s [-d sax driver] URL QBE" %
        sys.argv[0]
        sys.exit()

    matches = xTract(SAXDriver,remainder[0],remainder[1])

    print "%d fragment(s) match" % len(matches)
    for fragment in matches:
        print 'fragment'
```

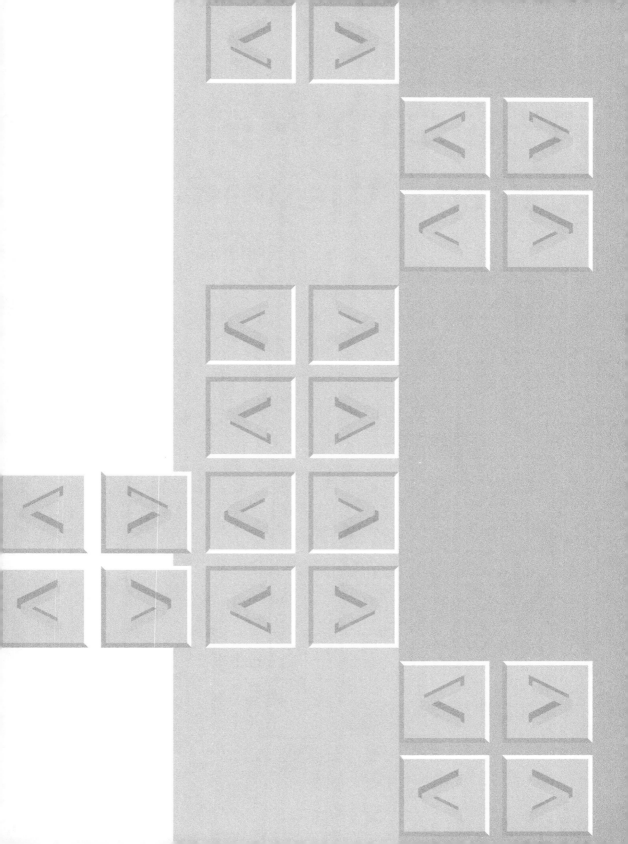

The C3 XML
Editor/Viewer

n this chapter, the C3 viewer introduced in chapter 4 is significantly enhanced to support :c3.

- Editing the tree structure with cut and paste
- Editing element names and data content
- Displaying and editing attribute names and values

We start with some screen shots of the new C3 in action.

Figure 17–1 is a screen shot of C3 with hamlet.xml loaded.

Figure 17–2 shows the PERSONAE element highlighted.

When Cut is selected from the edit menu, the PERSONAE element disappears, as shown in figure 17–3

In figure 17–4, the insertion point has been moved to the fm element.

In figure 17–5, the Paste option from the edit menu has been used to insert the previously cut PERSONAE element below the fm element.

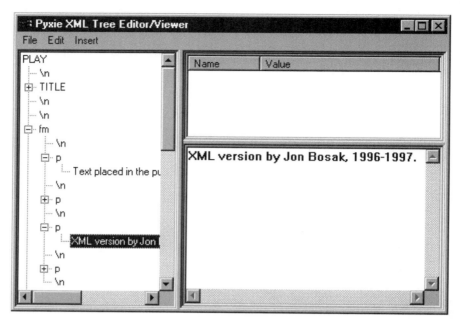

Figure 17–1   The C3 viewer displaying Hamlet.

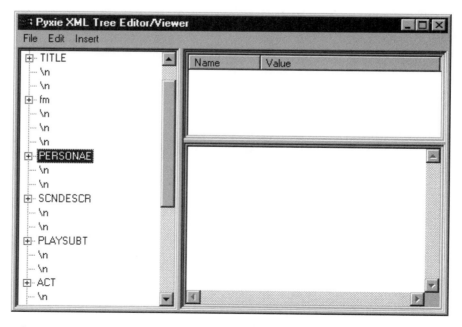

Figure 17–2   The C3 viewer highlighting PERSONAE element.

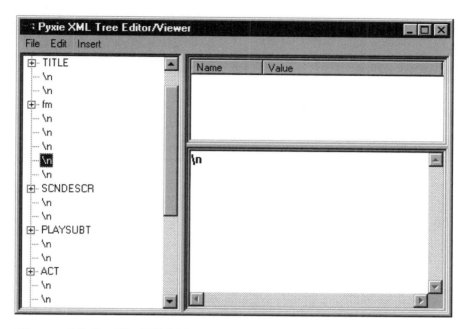

Figure 17–3 The PERSONAE element no longer visible.

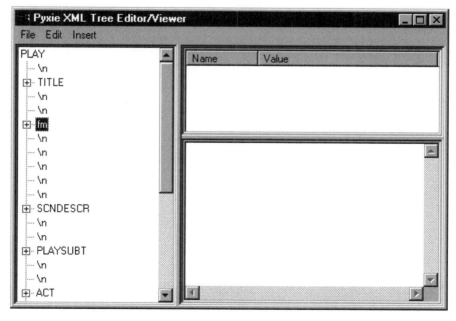

Figure 17–4 Moving the insertion point around the tree control.

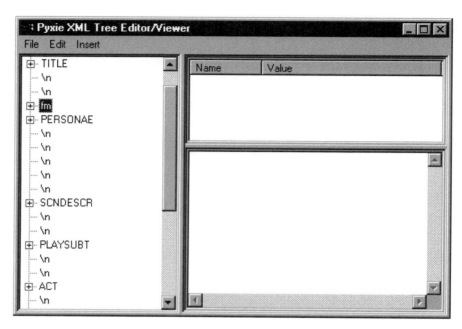

Figure 17–5   Hamlet after the PERSONAE element has been pasted.

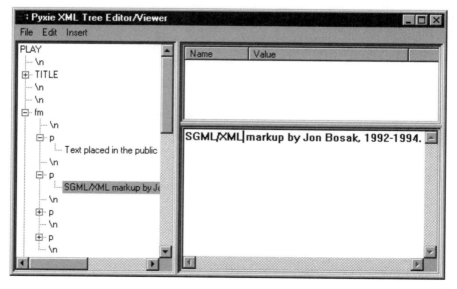

Figure 17–6   Displaying/editing character data.

The character data content can be edited both in the data character window (bottom right) and directly in the tree control. In figure 17–6, the text of a p element is displayed.

In figure 17–7, the text has been changed from SGML to SGML/XML, using the character data pane. Notice how the text in the tree control has changed to remain synchronized.

Figure 17–8 shows an XML file in which the first name element has an attribute x set to the value y.

By double-clicking on the attribute in the attribute pane, we can edit the name and the value of the attribute, as shown in figure 17–9.

When the Attribute Edit window is closed, the updated attribute name/value appears in the attribute pane, as shown in figure 17–10. New attributes can be added through the Insert-Attribute menu option.

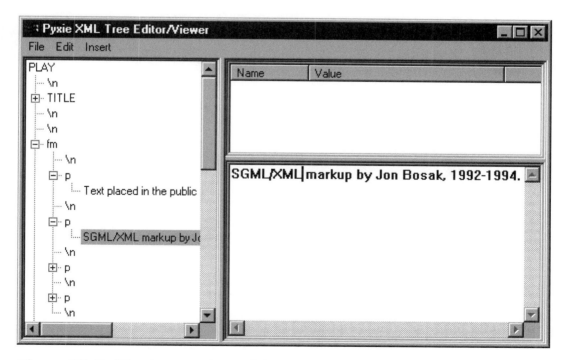

Figure 17–7   The character data and the tree control are kept in sync.

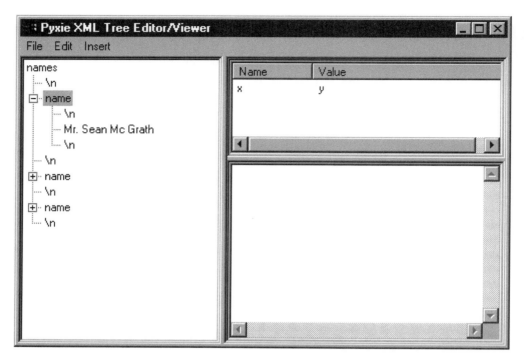

Figure 17–8   Attribute display in the attribute list window.

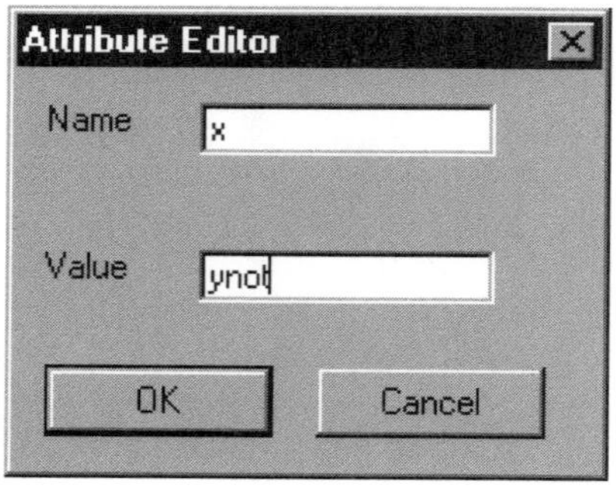

Figure 17–9   Editing attribute names and values.

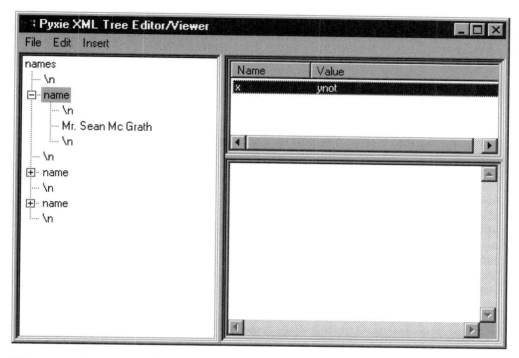

Figure 17–10   Updated attribute window after attribute edit.

17.1 | Developing wxPython Applications

The C3 viewer uses the wxPython GUI toolkit we installed in chapter 4. The wxPython toolkit is very powerful indeed. An entire book would be required to cover wxPython in the detail required to do it justice. In this chapter, we start with a simple "Hello World" application in wx-Python but then cut straight to the details of the C3 implementation. The best way to get familiar and productive with wxPython is by using it. I would suggest you proceed with the following steps.

1. Get the "Hello World" application below up and running on your machine.

2. Install and play with the enhanced C3 viewer. You will find the complete source code at the end of this chapter.

3. Read the comments and docstrings in the C3 source.

4. Read the detail sections in this chapter.

5. Execute the demo supplied with wxPython. Examine the code in the code tab provided.

17.2 | A "Hello World" wxPython Application

All wxPython applications take the same basic shape. Figure 17–11 is a screen shot of a simple wxPython application.

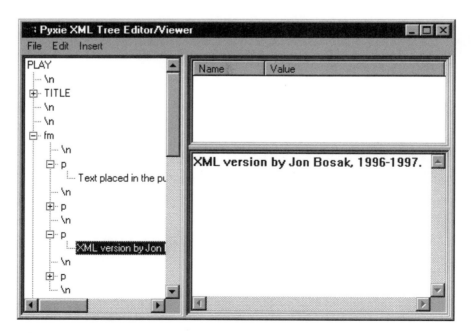

Figure 17–11   A very simple wxPython application.

Here is the code.

```
CD-ROM reference=17001.txt
# Import wxPython functionality
from wxPython.wx import *

class MyFrame(wxFrame):
    def __init__(self, parent, id, title):
        # Initialize wxFrame
        wxFrame.__init__(self, parent, -1,
                                  title,
                                  wxDefaultPosition,
                                  wxSize(450, 300))
        # Create File, Edit, and Insert menus and menu items.
        FileMenu = wxMenu()
        FileMenu.Append (1001,"Exit")
        menubar = wxMenuBar()
        menubar.Append (FileMenu,"File")
        self.SetMenuBar(menubar)
        # Center the frame on the screen.
        self.Centre(wxBOTH)
        self.Text = wxTextCtrl (
                self,-1,"Hello World",
                wxDefaultPosition,
                wxSize(100,100),
                wxTE_MULTILINE|wxHSCROLL)

        EVT_MENU(self, 1001, self.OnExit)

    def OnExit(self,event):
        """
        Handler for File_Exit
        """
        self.Close()

# Application base class used by wxPython
class MyApp(wxApp):
    def OnInit(self):
        self.frame = MyFrame(NULL, -1, "wxPython Hello
          World App")
        self.frame.Show(true)
        self.SetTopWindow(self.frame)
        return true

app = MyApp(0)
app.MainLoop()
```

Let us go through the code piece by piece. The first thing we need to do is import the wxPython library. The recommended way to do this is to import everything as follows.

```
CD-ROM reference=17002.txt
# Import wxPython functionality
from wxPython.wx import *
```

All wxPython applications will have at least one class derived from wxFrame. This is the class where the majority of the action takes place. It is where you create controls to display in the frame and also where you put handlers for events that occur in those controls. A lot goes on in the constructor of a wxFrame.

```
CD-ROM reference=17003.txt
        wxFrame.__init__(self, parent, -1,
                                title,
                                wxDefaultPosition,
                                wxSize(450, 300))
```

This method call initializes the wxFrame parent of the current class. It is passed a title for the frame, a default position, and the overall size of the frame.

```
CD-ROM reference=17004.txt
        # Create File, Edit, and Insert menus and menu items.
        FileMenu = wxMenu()
        FileMenu.Append (1001,"Exit")
        menubar = wxMenuBar()
        menubar.Append (FileMenu,"File")
        self.SetMenuBar(menubar)
```

You create menu objects by calling wxMenu(). Menu items are added to menu objects with the Append method. Each menu item has an associated unique number—1001 in the case of the Exit menu item above. This number serves to connect menu items with menu handlers, as we will see in a moment.

```
CD-ROM reference=17005.txt
        # Center the frame on the screen.
        self.Centre(wxBOTH)
```

Here the frame is centered on the screen both horizontally and vertically.

```
CD-ROM reference=17006.txt
            self.Text = wxTextCtrl (self,-1,"Hello World",
                wxDefaultPosition,
                wxSize(100,100),
                wxTE_MULTILINE|wxHSCROLL)
```

Here, a text control is created and stored in the instance variable `Text`. The construction of a control is similar to the construction of a frame. Controls typically are given titles and default positions. In the case of `TextCtrl` objects, we can specify that the control should allow multiple lines of text, `wxTE_MULTILINE`, and that it should have a horizontal scroll bar, `wxHSCROLL`.

The final job we need to do in the `wxFrame` constructor is to establish the connection between the Exit menu item (numbered 1001) and the handler for that method, which will be the instance method `self.OnExit`.

```
CD-ROM reference=17007.txt
            EVT_MENU(self, 1001, self.OnExit)
```

That concludes the constructor for the frame. The handler for the exit menu item is straightforward. It simply calls the `close` method to close down the application.

```
CD-ROM reference=17008.txt
        def OnExit(self,event):
            """
            Handler for File_Exit
            """
            self.Close()
```

As well as a frame, wxPython applications have an application class derived from `wxApp`. This class typically does nothing except create the application's main frame and then starts processing events for the application by calling `MainLoop`.

```
CD-ROM reference=17009.txt
# Application base class used by wxPython
class MyApp(wxApp):
    def OnInit(self):
        self.frame = MyFrame(NULL, -1, "wxPython Hello
            World App")
        self.frame.Show(true)
        self.SetTopWindow(self.frame)
        return true
app = MyApp(0)
app.MainLoop()
```

17.3 | Converting an xTree to a wxTree, and Vice Versa

The heart of C3 is the relationship between an xTree object used to manipulate XML and the wxTreeCtrl object used to display and edit XML. The wxTreeCtrl class is based around the idea that a tree is made up of a collection of Item objects. There is a single root Item that contains all other Item objects. Building a wxTreeCtrl object from an xTree object makes heavy use of the AppendItem method. Given the Item object representing the parent item, this method appends a new Item as the last child of that parent. The InsertwxTreeChildren method uses an xTree as a template hierarchy from which to create a wxTreeCtrl hierarchy. The algorithm works by traversing the xTree in a top-down, left-to-right fashion, creating Item objects and appending them as it goes.

Each Item has associated with it a wxTreeItemData object. This class allows arbitrary data to be associated with an Item in a wxTreeCtrl. In C3, this storage space is used to differentiate between element nodes and data nodes by means of a Python list structure. An element node will have the constant ELEMENT as the first item in the list. A data node will have the constant DATA as the first item in the list. For ELEMENT nodes, the second item in the list is a Python dictionary used to store any attributes associated with that element.

```
CD-ROM reference=17010.txt
    def InsertwxTreeChildren(self,wxTreeNode,PYXTree):
```

```
"""
Given an xTree, create a branch beneath the
current selection, using an xTree.
"""
PYXTree.PushPos()
for c in PYXTree.Children():
        PYXTree.Seek(c)
        if PYXTree.AtElement():
                NewwxNode = self.wxTree.AppendItem(
                        wxTreeNode,
                        PYXTree.ElementTypeName,
                        -1,-1,
                wxTreeItemData(
                        [ELEMENT,PYXTree.AttributeValues
                          .copy()]))
        else:
                NewwxNode = self.wxTree.AppendItem(
                        wxTreeNode,
                        PYXEncoder(PYXTree.Data),
                        -1,-1,wxTreeItemData([DATA]))
        # Recursive call to insert children of each child
        self.InsertwxTreeChildren(NewwxNode,PYXTree)
PYXTree.PopPos()
```

At the point where the contents of a `wxTreeCtrl` need to be converted back to XML, the `wxTree2PYXList1` method does the work. It uses a utility method, `wxTreeChildrenList`, to get the list of children for any given item. Using this list, it can perform a depth-first, left-to-right traversal of the `wxTreeCtrl` structure. It uses the `ItemData` associated with each item to determine whether the current item is an element or a data node as it traverses the `wxTreeCtrl`.

CD-ROM reference=17011.txt
```
    def wxTree2PYXList1 (self,item,res):
        """
        Recursive function to create a list of PYX events
        from a wxTree control
        The res list variable is accumulated list.
        """
        ItemData = self.wxTree.GetPyData(item)
        if ItemData[0] == ELEMENT:
            res.append ("(%s" % self.wxTree.GetItem
              Text(item))
```

```
                    Attributes = ItemData[1]
                    for (a,v) in Attributes.items():
                        res.append ("A%s %s" % (a,v))
                    children = self.wxTreeChildrenList(item)
                    for c in children:
                        self.wxTree2PYXList1(c,res)
                    res.append (")%s" % self.wxTree.GetItem
                      Text(item))
        else:
        res.append ("-%s" % self.wxTree.GetItemText(item))
```

17.4 | Dynamic Module Loading

From time to time, heavily used Python modules are translated to C if using the C version leads to a speed increase. The functionality of the string module, for example, has been reimplemented in C. When Python loads the string module, it checks to see if the optimized version known as strop is available. If it is, the optimized module is loaded instead. All references to the string module will work but will be implemented by the C optimized strop module.

Two other Python modules that have recently been optimized are sgmllib and StringIO. For sgmllib, the optimized module is known as sgmlop. For StringIO, the optimized module is known as cStringIO.

Depending on the platform and the version of Python your scripts are running on, these optimized modules may or may not exist. If they exist, it would be nice to use them, but we would equally like scripts to run with the nonoptimized versions. The c3 viewer uses the StringIO module. Here is how it deals with the possibility that the platform may or may not have the optimized module available.

CD-ROM reference=17012.txt

```
try:
    import cStringIO
    StringIO = cStringIO

except ImportError:
    import StringIO
```

The `import` statement is wrapped in a `try`/`except` block. If the import of `cStringIO` fails because the module is unavailable, an `ImportError` exception is raised. If this happens, the code imports the `StringIO` module instead. If the import succeeds, a variable `StringIO` is created that references the `cStringIO` module. That way, the body of the program can use `StringIO` as the name prefix, and it will work regardless of the presence or absence of `cStringIO`.

17.5 | The Complete Source Code for C3

```
CD-ROM reference=17013.txt
"""
C3 -- (Which is pronounced "See Tree" in Dublin) -- An XML
Tree Editor/Viewer

"""
import sys,string,os

# Import optimized cStringIO if available, otherwise StringIO.
try:
      import cStringIO
      StringIO = cStringIO
except ImportError:
      import StringIO
# Import wxPython functionality.
from wxPython.wx import *

# Import the Pyxie XML processing library.
from pyxie import *

# Useful constants for differentiating between Element nodes
# and data
# nodes in wxTreeCtrl controls
ELEMENT = 1
DATA    = 0

# The del key is "hooked" to delete branched from wxTreeCtrl
# controls.
DEL_KEY = 127
```

```
class AttributeEditorDialog (wxDialog):
    """
    Attribute editing modal dialog window
    """
    def __init__(self,parent,AV):
        """
        Create a modal wxDialog control. AV parameter
        is a list consisting
        of attribute name and attribute value. The modified
        values for these two variables can then be
        picked up from the list.
        """
        wxDialog.__init__ (self,
            parent,
            -1,
            "Attribute Editor",
            wxPoint(100,100),
            wxSize(200,160),
            wxDIALOG_MODAL|wxDEFAULT_DIALOG_STYLE)

        # Storage for the attribute name/value pair
        self.AV = AV

        wxStaticText(self, -1, "Name",wxPoint(10,10))
        wxStaticText(self, -1, "Value",wxPoint(10,60))

        self.AttributeNameTextControl = wxTextCtrl(
            self,
            -1,
            self.AV[0],
            wxPoint(60, 10),
            wxSize(100, 20))
        self.AttributeValueTextControl = wxTextCtrl(
            self,
            -1,
            self.AV[1],
            wxPoint(60, 60),
            wxSize(100, 20))

        # Hook changes to the two text controls.
        EVT_TEXT(self.AttributeNameTextControl,
                 self.AttributeNameTextControl
                 .GetId(),
                 self.AttributeNameTextChanged)
```

```
            EVT_TEXT(self.AttributeValueTextControl,
                    self.AttributeValueTextControl
                    .GetId(),
                    self.AttributeValueTextChanged)
        # Allow user to OK or Cancel the dialog.
        wxButton(self,
                wxID_OK,
                "OK",
                wxPoint(10, 100),
                wxSize(76, 24)).SetDefault()

        wxButton(self,
                wxID_CANCEL,
                "Cancel",
                wxPoint(100, 100),
                wxSize(76,24))

        EVT_BUTTON(self, wxID_OK, self.OnOK)

    def OnOK(self,event):
        """
        Handler for pressing OK button. End modal dialog.
        """
        self.EndModal(wxID_OK)

    def AttributeValueTextChanged(self,event):
        """
        Handler for changes to text control, update
        Attribute Value storage in AV[1].
        """
        self.AV[1] = self.AttributeValueTextControl
        .GetValue()

    def AttributeNameTextChanged(self,event):
        """
        Handler for changes to text control, update
        Attribute Name storage in AV[0].
        """
        self.AV[0] = self.AttributeNameTextControl
        .GetValue()


# Main application frame

class MyFrame(wxFrame):
```

```
def __init__(self, parent, id, title):
    # Initialize wxFrame.
    wxFrame.__init__(self, parent, -1,
                            title,
                            wxDefaultPosition,
                            wxSize(450, 300))
    # Create File, Edit, and Insert menus and menu items.
    FileMenu = wxMenu()
    FileMenu.Append (1001,"New")
    FileMenu.Append (1002,"Open")
    FileMenu.Append (1003,"Close")
    FileMenu.Append (1004,"Save")
    FileMenu.Append (1005,"Save As")
    FileMenu.Append (1006,"Exit")
    EditMenu = wxMenu()
    EditMenu.Append (2001,"Cut")
    EditMenu.Append (2002,"Copy")
    EditMenu.Append (2003,"Paste")
    EditMenu.Append (2004,"Delete")

    InsertMenu = wxMenu()
    InsertMenu.Append (3001,"Child")
    InsertMenu.Append (3002,"Attribute")
    menubar = wxMenuBar()
    menubar.Append (FileMenu,"File")
    menubar.Append (EditMenu,"Edit")
    menubar.Append (InsertMenu,"Insert")

    self.SetMenuBar(menubar)

    # Center the frame on the screen.
    self.Centre(wxBOTH)

    # Create splitter windows used for three-pane layout.
    self.splitter1 = wx.wxSplitterWindow (self, -1)
    self.splitter2 = wx.wxSplitterWindow (self
    .splitter1, -1)

    # Tree Control for the XML hierarchy
    self.wxTree = wxTreeCtrl (self.splitter1 ,
                -1 ,
                wxDefaultPosition,
                wxSize(100,100),
                wxTR_EDIT_LABELS|wxTR_HAS_BUTTONS)

    # List Control to display attribute names and values
    self.Attributes = wxListCtrl (self.splitter2,
```

```
                    -1,
                    wxDefaultPosition,
                    wxDefaultSize,
                    wxLC_REPORT|wxSUNKEN_BORDER|wxVSCROLL)

self.Attributes.InsertColumn (0,"Name")
self.Attributes.InsertColumn (1,"Value")
self.Attributes.SetColumnWidth(1,200)

# Text Control to display character data
self.CharacterData = wxTextCtrl (self.splitter2,
                        -1,
                        "" ,
                        wxDefaultPosition,
                        wxSize(10,10),
                        wxTE_MULTILINE|wxHSCROLL)

# Create the three-pane screen layout with
# splitter windows.
self.splitter1.SplitVertically (self.wxTree,self
.splitter2)
self.splitter1.SetSashPosition(180,true)
self.splitter2.SplitHorizontally (
        self.Attributes,self.CharacterData)
self.splitter2.SetSashPosition(100,true)

# Menu event handlers
# File menu
EVT_MENU(self, 1001, self.OnNew)
EVT_MENU(self, 1002, self.OnOpen)
EVT_MENU(self, 1003, self.OnClose)
EVT_MENU(self, 1004, self.OnSave)
EVT_MENU(self, 1005, self.OnSaveAs)
EVT_MENU(self, 1006, self.OnExit)

# Edit menu
EVT_MENU(self, 2001, self.OnwxTreeCut)
EVT_MENU(self, 2002, self.OnwxTreeCopy)
EVT_MENU(self, 2003, self.OnwxTreePaste)
EVT_MENU(self, 2004, self.OnwxTreeDelete)

# Insert menu
EVT_MENU(self, 3001, self.OnwxTreeInsertChild)
EVT_MENU(self, 3002, self.OnwxTreeInsertAttribute)

# Handler for edited labels in tree control
EVT_TREE_END_LABEL_EDIT (self.wxTree,
```

```python
                              self.wxTree.GetId(),
                              self.OnEndwxTreeLabelEdit)

        # Handler for change of selection in tree control
        EVT_TREE_SEL_CHANGED(self.wxTree,
                              self.wxTree.GetId(),
                              self.OnwxTreeSelChanged)
        # Handler for change in data in character data
        # text control
        EVT_TEXT(self.CharacterData,
                  self.CharacterData.GetId(),
                  self.OnCharacterDataChanged)

        # Handler for keystrokes in Tree Control
        EVT_CHAR(self.wxTree, self.OnwxTreeChar)

        # Handler for keystrokes in Attribute display
        # (used to hook DEL)
        EVT_CHAR(self.Attributes, self.OnAttributesChar)

        # Handler for change of selection in Attribute list
        EVT_LIST_ITEM_SELECTED(self,
            self.Attributes.GetId(),
            self.OnAttributeItemSelected)

        # Handler for double-click event in Attribute list
        EVT_LEFT_DCLICK(
              self.Attributes,
              self.OnAttributeItemDoubleClick)

        # Storage for currently loaded filename
        self.CurrentFilename = ""

        # Storage for clipboard (a PYXTree)
        self.Clipboard = None

        # Used to determine when application is closing down
        self.Closing = 0

    def OnAttributeItemDoubleClick(self,event):
        """
        Handle double-click in attribute list.
        Pop up attribute editing dialog.
        """
        # The AttributeCurrentItem variable keeps
        # track of the currently
```

```
        # selected attribute in the attribute list.
        AttributeName = self.Attributes.GetItemText(
            self.AttributeCurrentItem)

        # Pick up XML attributes for currently selected
        # element in tree control.
        Current = self.wxTree.GetSelection()

        # Each node in a wxTree has a list associated
        # with it.
        # Item 0 in the list is ELEMENT for element
        # nodes. Item 1 contains attribute storage
        # (dictionary).
        data = self.wxTree.GetItemData(Current)
        attrs = data.GetData()[1]
        AttributeValue = attrs[AttributeName]

        # Zap the name/value association for the
        # attribute we are about to edit.
        del attrs[AttributeName]

        # Create the list to pass into the modal dialog.
        pair = [AttributeName,AttributeValue]
        # Display the dialog.
        AttributeEditorDialog(self,pair).ShowModal()
        # Create a new association with the modified
        # attribute/value pair.
        attrs[pair[0]] = pair[1]

        # Force a refresh of the attribute window.
        self.OnwxTreeSelChanged (event)

def OnAttributeItemSelected(self, event):
    """
    Handler for change of selected attribute list
    control item
    """
    self.AttributeCurrentItem = event.m_itemIndex

def OnOpen(self,event):
    """
    Handler for File_Open
    """
    f = wxFileDialog(self,
            "Select a file",
            ".",
```

```
                            "",
                            "*.xml",
                            wxOPEN)

            if f.ShowModal() == wxID_OK:
                self.CurrentFilename = f.GetPath()
                wxBeginBusyCursor()
                pyxTree = PYX2xTree(
                        PYExpat2PYX(open(f.GetPath(),"r")))
                self.LoadwxTree (pyxTree)
                wxEndBusyCursor()
            f.Destroy()

    def OnClose(self,event):
        """
        Handler for File_Close
        """
        self.wxTree.DeleteAllItems()
        self.Attributes.DeleteAllItems()
    def OnExit(self,event):
        """
        Handler for File_Exit
        """
        self.Closing = 1
        self.Close()

    def OnwxTreeChar(self, event):
        """
        Handler for keystokes in the Tree control
        Cut, Copy, Paste, and DEL supported
        """
        key = event.KeyCode()
        if key == DEL_KEY:
            self.OnwxTreeDelete(event)
        elif key == ord("x") and event.ControlDown():
            self.OnwxTreeCut(event)
        elif key == ord("v") and event.ControlDown():
            self.OnwxTreePaste(event)
        elif key == ord("c") and event.ControlDown():
            self.OnwxTreeCopy(event)
        else:
            # Pass unprocessed event on to higher handlers.
            event.Skip()

    def OnAttributesChar(self, event):
        """
```

```
        Handler for keystrokes in Attribute list control
        """
        key = event.KeyCode()
        if key == DEL_KEY:
            self.Attributes.DeleteItem(
                self.AttributeCurrentItem)
        else:
            # Pass unprocessed event on to higher handlers.
            event.Skip()

def OnwxTreeCut(self,event):
        """
        Handler for Edit_Cut and Ctrl_x in tree control
        """
        # Create an xTree (PYXTree) from the currently
        # selected branch.
        self.Clipboard = self.wxTree2PYXTree(
            self.wxTree.GetSelection())
        # Zap the branch.
        self.OnwxTreeDelete(event)

def OnwxTreeCopy(self,event):
        """
        Handler for Edit_Copy and Ctrl_c in tree control
        """
        # Create an xTree (PYXTree) from the currently
        # selected branch.
        self.Clipboard = self.wxTree2PYXTree(
            self.wxTree.GetSelection())

def OnwxTreePaste(self,event):
        """
        Handler for Edit_Paste and Ctrl_v in tree control
        """
        if self.Clipboard:
            self.InsertPYXTreeIntowxTreeAsSibling(
                self.wxTree.GetSelection(),
                self.Clipboard)
            self.Clipboard.Home()

def OnwxTreeSelChanged(self,event):
        """
        Handler for change of selected item in tree control
        """
        if self.Closing:
            # Do nothing if the application is closing down.
```

```
                        return
            # Update attribute and character data windows.
            self.CharacterData.Clear()
            self.Attributes.DeleteAllItems()
            Current = self.wxTree.GetSelection()

            # Each node in a wxTree has a list associated
            # with it.
            # Item 0 in the list is ELEMENT for element nodes
            # and DATA for data nodes. For ELEMENT nodes, item 1
            # contains attribute storage (dictionary).
            data = self.wxTree.GetItemData(Current)
            type = data.GetData()[0]
            if type == ELEMENT:
                    attrs = data.GetData()[1]
                    pos = 0
                    # Insert attributes into Attribute list control.
                    for (a,v) in attrs.items():
                            self.Attributes.InsertStringItem
                              (pos, a)
                            self.Attributes.SetStringItem
                              (pos,0,a)
                            self.Attributes.SetStringItem
                              (pos,1,v)
                            pos = pos + 1
            else:
            # A data node; update the character data display.
            self.CharacterData.SetValue
            (self.wxTree.GetItemText(Current))

    def OnCharacterDataChanged(self,event):
        """
        Handler for change of character data — sync
          change in tree
        Control.
        """
        v = self.CharacterData.GetValue()
        Current = self.wxTree.GetSelection()
        self.wxTree.SetItemText(Current,v)

    def OnwxTreeInsertChild(self,event):
        """
        Handler for Insert_Child menu option
        """
        Current = self.wxTree.GetSelection()
        data = self.wxTree.GetItemData(Current)
        # If current node is a data node, make it
```

```
            # an element node because it is about to
            # have a baby.
            if data.GetData()[0] == DATA:
                    etn = self.wxTree.GetItemText(Current)
                    data.SetData([ELEMENT,{}])
            # Insert new node as child of this one.
            self.wxTree.PrependItem(
                    Current,
                    "temp",
                    -1,-1,
                    wxTreeItemData([ELEMENT,{}]))
            # Force refresh of tree control window.
            self.wxTree.Refresh()

    def OnwxTreeInsertAttribute(self,event):
            """
            Handler for Insert_Attribute menu item
            """
            Current = self.wxTree.GetSelection()
            data = self.wxTree.GetItemData(Current)
            # If current node is a data node, make it
            # an element node because it is about to
            # have an attribute attached.
            if data.GetData()[0] == DATA:
                    data.SetData([ELEMENT,{}])
            attrs = data.GetData()[1]
            # Create a blank attribute name/value pair for the
            # modal dialog edit.
            pair = ["",""]
            if AttributeEditorDialog(self,pair).ShowModal()
            == wxID_OK:
                # Update only if OK is pressed.
                attrs[pair[0]] = pair[1]
            # Force a refresh of the attribute window.
            self.OnwxTreeSelChanged (event)

    def OnSave(self,event):
            """
            Handler for File_Save
            """
            f = open (self.CurrentFilename,"w")
            root = self.wxTree.GetRootItem()
            f.write (`self.wxTree2PYXTree(root)`)
            f.close()

    def OnSaveAs(self,event):
            """
```

```
        Handler for File_SaveAs
        """
        f = wxFileDialog(self,
                    "Select a file",
                    ".",
                    "",
                    "*.xml",wxOPEN)
        if f.ShowModal() == wxID_OK:
            self.CurrentFilename = f.GetPath()
            out = open (self.CurrentFilename,"w")
            root = self.wxTree.GetRootItem()
            out.write (`self.wxTree2PYXTree(root)`)
            out.close()

    def OnNew(self,event):
        """
        Handler for File_New
        """
        # Create a "blank" xTree and load that into the
        # tree control.
        pyxTree = PYX2xTree(
            StringIO.StringIO("(blank\n_blank\n)
            blank"))
        self.LoadwxTree (pyxTree)

    def OnwxTreeDelete(self,event):
        """
        Handler for DEL key in tree control
        """
        self.wxTree.Delete(self.wxTree.GetSelection())

    def wxTreeChildrenList(self,item):
        """
        Given an item in a wxTreeCtrl control, create a list
        of its children items.
        """
        res = []
        item = self.wxTree.GetFirstChild(item,0)[0]
        while item.IsOk():
            res.append (item)
            item = self.wxTree.GetNextSibling(item)
        return res

    def wxTree2PYXTree (self,item):
        """
        Given an item in a wxTreeCtrl control, create an xTree.
```

```
        """
        res = self.wxTree2PYXList(item)
        return PYX2xTree (
            StringIO.StringIO(string.joinfields(res,
            "\n")))

def wxTree2PYXList1 (self,item,res):
    """
    Recursive function to create a list of PYX events
    from a wxTree control
    The res list variable is accumulated list.
    """
    ItemData = self.wxTree.GetPyData(item)
    if ItemData[0] == ELEMENT:
        res.append ("(%s" % self.wxTree.GetItem
        Text(item))
        Attributes = ItemData[1]
        for (a,v) in Attributes.items():
            res.append ("A%s %s" % (a,v))
        children = self.wxTreeChildrenList(item)
        for c in children:
            self.wxTree2PYXList1(c,res)
        res.append (")%s" % self.wxTree.GetItem
        Text(item))
    else:
        res.append ("-%s" % self.wxTree.GetItem
        Text(item))
def wxTree2PYXList (self,item):
    """
    Create a list of PYX events from an xTree control.
    wxTree2PYXList1 method does the recursive work.
    """
    res = []
    ItemData = self.wxTree.GetPyData(item)
    if ItemData[0] == DATA:
        # If the selected item is data, need a
        # wrapping element in order to construct a
        # valid xTree.
        res.append ("(!CUTTING")
        res.append ("-%s" % self.wxTree.GetItem
        Text(item))
        res.append (")!CUTTING")
    else:
        self.wxTree2PYXList1(item,res)
    return res
def OnEndwxTreeLabelEdit(self, event):
```

```
        """
        Handler for end of tree control label edit
        """
        Current = self.wxTree.GetSelection()
        self.wxTree.SetItemText(
            Current,event.GetLabel())
        self.CharacterData.SetValue(
            self.wxTree.GetItemText(Current))

    def InsertwxTreeChildren(self,wxTreeNode,PYXTree):
        """
        Given an xTree, create a branch beneath the
        current selection, using an xTree.
        """
        PYXTree.PushPos()
        for c in PYXTree.Children():
            PYXTree.Seek(c)
            if PYXTree.AtElement():
                NewwxNode = self.wxTree.AppendItem(
                    wxTreeNode,
                    PYXTree.ElementTypeName,
                    -1,-1,
                    wxTreeItemData(
                        [ELEMENT,
                        PYXTree.AttributeValues.
                        copy()]))
            else:
                NewwxNode = self.wxTree.AppendItem(
                    wxTreeNode,
                    PYXEncoder(
                        PYXTree.Data),
                    -1,-1,
                    wxTreeItemData([DATA]))
            # Recurisive call to insert children of
            # each child
            self.InsertwxTreeChildren(NewwxNode,PYXTree)
        PYXTree.PopPos()

    def InsertPYXTreeIntowxTreeAsSibling(self,wxTreeNode,
       PYXTree):
        """
        Given an xTree, create a branch as sibling of
        current selection, using an xTree.
        """
        if PYXTree.AtElement("!CUTTING"):
            PYXTree.Down()
```

```
                NewwxNode = self.wxTree.InsertItem(
                        self.wxTree.GetParent(wxTreeNode),
                        wxTreeNode,
                        PYXTree.Data,
                        -1,-1,
                        wxTreeItemData([DATA,PYXTree.Data]))
            else:
                NewwxNode = self.wxTree.InsertItem(
                        self.wxTree.GetParent(wxTreeNode),
                        wxTreeNode,
                        PYXTree.ElementTypeName,
                        -1,-1,
                        wxTreeItemData(
                            [ELEMENT,
                            PYXTree.AttributeValues
                            .copy()]))
            self.InsertwxTreeChildren(NewwxNode,PYXTree)
        self.wxTree.Refresh()

    def LoadwxTree (self,PYXTree):
        """
        Load an XML file.
        """
        wxBeginBusyCursor()
        self.wxTree.DeleteAllItems()
        PYXTree.Home()
        wxTreeNode = self.wxTree.AddRoot(
                PYXTree.ElementTypeName,
                -1,-1,
                wxTreeItemData(
                    [ELEMENT,PYXTree.AttributeValues
                    .copy()]))
        self.InsertwxTreeChildren(wxTreeNode,PYXTree)
        wxEndBusyCursor()

# Application base class used by wxPython
class MyApp(wxApp):
    def OnInit(self):
        self.frame = MyFrame(NULL, -1, "Pyxie XML Tree
        Editor/Viewer")
        self.frame.Show(true)
        self.SetTopWindow(self.frame)
        return true

def wxTree (pyx=None):
    """
```

```
    Main entry point for using C3 as a library
    """
    app = MyApp(0)
    if pyx:
        app.frame.LoadwxTree (
            PYX2xTree(PYExpat2PYX(open(pyx,"r")))))
    app.MainLoop()

if __name__ == "__main__":
    import sys
    try:
        if len(sys.argv) > 1:
            wxTree (sys.argv[1])
        else:
            wxTree()
    except PyxieException,e:
        print e.problem
```

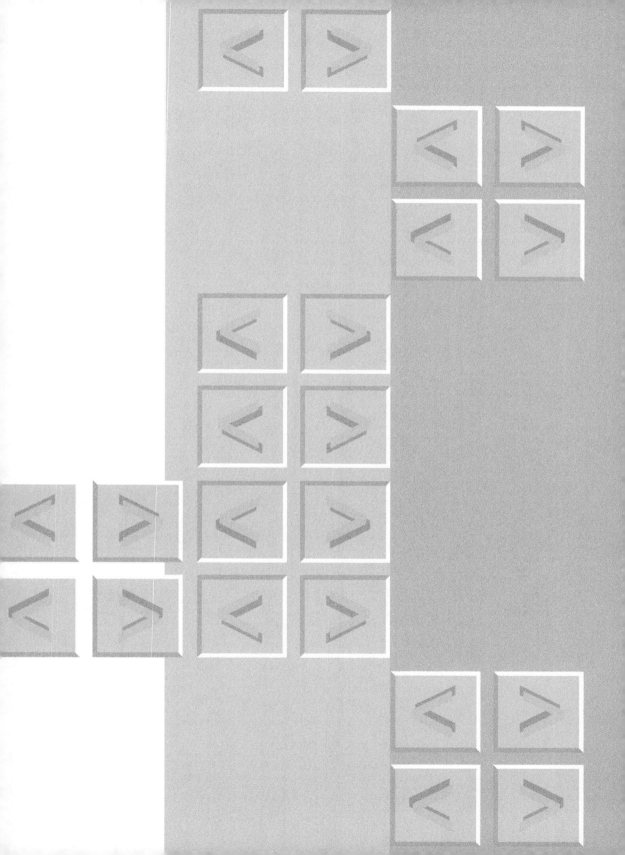

Appendix A
An Overview of Python for Java Programmers

The most important thing to realize about the relationship between Python and the Java programming language is that they are complementary tools. They have strengths at opposite ends of the programming spectrum and they both belong in your programming tool chest.

The key to understanding the relationship and synergy between the Java platform and Python is differentiating Java the virtual machine from Java the programming language.

The Java platform consists of two very different things:

- A virtual machine
- A programming language

The Java virtual machine is a program that reads and executes instructions expressed in Java Virtual Machine Code, known as Java bytecode. The Java programming language generates bytecode in the form of `.class` files. It is entirely possible to generate Java bytecode from languages other than Java. This has been done for Tcl, Awk, JavaScript and Scheme, for example.

503

It has also been done with Python in the form of JPython. JPython (http://www.jpython.org) is a 100% Pure Java™ implementation of the Python programming language. Using JPython, you can execute Python programs on any Java virtual machine. JPython provides tight integration with the JDK and Java classes in general. You can not only use Java classes from JPython, you can subclass them in JPython.

Comparing the Python and Java Programming Languages

The Java programming language is syntactically spartan. That is, it has a lean syntax for expressing control structures and some low-level data types such as integers and strings. Most of the richness and power of the Java development platform resides in the JDK rather than in the language itself.

The Python programming language is also syntactically quite spartan. Unlike the Java programming language, Python does provide native support for iterating data structures, manipulating strings and manipulating hierarchical data structures. Python is a higher-level programming language than Java, allowing complex data structures and control flows to be expressed in a more concise syntax than is possible in the Java programming language.

Java is a compiled language. That is, the source code .java files are compiled to produce .class files, which are then executed in a separate step. Python, on the other hand, is an interpreted language. It executes programs directly from their source code form. More accurately, Python *appears* to execute programs directly from their source code form. Behind the scenes, Python compiles your programs into an intermediate form that is then executed on the Python virtual machine. The Python virtual machine is analogous to the Java virtual machine.

Unlike Java, Python can be used interactively. That is, you can execute Python and find yourself in an interactive programming environment where you can do anything the Python language allows you to do: perform calculations, define classes, and so on.

Java is statically typed. That is, variables have associated types; that is, integer, string, array, and so on. If a program declares x to be an integer and then attempts to assign a string to it, the Java compiler will generate an error message. Similarly, a class that is declared to implement a particular interface will not compile unless it supports all the methods required by that interface. Python, on the other hand, is dynamically typed. A variable x can be an integer one minute and a string the next. Python will not complain. The concept known in Java technology as an interface is used extensively in Python. However, Python does not enforce implementation of interfaces at compile time as Java does.

Both the Java programming language and Python have automatic memory management and garbage collection. That is, you do not need to worry about allocating and deallocating memory for variables in Python. When the number of references to an object shrinks to zero, the space occupied by the object is reclaimed automatically.

There is one important difference between how Python and the Java programming language handle memory management. Periodically, the Java platform stops whatever it is doing and scans memory for reclaimable objects; Python looks for reclaimable objects as the number of references change in the course of executing code.

The Python memory management system does have one facet that can be troublesome. If two objects, x and y, reference each other and there are no other references to x and y, Python will not be able to reclaim the memory occupied by x and y because their reference counts will never be zero. If this form of mutual object references occurs in your Python program, you need to unlink the objects to allow Python to reclaim the memory used.

Both Java and Python are object-oriented programming languages. Java uses a single inheritance model combined with interfaces. Python supports single and multiple inheritance. Although the interface concept is not an explicit part of the Python syntax, it is extensively used in Python's type system.

Both the Java programming language and Python take an object-oriented approach to exception handling. The syntax differs but the concepts are very similar.

In conclusion, Java and Python have similarities as well as differences. Many of the differences are due to the different problem domains the languages excel in. Java is a low-level, statically typed, systems programming language. Python is a high-level, dynamically typed language. Python programs generally run slower than Java programs, but in my experience, are often five times shorter in length and about three times faster to write.

The JPython implementation of the Python programming language allows you to mix and match Java and Python to make the best use of the strengths of each language.

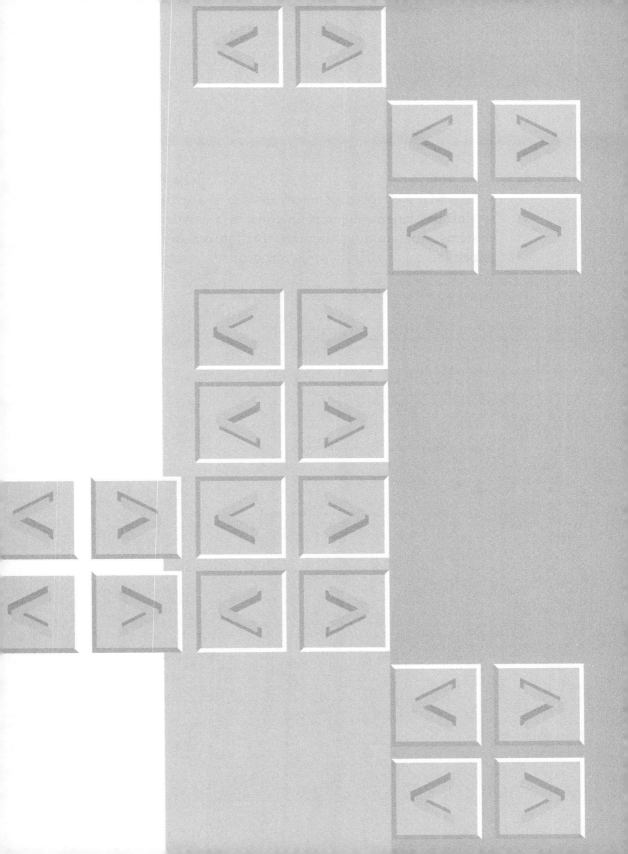

Appendix B
An Overview of Python for Perl Programmers

T here is a definite overlap in the problem domains in which both Python and Perl are used. The overlap is not complete, but it is sufficiently large that most developers choose to use Python or Perl in their work, but not a mixture of both.

Comparisons between Perl and Python are unavoidably subjective. Both languages have ardent supporters and ardent detractors. Unfortunately, comparisons between Perl and Python often lead to heated debate when published in public forums—especially the comp.lang.perl and comp.lang.python Usenet groups.

Both Python and Perl are interpreted programming languages. They are executed directly from their textual form without any (visible) compilation stage. Both languages are highly portable, running essentially on every computing platform in widespread use.

Both languages are written in C and both can be extended by the integration of third-party C modules. They also both have C style string interpolation similar to that used in the printf function.

Both languages are dynamically typed. That is, a variable x can be an integer one minute and a string the next. There is no need to declare variables or associate them with any particular data type.

In Perl, variables are prefixed with a dollar sign, for example, `$foo`. There is no special syntax for variables in Python.

Perl uses braces {} to group code statements together and a semicolon to separate statements. Python, on the other hand, uses the indentation of your code to determine the correct statement grouping. Python statements generally appear one per line, so there is no statement separator to correspond to Perl's use of the semicolon.

Both languages feature an extensive library of modules providing support for everything from database access to GUI development to artificial intelligence engines.

Although Perl has some object-oriented features, Python is more object oriented than Perl. Although Python does not require you to adopt an object-oriented programming style, it has a way of gently steering you toward taking an object-oriented approach.

Perl syntax is a lot bigger than the syntax in Python. There are a lot more special characters and more complex parsing rules in Perl than in Python.

Both languages have powerful regular expression support. It is built directly into the Perl language, whereas they are implanted as an external library module in Python. Python's regular expression syntax is modeled on that of Perl.

Perl has a syntax for handling references to objects. In Python, references are simply the way the language works. That is, x = y in Python makes x refer to the same object that y refers to.

With Perl references, it is possible to build hierarchical data structures. In Python, there is no need for special syntax for doing this because hierarchical structures (nested lists) are supported directly.

Both Perl and Python have a built-in hash table data structure. Perl's terminology for this structure is an associative array. In Python, it is referred to as a dictionary.

It is easier to write "one liners" in Perl. Perl also allows a complete program to be specified as a command-line parameter to the interpreter, but Python does not. This one-liner facility in Perl can be useful in Unix-style pipeline processing.

Both Python and Perl are set to continue to thrive for many years to come. It will come as no surprise that I, the author of this book, favor Python over Perl. In particular, I believe that Python is a better language for XML application development, which is what I spend my days doing. I have no doubt that there are application domains where Perl is better than Python, but they are beyond my experience.

Finally, I have a number of strictly business reasons for preferring Python to Perl. I have personal experience of having difficulty understanding the Perl code created by members of my programming team. Code that can only be understood and maintained by particular developers is bad for business.

I have personal experience of charging down the hall asking the developer who wrote a particularly impenetrable piece of Perl code to step forward, only to realize that I had written the code myself! Embarrassing and definitely bad for business.

That said, Perl and Python are, at the end of the day, just tools. It is important to remember that a bad programmer can write bad code in any language. Equally, programmers as skillful as Larry Wall or Guido van Rossum can write good code in any language.

For programmers of more modest skills, I believe Python to be a better choice.

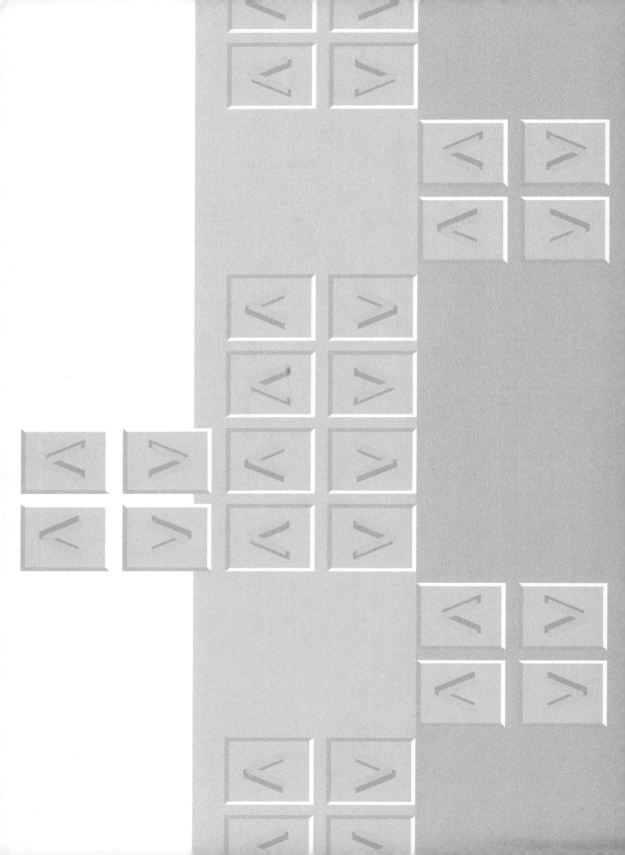

Index

Symbols

A

B

C

▌F

▌G

M

N

O

∎ *T*

LICENSE AGREEMENT AND LIMITED WARRANTY

READ THE FOLLOWING TERMS AND CONDITIONS CAREFULLY BEFORE OPENING THIS SOFTWARE MEDIA PACKAGE. THIS LEGAL DOCUMENT IS AN AGREEMENT BETWEEN YOU AND PRENTICE-HALL, INC. (THE "COMPANY"). BY OPENING THIS SEALED SOFTWARE MEDIA PACKAGE, YOU ARE AGREEING TO BE BOUND BY THESE TERMS AND CONDITIONS. IF YOU DO NOT AGREE WITH THESE TERMS AND CONDITIONS, DO NOT OPEN THE SOFTWARE MEDIA PACKAGE. PROMPTLY RETURN THE UNOPENED SOFTWARE MEDIA PACKAGE AND ALL ACCOMPANYING ITEMS TO THE PLACE YOU OBTAINED THEM FOR A FULL REFUND OF ANY SUMS YOU HAVE PAID.

1. **GRANT OF LICENSE:** In consideration of your payment of the license fee, which is part of the price you paid for this product, and your agreement to abide by the terms and conditions of this Agreement, the Company grants to you a nonexclusive right to use and display the copy of the enclosed software program (hereinafter the "SOFTWARE") on a single computer (i.e., with a single CPU) at a single location so long as you comply with the terms of this Agreement. The Company reserves all rights not expressly granted to you under this Agreement.

2. **OWNERSHIP OF SOFTWARE:** You own only the magnetic or physical media (the enclosed software media) on which the SOFTWARE is recorded or fixed, but the Company retains all the rights, title, and ownership to the SOFTWARE recorded on the original software media copy(ies) and all subsequent copies of the SOFTWARE, regardless of the form or media on which the original or other copies may exist. This license is not a sale of the original SOFTWARE or any copy to you.

3. **COPY RESTRICTIONS:** This SOFTWARE and the accompanying printed materials and user manual (the "Documentation") are the subject of copyright. You may not copy the Documentation or the SOFTWARE, except that you may make a single copy of the SOFTWARE for backup or archival purposes only. You may be held legally responsible for any copying or copyright infringement which is caused or encouraged by your failure to abide by the terms of this restriction.

4. **USE RESTRICTIONS:** You may not network the SOFTWARE or otherwise use it on more than one computer or computer terminal at the same time. You may physically transfer the SOFTWARE from one computer to another provided that the SOFTWARE is used on only one computer at a time. You may not distribute copies of the SOFTWARE or Documentation to others. You may not reverse engineer, disassemble, decompile, modify, adapt, translate, or create derivative works based on the SOFTWARE or the Documentation without the prior written consent of the Company.

5. **TRANSFER RESTRICTIONS:** The enclosed SOFTWARE is licensed only to you and may not be transferred to any one else without the prior written consent of the Company. Any unauthorized transfer of the SOFTWARE shall result in the immediate termination of this Agreement.

6. **TERMINATION:** This license is effective until terminated. This license will terminate automatically without notice from the Company and become null and void if you fail to comply with any provisions or limitations of this license. Upon termination, you shall destroy the Documentation and all copies of the SOFTWARE. All provisions of this Agreement as to warranties, limitation of liability, remedies or damages, and our ownership rights shall survive termination.

7. **MISCELLANEOUS:** This Agreement shall be construed in accordance with the laws of the United States of America and the State of New York and shall benefit the Company, its affiliates, and assignees.

8. **LIMITED WARRANTY AND DISCLAIMER OF WARRANTY:** The Company warrants that the SOFTWARE, when properly used in accordance with the Documentation, will operate in substantial conformity with the description of the SOFTWARE set forth in the Documentation. The Company does not warrant that the SOFTWARE will meet your requirements or that the operation of the SOFTWARE will be uninterrupted or error-free. The Company warrants that the media on which the SOFTWARE is delivered shall be free from defects in materials and workmanship under normal use for a period of thirty (30) days from the date of your purchase. Your only remedy and the Company's only obligation under these limited warranties is, at the Company's option, return of the warranted item for a refund of any amounts paid by you or replacement of the item. Any replacement of SOFTWARE or media under the warranties shall not extend the original warranty period. The limited warranty set forth above shall not apply to any SOFTWARE which the Company determines in good faith has been subject to misuse, neglect, improper installation, repair, alteration, or dam-

age by you. EXCEPT FOR THE EXPRESSED WARRANTIES SET FORTH ABOVE, THE COMPANY DISCLAIMS ALL WARRANTIES, EXPRESS OR IMPLIED, INCLUDING WITHOUT LIMITATION, THE IMPLIED WARRANTIES OF MERCHANTABILITY AND FITNESS FOR A PARTICULAR PURPOSE. EXCEPT FOR THE EXPRESS WARRANTY SET FORTH ABOVE, THE COMPANY DOES NOT WARRANT, GUARANTEE, OR MAKE ANY REPRESENTATION REGARDING THE USE OR THE RESULTS OF THE USE OF THE SOFTWARE IN TERMS OF ITS CORRECTNESS, ACCURACY, RELIABILITY, CURRENTNESS, OR OTHERWISE.

IN NO EVENT, SHALL THE COMPANY OR ITS EMPLOYEES, AGENTS, SUPPLIERS, OR CONTRACTORS BE LIABLE FOR ANY INCIDENTAL, INDIRECT, SPECIAL, OR CONSEQUENTIAL DAMAGES ARISING OUT OF OR IN CONNECTION WITH THE LICENSE GRANTED UNDER THIS AGREEMENT, OR FOR LOSS OF USE, LOSS OF DATA, LOSS OF INCOME OR PROFIT, OR OTHER LOSSES, SUSTAINED AS A RESULT OF INJURY TO ANY PERSON, OR LOSS OF OR DAMAGE TO PROPERTY, OR CLAIMS OF THIRD PARTIES, EVEN IF THE COMPANY OR AN AUTHORIZED REPRESENTATIVE OF THE COMPANY HAS BEEN ADVISED OF THE POSSIBILITY OF SUCH DAMAGES. IN NO EVENT SHALL LIABILITY OF THE COMPANY FOR DAMAGES WITH RESPECT TO THE SOFTWARE EXCEED THE AMOUNTS ACTUALLY PAID BY YOU, IF ANY, FOR THE SOFTWARE.

SOME JURISDICTIONS DO NOT ALLOW THE LIMITATION OF IMPLIED WARRANTIES OR LIABILITY FOR INCIDENTAL, INDIRECT, SPECIAL, OR CONSEQUENTIAL DAMAGES, SO THE ABOVE LIMITATIONS MAY NOT ALWAYS APPLY. THE WARRANTIES IN THIS AGREEMENT GIVE YOU SPECIFIC LEGAL RIGHTS AND YOU MAY ALSO HAVE OTHER RIGHTS WHICH VARY IN ACCORDANCE WITH LOCAL LAW.

ACKNOWLEDGMENT

YOU ACKNOWLEDGE THAT YOU HAVE READ THIS AGREEMENT, UNDERSTAND IT, AND AGREE TO BE BOUND BY ITS TERMS AND CONDITIONS. YOU ALSO AGREE THAT THIS AGREEMENT IS THE COMPLETE AND EXCLUSIVE STATEMENT OF THE AGREEMENT BETWEEN YOU AND THE COMPANY AND SUPERSEDES ALL PROPOSALS OR PRIOR AGREEMENTS, ORAL, OR WRITTEN, AND ANY OTHER COMMUNICATIONS BETWEEN YOU AND THE COMPANY OR ANY REPRESENTATIVE OF THE COMPANY RELATING TO THE SUBJECT MATTER OF THIS AGREEMENT.

Should you have any questions concerning this Agreement or if you wish to contact the Company for any reason, please contact in writing at the address below.

Robin Short
Prentice Hall PTR
One Lake Street
Upper Saddle River, New Jersey 07458

About the CD-ROM

The CD-ROM contains the following software packages.

Windows

py152.exe	The core Python distribution
PythonXML.exe	The Python XML library from the XML-SIG
win32all-125.exe	Mark Hammond's Win32 extensions to Python
wxPython-2.1b3.exe	The wxPython GUI library
xmln.exe	The xmln PYX generating utility.
xmlv.exe	The xmlv PYX generating utility
pythlp.chm	The Python 1.5.2 manuals in compiled help format
mysql-shareware-win32-1 1.zip	Shareware version of MySQL for Windows
libmySQL.dll	DLL providing access to MySQL database engine
MySQL.pyd	Python module providing access to MYSQL
MySQLdb-0.0.3.tar.gz	Source code for the Python MySQL module

Linux

python-1.5.2-2.i386.rpm	Python 1.5.2 for Linux (RPM format)
python-base_1.5.1-7.deb	Python for Linux (Debian format)
python-xml-0.5.1-2.i386.rpm	XML Library for Python from the XML-SIG (RPM format)
xmln	The xmln PYX generating utility
xmlv	The xmlv PYX generating utility
wxPython-2 1b1-2 i386.rpm	The wxPython library (RPM format)
MySQL-client-3.22.25-1.i386.rpm	MySQL client for Linux (RPM format)
MySQL-3.22.25-1.i386.rpm	MySQL server for Linux (RPM format)

Generic Unix

xml-0 5 1.tgz	XML SIG distribution for generic Unix

Miscellaneous

xmln.c	Source code for the xmln utility
xmlv.c	Source code for the xmlv utility
testpyexpat.py	Test program for the PyExpat XML parser
testsax.py	Test program for SAX processing

Technical Support

Prentice Hall does not offer technical support for this software. However, if there is a problem with the media, you may obtain a replacement copy by e-mailing us with your problem at: disc_exchange@prenhall.com.